Sex and Manifest Destiny

Also by Martin Naparsteck

Richard Yates Up Close: The Writer and His Works (McFarland, 2012)

Sex and Manifest Destiny
The Urge That Drove Americans Westward

Martin Naparsteck

McFarland & Company, Inc., Publishers
Jefferson, North Carolina, and London

LIBRARY OF CONGRESS CATALOGUING-IN-PUBLICATION DATA

Naparsteck, M. J. (Martin John), 1944–
    Sex and manifest destiny : the urge that drove Americans westward / by Martin Naparsteck.
       p.   cm.
    Includes bibliographical references and index.

    ISBN 978-0-7864-6654-2
    softcover : acid free paper ∞

    1. United States — Territorial expansion — Social aspects.   2. Sex and history — West (U.S.)   3. Frontier and pioneer life — West (U.S.)   4. Indians of North America — Sexual behavior.   5. Whites — Relations with Indians.   6. Polygamy — West (U.S.) — History.   7. Polygamy — Religious aspects — Mormon Church.   I. Title.
E338.N37 2012
306.70978 — dc23   2012034105

BRITISH LIBRARY CATALOGUING DATA ARE AVAILABLE

© 2012 Martin Naparsteck. All rights reserved

No part of this book may be reproduced or transmitted in any form or by any means, electronic or mechanical, including photocopying or recording, or by any information storage and retrieval system, without permission in writing from the publisher.

On the cover: *Sacajawea Guiding Lewis and Clark,* Newell Convers Wyeth, 1939 (PicturesNow)

Manufactured in the United States of America

McFarland & Company, Inc., Publishers
  Box 611, Jefferson, North Carolina 28640
    www.mcfarlandpub.com

For Mom and Dad
And for my brothers
Bob, Ron, Ken, Howard

[It] is by right of our manifest destiny to overspread and to possess the whole of the continent which Providence has given us for the development of the great experiment of liberty and federated self-government entrusted to us.

—John L. O'Sullivan, 1845

Table of Contents

Preface   1
Introduction: Rethinking Manifest Destiny   5

1. Lewis and Clark: Exploring for Sex   13
2. Mountain Men: Escaping to Sex   31
3. The Missionary: Saving Indians from Sex   58
4. Presidential Sex   89
5. Saving White Women from Indians   104
6. Sexual Exodus   161
7. End of the Sex Drive   184

Appendices
    A. "Annexation" by John O'Sullivan: The First Mention of "Manifest Destiny"   187
    B. Thomas Jefferson's Letter of Instructions to Meriwether Lewis   192
    C. Meriwether Lewis's Invitation to William Clark   195
    D. Excerpts from Letters Written by Marcus Whitman   196
    E. Fanny Kelly's Petition to Congress   197
    F. Joseph Smith's Revelation on Plural Marriage   199
    G. Mormon Church Ban on Polygamy   201

Chapter Notes   203
Selected Bibliography   215
Index   223

Preface

This book seeks to prove that the natural human sex drive contributed to the drive to expand the United States westward across the entire continent, a process that is generally known as the fulfillment of Manifest Destiny. Sex is so elemental a human activity that I was surprised a few years ago to be unable to find, despite an extensive library and bibliographic search, a single book or scholarly article that made the point about sex contributing to the fulfillment of Manifest Destiny. I also scanned numerous American history volumes in used and new bookstores, spoke with friends who are professional historians, and in general was unsuccessful in finding anyone, professional or amateur historian, who proposed sex as a manifest part of American westward expansion.

Not that sex remains un-discussed in American history texts. Quite the opposite. There are dozens of books, hundreds of articles, movies, TV shows, paintings, and other depictions of sex while America was expanding westward. But mostly these are either histories of sex (for example, histories of prostitution) or acknowledgment that sexual relations occurred. But an argument that the sex drive *contributed* to Americans moving westward is, as far as I can tell, non-existent (prior to this book).

Many motivations for American westward expansion have been presented in hundreds, even thousands, of books and articles. These include economic, military, political, sociological, even philosophical and religious arguments. (Some of these are briefly discussed in the Introduction to this volume.) And, often, excellent cases are made to prove the points. The central argument of this book is not that the sex drive was the most important motivating factor in making the United States a continent-wide country. There is no attempt in this volume to rank the importance of sex in motivating Americans to go to the West. But my hope (and belief) is that I've presented enough evidence to convince even skeptics that sex was a significant motivating factor in that movement.

I have accordingly divided this volume into six distinct chapters, which are preceded by an Introduction that presents the history of the term Manifest Destiny, defends the general concept of revising history, explains what is not in this volume, and in general seeks to prepare the reader for the facts and arguments that are presented.

The first chapter focuses on the Lewis and Clark Expedition and argues that one of many reasons Thomas Jefferson sent them on their mission was because he had a scientific interest in the sex habits of Native American tribes. This chapter also explores the possibility that Meriwether Lewis was gay (a proposition believed by some biographers and historians but not fully accepted by all) and how that might have contributed to the success of his mission.

The second chapter discusses mountain men, a group that constituted the first significant number of whites to spend extended periods in the West, although there were never more than about a thousand of them. Many of the mountain men did not fit in well in the social restraints of the East, including those imposed on male-female relations. Many of them married or lived with Indian women. In fact, part of the appeal of the West for these men was the sex lives they expected to have with Indian women.

That is followed by a chapter on missionaries, both Catholic and Protestant, who went west to convert Indians to their religions. They were seeking to save the souls of Native Americans, and among the reasons they believed those souls needed saving were the sexual practices of many of the tribes, which sometimes included polygamy, encouragement or toleration of premarital sex, easy divorce, wife swapping, and other cultural norms the white missionaries found unacceptable.

Next is a chapter on presidential sex. This is not an examination of the sex lives of all presidents, but is instead limited to two presidents, Andrew Jackson and Sam Houston (who was president of the short-lived Republic of Texas). Jackson's bitterness at the way his wife was treated contributed to a personality that encouraged Westward expansion, including initiating what would become known as the Trail of Tears, the forced removal of Cherokees from the Southern U.S., to what is now Oklahoma. In Houston's case, a wound to his genital area that he received while serving in the Army under Jackson contributed to the breakup of his marriage, resulting in his fleeing to the West, where he helped secure Texan independence from Mexico, which eventually led to Texas becoming part of the United States.

As white Americans established communities farther and farther west, they met more and more resistance from the people already living there, Native Americans. Official U.S. government policy towards Indians was always ill-defined, but tended to vacillate among three general alternatives: assimilation (make them as white as possible), isolation (put them on reservations), and extermination. The last of these, extermination, has received a great deal of attention although it was never official government policy, was widely condemned by most influential white leaders, and was the least effective of the three approaches in actually subduing the Indian tribes. Yet it is part of the story of American westward expansion, and whites found it necessary to develop a moral justification for the killings. Much of that justification revolved around a fear, usually but not always poorly founded, that white women were in danger of being raped by Indian men or forced to become their wives. The development of that defense of extermination contributed to the country's conquest of the Indian tribes.

The sixth chapter focuses on the Mormon exodus to what is now Utah. Mormons left upstate New York, where the church was founded, and moved, first to Kirtland, Ohio, then Western Missouri, next to Illinois, and finally, because of hostility from neighbors, to the Great Salt Lake Valley in what is now Utah. In Missouri the governor issued an order saying all Mormons who did not leave the state were to be exterminated. In Illinois, the church founder and leader, Joseph Smith, was assassinated. Much of the hostility Mormons faced resulted from hostility to their practice of what they called plural marriage, a form of polygamy. They fled to Utah to be able to engage in plural marriage, which of course involves sexual relations.

The main text concludes with a discussion of how the sex drive ceased to be a motivating factor in American westward expansion in the late 19th century, largely because that expansion had been completed. It is consistent with Frederick Jackson Turner's thesis that the end of the frontier in American history essentially altered the American character.

After the main text, I've included appendices containing some of the key documents I used to base my thesis. These include Thomas Jefferson's letter to Meriwether Lewis instructing him on what to look for during his expedition; Lewis's letter to William Clark inviting him to join the expedition; excerpts from letters written by Marcus Whitman, one of the most famous missionaries in the 19th century American West; a petition to Congress written by Fanny Kelly, among the most famous women to be captured by Indians; and two key Mormon documents regarding polygamy. (Excerpts from numerous other primary sources appear throughout the text.)

The essential methodology is an accumulation of detail demonstrating that people who played a role in making the United States an Atlantic-to-Pacific country made some key decisions with sex in mind. No one detail is convincing in itself. It's the accumulation that leads to the conclusion.

Introduction: Rethinking Manifest Destiny

This is a revisionist history. For some readers, historical revisionism is a vice, but much of history is badly in need of revising. Much of what we've been told about the past, we've been told for political or religious reasons. In American history few concepts have been as much in need of revision as Manifest Destiny.

John L. O'Sullivan, one of the most important commentators on politics and literature in the mid–19th century United States, and now almost forgotten, was the first to use the term "manifest destiny." It first appeared in his essay titled "Annexation" in the July–August 1845 issue of the *Democratic Review*, a magazine he co-founded in 1837 (the full title of the magazine was *The United States Magazine and Democratic Review*, but it was generally known by the second half of its long name). In that essay he defended the decision to annex the Republic of Texas as a state, effectively and forever ending Mexico's claim to the area. O'Sullivan wrote that it was America's "manifest destiny to overspread the continent allotted by Providence for the free development of our yearly multiplying millions" (the full text of O'Sullivan's "Annexation" appears in Appendix A).

In other words, the westward expansion of the United States was both clear (manifest) and inevitable. At the time, no one seemed to notice the phrase, even though the *Democratic Review* was considered the leading literary voice of what might be called the liberal wing of the Democratic Party. *The North American Review* was its chief intellectual and conservative rival among political magazines. O'Sullivan liked the phrase well enough to use it again, four months later. This time the occasion was an article in the December 27, 1845, issue of the *New York Morning News,* and he was writing about the annexation of Oregon Territory, which was then jointly administered by the United States and Great Britain. O'Sullivan wrote, "That claim is by right of our manifest destiny to overspread and to possess the whole of the continent which Providence has given us for the development of the great experiment of liberty and federated self-government entrusted to us."

O'Sullivan in his lifetime was known as an advocate for creating an American literature free of European influences, for abolition of the death penalty, and for Cuba's right to be independent of Spain. Even while he was alive, few people seemed to know he originated the term "manifest destiny." The concept behind it — the inevitability of the United States becoming a country stretching from the Atlantic to the Pacific Ocean — was, of course, not original with O'Sullivan. It existed from the earliest days of the republic. O'Sullivan did not advocate the use of force to impose that expansion on unwilling populations. Rather, he thought the American form of democracy so obviously superior to all other forms of government that the Spanish and Mexicans in the Southwest, the British settlers in the Northwest, and everyone else would want the land they lived on to be part of the United States. He largely ignored the question of how Native Americans would fit into the expansion, and he was inconsistent in what he said about the millions of black slaves in the South. Early in his career as a writer and editor he mildly opposed slavery and favored adding more free states to the union. But when the Civil War began, he supported the Confederacy, arguing that the presidency had acquired too much power and that blacks and whites could not coexist in the same land without slavery. He may, in fact, have been employed by the Confederacy to write pamphlets supporting its cause. After the Civil War, however, whatever influence he had as a political commentator evaporated.

When he died in New York City in 1895, hardly anyone noticed. His famous two-word phrase was far better known than he was. In 1927 historian Julius Pratt did extensive research to find out who originated the phrase and proved it was O'Sullivan. Today, of course, nearly every American has heard or read the phrase in a high school or college history class. Few have heard or read about O'Sullivan.[1]

The term Manifest Destiny has come down to us in its most negative connotation, and it is now inseparable from concepts of genocide, greed, empire, and cultural bigotry. Mostly, it deserves the ill treatment it has received. But we should also always be willing to newly examine the concepts behind our beliefs. This book attempts to do that, to offer a view of one aspect of Manifest Destiny that historians have ignored, the relation between the oldest of human drives, sex, and the drive to make the United States a continental country.

To help clarify the point being made, three other factors often associated with American westward expansion will be briefly examined. These include (1) the widespread cultural assumptions that violence was both needed and widely used to make the West inhabitable by white Americans; (2) the depiction of employment in the earliest days of white settlements in the West was dominated by ranches and small business districts in scattered towns; and (3) the concept of seeking religious freedom was largely a phenomenon restricted to colonial settlement along the Atlantic Coast. All of these should be recognized as important factors in American westward expansion. A brief, single-sample-based discussion of each, however, offers three opportunities to reexamine how we think about Manifest Destiny.

First, consider the movies *High Noon* and *Rio Bravo*. Violence and American westward expansion are so interlocked in American cultural representation of that expansion that it's difficult to think of one without thinking of the other. Cowboy movies, novels, songs, poetry, and paintings frequently depict Western settlement by whites as a conflict: between whites and Indians, between good and bad, between ranchers and farmers, between the genteel and the wild. Sometimes Indians are savage aggressors. More recently, they are just as likely to be portrayed as noble defenders of cultures under attack. Sometimes the good guys are the sheriffs and marshals and the Army. Often the outlaw is praised: Billy the Kid, Jesse James, Geronimo, and Sitting Bull — law-breakers all — are just as likely to be depicted today as noble as they once were depicted as evil. The depictions often simply reflect changing cultural trends, and, just as often, ignorance (or disregard) of history. Sometimes, however, the differing depictions reflect political attitudes.[2]

Both *High Noon* and *Rio Bravo* are widely considered among the best Western films ever made, but today much of the controversy surrounding them has been forgotten or relegated to footnotes. When the films were made in the 1950s, however, the first, *High Noon*, released in 1952, was seen as a liberal statement, primarily as an attack on McCarthyism, while *Rio Bravo*, released in 1959, was often called a conservative response to the earlier movie.

The similarities are striking. Anyone watching them back-to-back on DVD is likely to conclude that *Rio Bravo* is a mirror image of *High Noon*, a reversal of everything in the earlier movie. In both movies a lawman waits for bad men to arrive in town, with the expectation that he will face them with inferior force. As almost always happens in Hollywood's version of how the West was won, the good guys win in the end.

The differences are more striking. In *High Noon* a Mexican woman who owns a hotel complains that she is the victim of discrimination. In *Rio Bravo*, a Mexican man who owns a hotel is loved by everyone in town. In *High Noon*, when the marshal asks townspeople for help, almost all of them turn him down out of fear. In *Rio Bravo* the sheriff has little difficulty recruiting help. In *High Noon*, the town drunk offers to help, but is rejected by the marshal, who worries that the drunk will be a liability. In *Rio Bravo*, the town drunk is recruited by the sheriff, who hopes this will help him stop drinking.

The differences are not coincidental. *Rio Bravo* producer and director Howard Hawks and its star, John Wayne, both intensely disliked *High Noon*. Both viewed it as an attack on the conservative political views they held. They deliberately made *Rio Bravo* as a corrective.

High Noon, partly based on the short story "The Tin Star" by John Cunningham, focuses on Marshal Will Kane, played by Gary Cooper, who gets married in an early scene. His replacement is not scheduled to arrive until the next day, but Kane and his bride, Amy, played by Grace Kelly, plan to leave town and settle elsewhere. Then word arrives that Frank Miller, a convicted murderer, has been released from prison and is scheduled to arrive in town, Hadleyville (probably in New Mexico Territory, although that's not specified). Kane decides to stay and protect the town from Miller, although his new wife and town officials want him to leave. Amy, a Quaker, abhors violence. Town officials fear a violent confrontation will be inevitable.

Significantly, in the Cunningham short story, the Kane character (Cunningham called him Duane) is a sheriff, a man elected to his position and not directly answerable to the wishes of the town's other elected officials. Duane, in fact, says that as sheriff he doesn't have to do what they want him to. Kane, as a marshal, is appointed, and in staying in town over the objections of the elected officials, is deliberately defying authority. That is one of the clearest messages in the movie: good citizens must resist incompetent authority, even if it requires breaking the law. Or, put in the context of the movie's real message, good citizens must resist the red-baiting, the often careless charges of affiliation with the Communist Party that was a hallmark of Wisconsin Senator Joseph McCarthy and the House Un-American Activities Committee in the early 1950s. Kane turns to one town resident after another to join a posse to help him. Everyone turns him down, each for a different reason. But clearly, most are just scared, just as so many good people didn't defend their friends during the red-baiting of the early 50s.

Much that is in *High Noon* is not in "The Tin Star" (for example, the wedding and the character Amy; Duane's wife being deceased, and his visits to her grave in the town cemetery), but a significant piece of the film's dialogue is very close to being lifted directly from the short story. In the movie, when Kane asks the retired marshal, Martin Howe (played by Lon Chaney, Jr.), to help, he's turned down; Howe says he would be a liability, because of the arthritis that afflicts his hands. But Howe adds, "You risk your skin catching killers and the juries turn them loose so they can come back and shoot at you again. If you're honest you're poor your whole life and in the end you wind up dying all alone on some dirty street. For what? For nothing. For a tin star." In the short story, the sheriff, Duane, says to his deputy, Toby, "They don't hang the right ones. You risk your life catching somebody, and the damned juries let them go so they can come back and shoot at you. You're poor all your life, and you got to do everything twice, and in the end they pay you off in lead. So you can wear a tin star. It's a job for a dog, son" (Cunningham, p. 72).

It reflects a view that both conservatives and liberals then and now could share, that police officers (and soldiers) are not appreciated enough. But the last two lines from the movie and short story quotes at least hint at a disdain for the job. Very near the end of the movie, after Kane has triumphed over Miller and his henchmen, he takes the tin star off his vest and flips it into the dirt at his feet. It is clearly an act of disdain. (John Wayne hated *High Noon* and often claimed, incorrectly, that Kane stepped on the tin star.)

A key scene has Amy arming herself and killing one of the bad guys to save her husband's life. Thus, the story line argues, even a peace-loving Quaker woman will recognize the need to sometimes use force to stand up for what is right.

Wayne called *High Noon* "the most un–American thing I've seen in my whole life" (see Weldhorn, "High Noon"). Howard Hawks, producer and director of *Rio Bravo*, said, "I made *Rio Bravo* because I didn't like *High Noon*. Neither did Duke [Wayne]. I didn't think a good town marshal was going to run around like a chicken with his head cut off asking everyone to help. And who saves him? His Quaker wife. That isn't my idea of a good Western" (Munn, p. 148).

In *Rio Bravo*, Sheriff John T. Chance (played by Wayne) arrests a murderer, and the murderer's friends plan to come to town to free him from jail. Chance asks for help only from those capable of and willing to provide it. He rejects offers of help from those not capable of providing it, saying they are amateurs. His love interest, a dance hall girl named Feathers, played by Angie Dickinson, helps at one point by throwing a flower pot out a window to distract the bad guys, but, unlike Amy in *High Noon*, she does no shooting.

In the end, in both movies, the good guys win, but Chance remains sheriff, proud of the job he has done, while Kane discards his tin star in disdain.

Generally, in the 50s, liberals praised *High Noon* and condemned *Rio Bravo*, and conservatives expressed exactly the opposite view. That distinction is mostly lost on modern audiences. What is not likely to be lost, however, is that in both cases, the "liberal" and the "conservative" film, is that the good guys must use force to defeat the bad guys. That view permeates Hollywood's view of how the West was won.

Second, think about cowboys and miners. On January 24, 1848, when John Marshall noticed some yellow flakes in the American River, a stream that ran through the property of his employer, Johan (John) Sutter, he set in motion one of the greatest voluntary migrations in world history, the California Gold Rush. Within two years, 300,000 people flocked to California. They came from China, from Mexico and South America, but mostly they came from the American East and today's Midwest.[3] Between 1847 and 1870, the population of San Francisco increased from 500 to 150,000. Similar figures clearly show that the work that most attracted settlers to the West, from the Rockies to the Pacific Coast, was mining. Gold, silver, copper, and later uranium drew Americans and foreigners by the hundreds of thousands. Farming, ranching, and retailing all attracted some people, but no occupation came close to matching the pull of mining. The completion of the first transcontinental railroad in 1869 opened the interior lands to migration, and only then did the ranching industry grow significantly, because it allowed the shipping of cows from the West to the Midwest and East to be slaughtered. The railroads led to the growth of towns, places where families could live in proximity to each other and provide needed commercial services like stores, restaurants, laundries, lawyers, newspapers, and dozens of others. Mining and railroads populated the West, not ranching. Yet, in the popular imagination cowboying was the principal occupation in the West in the final three decades of the 19th century. In reality, U.S. Census figures show that cowboys never constituted more than one percent of the population in any Western state during that period.[4]

There is a conflict between the reality and popular conception when it comes to thinking of what Westerners did to earn their living in the later decades of the 19th century.

Third, think about the American quest for religious freedom. In the popular mind, European colonization of what became the United States is strongly associated with a quest for religious freedom. The Puritans, particularly, are a symbol, especially among religious conservatives, so interlinked with the founding of America that they are often spoken and written about as if they are the same phenomenon. What is often omitted in the discussion is the reality that many religious groups in the United States believed they did not have true religious freedom and often moved west to find it. This will be a key point in the chapter on Mormon westward movement, but it applies also to other religious groups. For example, Hasia R. Diner writes in "American West, New York Jewish," that as early as the late 19th century, "the West has functioned as the place from which they [American Jews] emphasize their embrace of America and its transformative power" (Diner, p. 50). Diner notes that as early as 1880, San Francisco had the second largest Jewish population in the country, outnumbered only by New York.[5]

In each of these three examples, there is no need to fully reject the popular assumption about the American West of the second half of the 19th century. Rather, we need only slightly revise those assumptions to make them a little more true.

These three points might be stated more accurately: (1) both liberals and conservatives view violence as having been necessary for successful Westward expansion; (2) mining and railroads provided the principal early occupations for whites who migrated to the West in the second half of the 19th century, not cowboying; and (3) Easterners often sought religious freedom by moving to the West. These can easily and usefully be beginning points for revising popular view of how the West became American.

And part of the revision should be an examination of the role sex played.

Numerous other factors played roles, of course. Pre–Civil War Southern slave owners wanted to increase their representation in Congress by adding more slave-holding states (an especially important factor in American migration into Mexican Texas). The availability of cheap land attracted speculators and families too poor to afford the more expensive Eastern lands. People were further encouraged by federal government enticements to populate the West with American citizens as a way of preventing other countries — particularly Spain, France, and England — from establishing successful rival claims. And the region held potential for vast profits (think again of mining and railroading) and even an allure for those with a desire for personal adventures. The list could go on. And on.

There is no shortage of factors that contributed to the United States fulfilling its Manifest Destiny. This book simply adds one more to a long list.

1

Lewis and Clark
Exploring for Sex

Sex drove Lewis and Clark west. Thomas Jefferson planned for a decade to send someone,[1] and in 1793, an expedition was sponsored, at Jefferson's suggestion, by the American Philosophical Society and funded by subscribers, including George Washington and Alexander Hamilton. It would head west by a southern route to gather information about natural history and the cultures of Indian tribes. Andre Michaux, a French botanist, led it, but about the time it reached Kentucky, Jefferson learned Michaux intended to form a militia of Americans to attack the Spanish west of the Mississippi.[2] Jefferson, at the time secretary of state in George Washington's Cabinet, demanded the French government order Michaux to return to the East. The French, anxious for American support in its war with England, agreed.

Earlier, in 1783, right after the Revolution ended, Jefferson corresponded with General George Rogers Clark, a Revolutionary War hero (and older brother, by 18 years, of William Clark), about the possibility of an expedition to the West, perhaps to California.[3] Jefferson worried that a group of British investors might get there first and establish settlements in areas he hoped would eventually become part of the United States. Jefferson wanted a large expedition. Clark, fearing that would alarm the Indian nations they passed through, wanted a much smaller one. Because of a failure to reach an agreement on the details of the trip, the expedition never got underway. In 1786, Jefferson supported an odd plan by John Ledyard, who wanted to travel to Europe, across Siberia, cross the Bering Sea, and walk south and then east across the American continent.[4] For companions he took two dogs. He got as far as Siberia when the Russian empress, Catherine the Great, ordered him arrested and deported.

In 1806, before Lewis and Clark returned from their epic trip to the Pacific Northwest, and during a time when many in the East feared they might have been killed, another expedition to the West, one almost totally forgotten today, set out on a southern route. Jefferson sent a party of about 50 men to see if a southern water route across the continent existed.[5] It was under the command of Captain Richard Sparks but known as the Freeman-Custis expedition, named for the two men who kept journals on the trip, Thomas Freeman, an engineer, and Peter Custis, a naturalist and a relative of Martha Custis, who married George Washington. However, James Wilkinson, governor of Upper Louisiana Territory and possibly part of a plot led by Vice President Aaron Burr to seek Spanish support for creating their own country in the interior of the continent, informed the Spanish of the expedition and a small Spanish army intercepted them in what is now East Texas and ordered them to turn back, which they did.

On each of the expeditions, Jefferson instructed the leaders to prepare maps and to make careful measurements of distances and locations, all useful information for future trade routes. But Jefferson's interests extended to the collection of scientific data.[6] In seeking funding, either from the Philosophical Society, or later from Congress, information useful for commerce was emphasized. But reading Jefferson's writings on the expeditions, it's clear his interests focused on scientific matters. His strongest scientific interests lay in botany, astronomy and in ethnology. It is that interest in ethnology—the study of cultures—that encompassed his interest in the sexual practices of American Indians.

France once claimed the Louisiana Territory but ceded it to Spain. But then Napoleon conquered Spain and installed his brother on the Spanish throne. In return, the brother gave the Louisiana Territory back to France. Jefferson, now president and worried French control of New Orleans would impede American trade along the Mississippi River, sent a delegation to France to offer to buy the city for $2,000,000. Napoleon's acceptance of the offer seemed unlikely. New Orleans was a small city at the time, but its location at the mouth of the Mississippi gave it great importance. Napoleon, however, surprised the American delegation, to state their reaction mildly, when he offered to sell the Americans the entire Louisiana Territory, which would roughly double the size of the young United States, for a mere $15,000,000. When Jefferson heard of the offer, he hesitated. He thought the U.S. Constitution did not authorize the purchase of foreign-owned lands. His friend and secretary of state, James Madison, the principal author of the Constitution, agreed. Jefferson planned to seek a Constitutional amendment to make certain he did nothing in violation of the law. But he thought better of that, thankfully for the future growth of the United States. He realized that would delay the purchase by, at the least, months.

Napoleon, meanwhile, reconsidered his offer but did not immediately retract it. Any delay, Jefferson sensed, almost certainly meant a withdrawal of

Napoleon's offer. The French emperor wanted the money to finance his European wars, but he knew the value of the land he offered exceeded his asking price by amounts too vast to calculate. Jefferson overcame his initial hesitation, asked Congress for the money, Congress agreed, and the United States and France sealed the deal. (Most scholars agree Jefferson's initial reaction was right, that indeed nothing in the Constitution permitted the purchase of the Louisiana Territory. Put another away, the single most important event leading to the United States' becoming a continental power violated the Constitution.)[7] Even before the deal closed, even before Napoleon made his offer, even before Jefferson offered to buy New Orleans, Jefferson planned still another expedition.

For this new expedition, Jefferson recruited his personal secretary, who was also a close friend despite 31 years difference in age, and Virginia neighbor, Meriwether Lewis. The two men developed their friendship after they met while wandering in the woods studying trees and flowers near their homes in central Virginia. Because the two men shared that friendship, because Lewis as Jefferson's personal secretary also became his confidant, they talked for hours about what Lewis should look for. Jefferson provided Lewis with almost the equivalent of a college education in the sciences, physical and social. He also sent Lewis to Philadelphia to consult with America's leading scientists. Exactly what Jefferson and Lewis talked about remains unrecorded, but some educated guesses can be made.[8]

A formal letter of 2,407 words written by Jefferson outlines what he wanted Lewis to look for. That letter, dated June 20, 1803, contains a long series of instructions.[9] (Extended excerpts from the letter appear in Appendix B.) These include, of course, seeking a water route to the Pacific Ocean. Also, Jefferson instructed Lewis to make extensive notes and to write them "distinctly & intelligibly for others as well as yourself." He evidently didn't think much of Lewis's handwriting. He instructed Lewis to make several copies of his notes, in case some became lost. In particular, Jefferson told Lewis to note the "traditions" of the Indians he met, and to make notes on their "domestic accommodations," and to observe what "diseases [are] prevalent among them, & the remedies they use; moral & physical circumstances which distinguish them from the tribes we know; peculiarities in their laws, customs & dispositions." Further, he wanted Lewis "to acquire what knolege you can of the state of morality, religion, & information among them."

Can this reasonably be interpreted to mean Jefferson wanted Lewis to study the sex lives of American Indians? This deduction is logical because Lewis consistently obeyed Jefferson's other instructions, such as making careful measurements of distances and locations of landmarks, and we can assume anything noted extensively in his journals must be there because Jefferson wanted it there. And there are dozens of references to the sex lives of the Indians.

Thomas Jefferson's interest in the sex lives of Indians helped drive Meriwether Lewis west.

The Lie

While serving in the Indian wars in Ohio in the 1790s, Meriwether Lewis developed a friendship with William Clark. He wrote to Clark and asked him to accompany him on the expedition to the Pacific.[10] He promised Clark a rank as an equal co-commander. Jefferson authorized the expedition as a military undertaking, called the Corps of Discovery. Jefferson, as commander in chief, arranged a commission as a captain in the Army for Lewis, and Lewis assumed the same rank as Clark. The Army, however, made Clark a lieutenant, but Lewis lied to the men on the expedition. He introduced Clark to them as a captain. Equal co-commanders, he said. Perhaps Lewis felt a sense of dishonor if he did not, in some way, keep his word. Of course, anyone familiar with the military knows equal co-commanders is inconsistent with both military tradition and common sense. But the lie held. Was it the only lie Lewis told, or was there something else about his relationship with Clark lost to history?

Venereal Diseases and the Corps

The men in the Corps of Discovery first contacted venereal disease from Indians in October 1804. But the disease they worried about at the time, and with good reason, was far more deadly than syphilis or gonorrhea. Smallpox killed, throughout recorded history, more people than all wars, than all accidents, than any other disease.[11] Six months earlier, in May, the Corps started out from Camp Wood on the Mississippi River, just north of St. Louis. They reached the Arikaras where the Missouri River meets the Grand in present-day north-central South Dakota.

Three decades earlier, anthropologists tell us, probably more than 30,000 Arikaras lived there. Contact with whites, especially French traders, brought smallpox to the tribe. Smallpox did not exist in the Americas before Columbus arrived, and none of the peoples living there developed an immunity to it. A smallpox epidemic swept through at least 20 distinct Arikara villages in the 1780s, killing about 25,000 members of the tribe. In the winter before Lewis and Clark arrived, a second smallpox epidemic reduced the tribe to three villages totaling about 2,000 people. But no evidence exists indicating any of the men in the Lewis and Clark expedition contacted smallpox from the Arikaras.

They did contact venereal disease. Whether it was syphilis or gonorrhea remains uncertain. Before reaching the Arikaras, the expedition met some Tetons. Clark wrote in his journal that the Tetons "offered us some women, which we did not except" (Clark, *Journals*, September 26, 1804).[12] ("Except" should not be read as a sign Clark was a bad speller, but rather as a recognition that the concept that a word should always be spelled the same way is largely an invention of the second half of the 19th century. Prior to that, if a word was spelled something like it sounded, the reader was expected to figure out what the word was, and if he couldn't that was a reflection on his poor reading skills rather than on the writer's poor spelling.)

The Arikaras believed if a woman had sex with a strong man, any other man having sex with that woman was likely to gain some of his strength. Since whites were generally a few inches taller than Native Americans—and besides, they had cannons, something the Arikaras had never before seen or heard (the whites fired several volleys to impress the Indians), and cannons were certainly strong—the husbands of Arikara women usually tolerated, and sometimes encouraged, sex between their wives and the strong visitors. York, Clark's black slave, was among the biggest and most muscular of the visitors, and one husband guarded his lodge's entrance while York copulated with his wife.

Why did the whites have sex with the Arikaras but not the Tetons? Hard to tell, but Clark's journal offers a strong clue. Of the Tetons, he wrote, "The Squaws are Chearfull fine lookg womin not handson" (Clark, *Journals*, September 26, 1804). He also described Tetons, both men and women, as "generally ill looking & not well made their legs & arms Small.... They Grese ... themselves with coal when they dress" (Clark, *Journals*, September 26, 1804). Clearly, he did not find Tetons attractive. However, Sergeant Patrick Gass, who kept his own journal, described the Arikaras as "cleanly Indians," "handsome," and "the best looking Indians I have ever seen" (Gass, *Journal*, pp. 47–48).[13] Beauty looked different to the eyes of a sergeant than the eyes of a lieutenant. Gass and other enlisted men found Arikara women good looking enough to overcome even a fear of smallpox.

Although the journals of both Lewis and Clark clearly indicate that nearly every man in the Corps suffered at some point from venereal disease, they make few direct references to the disease. Medical doctors who studied the journals, however, tend to agree most of the men contacted syphilis.[14] Maybe none of them suffered from gonorrhea. In either case the treatment consisted of a mercurous chloride pill, called calomel. The symptoms of syphilis usually take three weeks, sometimes six weeks, to appear and most often evidence themselves by the appearance of a chancre, or small lesion. The lesion often leaks a highly contagious fluid. Six weeks after the first appearance of chancres, a rash usually appears, and then ulcers inside the mouth. Three weeks to three months later, the visible symptoms disappear, but the disease can remain latent in the victim for up to three decades.

The first telltale symptom indicating gonorrhea, by contrast, is a discharge of pus from the urethra (the channel in the penis through which urine and semen pass[15]). Although in the early 19th century written references to venereal diseases seldom made clear distinctions between syphilis and gonorrhea, the symptoms are distinct enough that Lewis probably could tell them apart. And he does — later in his journals, when he reports on his examination of the Shoshoni in what is present-day Montana and Idaho — make a clear reference to both diseases, indicating he could distinguish between them.

The first reference to using mercury pills comes in December 1804, when the expedition visits Mandan Indians in what is now south-central North Dakota.[16] The references to sex with the Arikara comes two months earlier. The timing is right for the symptoms of syphilis to appear and not disappear, convincing Lewis, as the Corps medical officer, that he needed to do some doctoring.

He no doubt was unaware of the long-term effects of mercury. As Stephen Ambrose writes in *Undaunted Courage*, his best-selling book about Lewis and Clark, "'mad as a hatter' referred to hatmakers who used mercury in the process of their work and became a bit crazy from breathing in all those fumes" (Ambrose, p. 197).[17] There were worse problems than a little craziness.

The Corps spent the winter of 1804–1805 with the Mandans. Clark wrote at the end of March 1805 that the men were "generally healthy except venerials complains which is verry Commion" (Clark, *Journals*, March 31, 1805). Clearly Clark and Lewis expected venereal disease to be a problem on the journey. They accepted it as inevitable, which is why Lewis brought mercury pills and why Clark, in his March 1805 journal entry, did not even hint venereal disease among the men would in any way slow their travels.

Why are there no references in the journals to Lewis or Clark suffering from venereal disease? One possibility, of course, is that they did but thought it unbecoming for officers and gentlemen (both were from well-to-do families) to admit to having sex with women they had not married. There may have been other reasons. One of them may be that while with the Mandans they met Sacagawea.

There are dozens of references to venereal disease among the men of the expedition in the journals of Lewis and Clark, although Ambrose notes (*Undaunted Courage*, p. 223) that "veneral disease, including syphilis, was so common it was scarcely commented upon." Sometimes the references are indirect (for example, a note might be made that a man was treated with mercury pills), but often they are direct. Among the direct references are entries by Clark on March 31, October 17, and November 21, 1805, and January 27, March 8, and March 15, 1806, and by Lewis on August 15 and 19, 1805, and January 27 and March 8 and 15, 1806.[18] Note that most of the direct references to the presence of venereal disease among the men are made during the second half of the expedition, suggesting that Lewis and Clark became more willing to acknowledge the disease as their time in the wilderness progressed, or that the men more frequently came in contact with Indians who were infected as their trip progressed, or that Lewis and Clark became better at diagnosing it.

Janey

Sacagawea spoke Shoshoni and Hidatsa. While she may have learned a few words of English during the almost two years she spent with the Corps of Discovery, she never learned enough, nor did any white member of the Corps learn enough of the languages she knew, for her to carry on a direct conversation with Lewis, Clark, or any enlisted man in the expedition. Her husband, Toussaint Charbonneau, a French Canadian trader, spoke French and Hidatsa. Private Francis Labiche spoke French and English. The only language anyone else in the party spoke with fluency was English. So anything we know about Sacagawea was spoken in Hidatsa to her husband, who translated it into French to Private Labiche (or Private George Drouillard, who also spoke a little French), who translated it into English. Certainly some things must have been lost or misunderstand in the translations. In addition, there were vast differences in cultures that neither she nor the men, nor we, ever came to fully understand.

What is known, or supposed,[19] about Sacagawea as a result of those multilayered translations is this. She was born about 1788, give or take one or two years, probably in what is now southeastern Idaho. In 1800, give or take a year, when she was 12, give or take one or two years, she was kidnapped by a raiding party of Hidatsa and taken across what is present-day Montana and half of North Dakota. She was kept in a Hidatsa village for a year or two or three, perhaps as a slave, more likely as a member of an adoptive family. She was sold or lost in a gambling match or, most likely, given, with the payment of some dowry, to Charbonneau, who either married her in a ceremony or simply treated her as a wife. He already had another wife, Otter Woman, who was also Shoshoni, whom he may have purchased or won or married at the same time Sacagawea entered his life. Or maybe he was already married to Otter Woman, who may have been about the same age or may have been four or six or eight years older than Sacagawea. Nothing is known with certainty.

Eleven days after Lewis and Clark entered the Mandan village, they met Charbonneau, who wanted to be hired as a guide or interpreter. When he told them he had two wives who spoke Shoshoni, they hired him immediately, on the condition he bring one of his wives with him. They expected to have to buy horses from the Shoshoni to cross the Rocky Mountains. Besides, Lewis, following Jefferson's instructions to find out as much as possible about the lives of Indians, wanted to study the sex lives of the Shoshoni. They probably had not had contact with whites, Lewis believed, and examining them to see if they suffered from venereal diseases might help determine if syphilis and gonorrhea originated in Europe or the Americas, a question that greatly interested Lewis's boss, the president of the United States. Charbonneau said his younger wife was the one who would have to go, because she was pregnant. So, without knowing anything else about her, Lewis made the decision Sacagawea would join the Corps on its trip to the Pacific. Lewis would come to greatly admire her. Clark would fall in love with her. He gave her a white woman's nickname: Janey.

Doctor Lewis

As the party traveled farther west, they either took syphilis with them or kept contacting it anew, or both. In late May, Lewis noted in his journal that many men complained about sore eyes. He attributed that to sand blown by wind, but some medical experts think it could be a symptom of syphilis. (Other medical experts lean towards a third possibility, the sun's constant glare.) Lewis treated the sore eyes with an eyewash that included some zinc and lead, which probably did no harm but is unlikely to have cured anything caused by syphilis.[20]

In mid–June the expedition experienced its first likely case of gonorrhea.[21] The patient was, surprisingly, Sacagawea. Lewis and Clark had camped at the large waterfalls of the Missouri River, at present-day Great Falls, Montana. Lewis had taken a side trip to explore some of the area north of there, and when he returned Clark told him Sacagawea had been very ill for nearly a week. He had bled her, put a mixture containing Peruvian bark on her pelvic area, and given her laudanum (an opium-laced medicine often used in the 19th century to ease pain). Nothing seemed to work. Clark complained in his journal that the young woman resisted his attempts to doctor her until her husband insisted she take her medicine. Without explaining his logic, Clark wrote, "If She dies it will be the fault of her husband as I am now convinced" (Clark, *Journals*, June 16, 1805). The logic, however, isn't hard to understand. His attraction to Sacagawea led to an intense dislike of and fault-finding in everything about Charbonneau.

When Lewis returned, he took over the doctoring. He gave her a more thorough examination than Clark had, including taking a close look at her vagina. It's possible Sacagawea's hesitancy to take the medication Clark prescribed was based on a refusal to allow him to examine her as closely as she allowed Lewis to. And perhaps an attempt by Clark to get Charbonneau to talk her into such an intimate examination was rebuffed by the Frenchman. Lewis, despite having had only a few days of medical training in Philadelphia prior to commencing on his epic journey, was more accepted by the men, and no doubt by Sacagawea and her husband, as being closer to a real doctor. Whatever the reason, Lewis deduced "her disorder originated principally from an obstruction of the mensis [i.e., vaginal discharge] in consequence of taking could" (Lewis, *Journals*, June 16, 1805). He gave her sulfur water on the theory Clark's bleeding of the patient had drained her of needed minerals. He also gave her some medicines consisting largely of the same Peruvian bark and opium Clark had used. He also bled her some more and continued to apply the same poultices to her pelvic area that Clark had. One of her symptoms, a twitching of her fingers and arms, was probably caused by the bleedings, but Lewis's treatment, although it doesn't seem all that different from Clark's, seemed to work.

The physician considered the leading medical historian on the Lewis and Clark trip, Eldon Chuinard, has high praise for Lewis's doctoring abilities. In his 1980 book, *Only One Man Died: The Medical Aspects of the Lewis and Clark Expedition*, he writes that Lewis's treatment of Sacagawea was as good as any doctor in the early 19th century. He suggests, in fact, that he saved her life. Chuinard also says Sacagawea's symptoms were consistent with someone suffering from gonorrhea. If that is the case she must have contracted it from her husband, because there is no evidence, or even a likelihood, she had sex with anyone else (some historians assert, without evidence, that Hidasta men raped her). The fact neither Clark nor Lewis guessed a venereal disease was the true cause of her illness probably kept the two men from increasing their disdain, if that was possible, for Charbonneau.

Sacagawea improved quickly and in a few days her fever was gone, the twitching had ceased, her pulse was strong, and she was up and walking around. Lewis instructed her to limit her diet, but walking outside the camp she gathered some roots known as white apples and ate them, and then ate some fish. Her fever shot up and she complained of feeling sick. Lewis, of course, blamed her husband: "I rebuked Sharbono severly for suffering her to indulge herself with such food he being privy to it and having previously told what she must only eat" (Lewis, *Journals*, June 19, 1805). He gave her saltpeter, which was used to treat both fever and gonorrhea, although he probably had in mind only her fever, since there is no indication he suspected she suffered from a venereal disease. That, may have been a bit of self-delusion by Lewis, who viewed Sacagawea as pure and therefore beyond catching a sex-related disease.

Sacagawea was immensely useful to the expedition. At one point in what is now Eastern Montana, one of the expedition's pirogues — big, clumsy boats — tilted in a wind, almost capsizing, taking on water. The boat contained maps, the journals, and small instruments, and many of these washed overboard. Lewis, who at the time was walking on shore, later wrote that he considered these items so valuable that he was prepared to give his life to save them. While the men on the boat struggled to right the vessel and bail out water, Sacagawea, her three-month-old baby strapped to her back, calmly reached over the side and retrieved item after item. Lewis later wrote, "The Indian woman to whom I ascribe equal fortitude and resolution, with any person onboard at the time of the accedent, caught and preserved most of the light articles which were washed overboard" (Lewis, *Journals*, May 16, 1805).

About three months later the expedition encountered a party of Indian warriors who didn't seem to like the presence of the white men. This was the closest in all the months of the journey that the expedition came to a serious military encounter. What saved them was a scene that, many historians have noted, not even the most brazen Hollywood scriptwriter would have written. The leader of the Shoshoni, Cameahwait, looked at the Indian girl with Lewis and Clark and she looked at him. Suddenly she ran to him and they embraced. They were big brother and little sister and had not seen each other in at least four years. The location of this most fortunate of reunions, close to the present-day Montana-Idaho line, was later named Camp Fortunate. Sacagawea also helped in gathering food and with chores around the camps. Lewis, Clark, and all the men of the expedition came to admire her. Clark came to love her.

Both Clark and Lewis wrote about a root called a white apple, that Sacagawea dug up but Lewis never mentioned it was the girl who prepared it for a meal, while Clark did. Lewis, in commenting on Sacagawea's kidnapping by Hidatsas, wrote, "I cannot discover that she shews any immotion of sorrow in recollecting this event or of joy in being again restored to her native country; if she had enough to eat and a few trinkets to wear I believe she would be perfectly content anywhere" (Lewis, *Journals*, July 28, 1805). It was similar to comments many slave owners made about blacks. Its bigotry is glaring. Throughout the journals, Lewis's preeminent attitude towards Sacagawea is one of praising her for her hard work and competence. As a Southern aristocrat from a slave-holding family, he no doubt praised some slaves for the same qualities. It's not an attitude that recognizes humanity; it's an attitude that recognizes contributions to the master.

Clark, conversely, although he too was a slave-owner (one of his slaves, York, accompanied the expedition), had a decidedly emotional response to Sacagawea. Consider, for example, his nickname for her — Janey.[22] Before he left on the historical journey, he was hoping to marry his cousin, Julia Hancock, who was 19 years his junior. Perhaps the similarity in ages led him to give the Indian girl a nickname with the same first letter as his beloved Julia. He and Julia did later marry and have five children. After the expedition Clark arranged for Sacagawea's son, Jean-Baptiste, whom he nicknamed Pomp, and her daughter, Lizette, born after the expedition ended, to live with him in St. Louis.

While the *Journals of Lewis and Clark* support a view that Clark loved Sacajawea, there is nothing in those journals, beyond his clear admiration of the role she played on the expedition, to suggest he in any way let her know of that love, or that she was aware of it. The idea that he loved her is a key plot element in the 1955 movie *The Far Horizons*, a remarkably inaccurate, even by Hollywood standards, portrayal of the Lewis and Clark expedition. In the movie, Clark, played by Charlton Heston, clearly loves Sacajawea, played by Donna Reed. Very near the end of the movie, Julia, Clark's future wife, reads him a letter she says was dictated by Sacajawea. In it, the Shoshoni woman says she appreciates the kindnesses shown to her by whites, but notes that she is not white and that she is not a member of the same nation he is. "Have happy memories," she dictates, "like ours were, my love all the days of your life." The letter has absolutely no historical basis.[23]

Clark and Lewis did not project their lofty opinion of Sacagawea onto her people, the Shoshoni. The Shoshoni of the early 19th century probably had less contact with whites than any other tribe in what is now the lower 48 states. They had a few rifles and horses, which, of course, they would not have had without at least indirect contact with whites. Lewis wrote that they were short and had fat ankles. They were, he said, "illy formed, at least much more so in general than any nation of Indians I ever saw" (Lewis, *Journals*, August 19, 1805). They were the Indian nation he spent the most time with since leaving the Mandan village where he met Sacagawea.[24] There is nothing in his or Clark's journals that gives a clear picture of what either thought of Sacagawea's physical appearance. The legend that has formed around her in the last two centuries seems to assume she was beautiful, but if she was, chances are Lewis or Clark would have indicated that, and, in addition, that would have been inconsistent with Lewis's view of the physical appearance of her kinspeople, whom she must have resembled.

He asked the Shoshoni questions about venereal diseases. That is, in English he asked a question to Private Francis Labiche, who then, speaking French, asked it of Charbonneau, who then, speaking Hidatsa, asked Sacajawea, who then, speaking Shoshoni, asked one of the Shoshoni. The answer went from Shoshoni to Hidatsa to French to English. To assume many things were distorted during the translation is common sense.

Among the things Lewis wrote that he learned was that Sacagawea had been promised to a Shoshoni man before she was kidnapped by the Hidatsa and that he (his name was not recorded) was now more than 30 years old and had two wives and, because Sacagawea had a baby by another man, he no longer wanted her as a wife. Lewis and Clark must have enjoyed hearing that, because she had proven herself a valuable member of the expedition. For Clark there was a second reason: his growing attachment to her. If the Shoshoni man still claimed her as his wife, under Shoshoni custom she would have been required to stay with him. The marriage to Charbonneau would have been less than insignificant, a white man's technicality.

Lewis wrote also that Shoshoni men treated Shoshoni women as little more than slaves, making them do all the work, including gathering food, making clothes, and everything else other than taking care of the horses and fighting the wars. His judgments, of course, may be suspect, since, as with Clark's view of Charbonneau, his admiration of the Shoshoni girl would be projected as a disapproval of any other man who was interested in her.

Lewis had instructions from Jefferson regarding the Shoshoni and all Indians. Lewis wrote, "I am anxious to learn whether these people had the venerial" (Lewis, *Journals*, August 19, 1805). Part of the reason was that he worried about the health of his men, although he realized he could not keep them from having sex with Shoshoni women. He did order them, however, not to engage in sex with any woman unless her husband knew and approved of what was happening. He was unable to learn how the Shoshoni treated venereal disease and learned that many of them died from it. He concluded that both syphilis and gonorrhea existed in the Americas before Columbus arrived.[25] His reasoning was that the Shoshoni had too little contact with whites to have caught it from them. His reasoning was flawed. The question of whether syphilis and gonorrhea originated in the Americas and was brought to Europe or whether the reverse happened, is, even today, far from scientifically settled. However, there is something close to a consensus in the scientific community on several points: (1) syphilis probably originated in North or Central America and was brought back to Europe by one or more men on Columbus's first voyage to the Caribbean;(2) gonorrhea existed in Europe before Columbus; and (3) whether gonorrhea existed in the Americas before Columbus cannot be determined.

Lewis realized his logic might be faulty. He noted that the Shoshoni suffered from smallpox and he knew that Europeans had brought that across the Atlantic, so it was at least possible, he felt, they also brought venereal diseases. However, his concluding thought on the subject was that the Shoshoni were "so much detached on the other ha[n]d from all communication with the whites that I think it most probable that those disorders are original with them" (Lewis, *Journals*, August 19, 1805). He makes no reference to wondering if Sacagawea was even a little embarrassed to have to pass questions and answers back and forth on the subject. Certainly he would not have asked a white woman to discuss the same subject.

The next encounter with venereal disease came during the winter of 1805–1806 at Fort Clapsop, near the mouth of the Columbia River. As they had done among the Mandans and the Shoshoni, the men had sex with Chinook women, paying for it with trinkets and venereal disease. Lewis wrote at one point that he treated infected men "by the uce of murcury" (Lewis, *Journals*, January 27, 1806). At least a dozen members of the expedition and maybe two dozen or more received mercury from Lewis during the trip to and from the Pacific. Venereal disease was the price they paid for the liberal sexual practices of the Mandans, Shoshoni, and Chinooks. The price they paid for being cured was greater.[26]

Lewis's January 26, 1806, entry in his journal is one of many examples that emphasizes his preoccupation with venereal disease, both as the Corps physician and, perhaps, for other reasons:

> Goodrich has recovered from the Louis veneria [syphilis] which he contracted from an amorous contact with a Chinnook damsel. I cured him as I did Gibson last winter by the uce of murcury. I cannot learn that the Indians have any simples which are sovereign specifics in the cure of this disease; and indeed I doubt very much wether any of them have any means of effecting a perfect cure. When once this disorder is contracted by them it continues with them during life; but always ends in decipitude, death, or premature old age; tho' from the uce of certain simples together with their diet, they support this disorder with but little inconvenience for many years, and even enjoy a tolerable share of health ... not withstanding that this disorder dose exist among the Indians on the Columbia yet is it witnessed in but few individuals, at least the males who are always sufficiently exposed to the observations or inspection of the phisician. In my whole rout down this river I did not see more than two or three with the gonnaerea and about double that number with the pox [syphilis] [Lewis, *Journals*, January 26, 1806].

Lewis was clearly going out of his way to observe, and in some cases inspect, the sexual organs of male Indians, but he doesn't seem to have put the same effort into observing or inspecting female Indians.

His claim that he cured Privates Sills Goodrich and George Gibson is, inaccurate. The mercury he gave them would probably have covered the symptoms for a while but would not have rid their bodies of the disease. However, as Lewis notes, many of the Indians with syphilis seemed to live pretty normal lives despite the disease. The real damage done to poor Goodrich and Gibson would have come from the mercury. Almost certainly it would do serious damage to their kidneys. It's impossible to tell from the journals kept by members of the Corps which men received mercury pills, but certainly more than those specifically mentioned. We can tell that because of several references to the men in general suffering from venereal disease and to the fact that every specific time a treatment is mentioned for the disease, the treatment is a mercury pill. The mercury in the calomel pills Lewis dispensed so freely was inorganic mercury (which also comes in elemental and organic forms). How dangerous is it? A 2010 posting on the Web site of the California poison hotline[27] said, "Inorganic mercuric salts are corrosive and they damage the kidneys. Following ingestion, symptoms include nausea, vomiting blood, burns and tissue death in the throat and stomach, abdominal pain, bloody diarrhea, decreased urination and kidney failure."

What effect did the mercury pills have on the men known to have taken them? That is impossible to determine with certainty, but several of them are known to have died not long after the Corps returned as a result of unspecified illnesses. Gibson, for example, died in the first half of 1809 (the exact date is not known). Others whose deaths might have been related to mercury poisoning include Privates John Colter, Reuben Field, Thomas Proctor Howard, Francois William Labiche, Jean-Baptise Lepage, Hugh McNeal, George Shannon, John Shields, William Werner, Joseph Whitehouse, and Richard Windsor, and Sergeants John Ordway and Nathaniel Pryor. (Goodrich probably died in the mid–1820s and nothing about his death is known today: date, cause, location.)

That's 14 out of a total of 34 people who are usually listed as part of the expedition. But that 34 includes Lewis and Clark, who seem not to have engaged in sex during the two-plus years the journey lasted; Sacagawea; her husband, Toussaint Charbonneau; their child, Jean-Baptiste; and Sergeant Charles Floyd, who died, possibly of a burst appendix, in August 1804, before any members of the Corps had sexual relations with Indian women (he was the only member of the expedition to die before it returned to St. Louis in September 1806). So 14 out of 28 members of the expedition may have died early deaths as a result of being given mercury pills to treat venereal disease.[28]

The Lie

When Chief Joseph gave his famous "From where the sun now stands, I will fight no more, forever" speech in 1877, some members of his Nez Percé tribe, according to tribal tradition, pointed to one of their elderly men and said to some of the white soldiers under General Nelson Miles's command that he was the son of William Clark. The tribal tradition, that Clark had sex with a Nez Percé woman in 1806 on the expedition's return voyage, has persisted for two centuries. There is nothing in the journals or other writings of anyone in the Corps to support the story, although, of course, that does not prove it is not true. According to the tradition, Clark never learned he had the son, whose name was Tsayahha, or Daytime Smoker. Tsayahha is known to have claimed he was Clark's son, and he had blue eyes and reddish hair, suggesting his father was white. Some members of the Corps certainly had sex with some Nez Percé women in 1806, but most historians believe there isn't anything close to enough evidence to confirm Clark was one of them.[29]

Given even less credibility are two claims that Lewis fathered two children by Indian women. One of these was a man named Martin Charger, a member of the Teton Sioux tribe that the Corps encountered in what is now north-central South Dakota. This is the tribe that Clark wrote was "generally ill looking & not well made their legs & arms Small.... They Grese ... themselves with coal when they dress" (Clark, *Journals*, September 26, 1804).[30] They were not, by Lewis's standards, very good looking. (Martin Charger's great-great-grandson, Harry Charger, denounces the claim for another reason: "What they're doing is calling us bastards," he says of those who support the claim.[31]) On the Lower Brule Sioux reservation in South Dakota is an epitaph on a tombstone that reads, "Joseph Lewis DeSmet, born 1805, died 1889, son of Meriwether Lewis of the famed Lewis and Clark expedition." Again, there is no historical evidence to support the claim (a baptismal record signed by a Catholic priest that supports the claim was not created until 1872, so it's not very convincing).[32]

The claims that both Lewis and Clark fathered Indian children are significant in another way. Even if, as is likely, they are inaccurate, they help to raise questions about the sex lives of the leaders of the Corps of Discovery. None of the written documentation of the expedition (largely the journals kept by Lewis and Clark) even hints either man had sex with Indian women. Those journals contain dozens of references, direct and indirect, to most of the other members of the Corps having sex with Indian women. Did the two leaders simply think it was unbecoming to record their own sexual activities? Did they not have particularly strong sex drives? Maybe they had extremely good self-control. Lewis was 29 when the Corps started up the Missouri River, Clark four years older. There's no reason to believe either lacked a sex drive. Maybe there was something else going on.

There has long been speculation these two men may have been homosexual. The speculation is particularly strong in relation to Lewis and far less convincing with Clark.

The way the speculation usually is presented, or at least the way it is most convincingly presented, is like this: Lewis was homosexual in an era and place when acknowledging that was virtually unheard of, and dangerous. As early as 1566 a Frenchman was executed by the Spanish in Florida for engaging in one or more homosexual acts. In 1620 a law passed in Virginia called for the death penalty for anyone who had homosexual relations. Some things had changed by the time Lewis and Clark were born. By then people were imprisoned and socially chastised, not executed, for homosexuality,[33] male-male or female-female sexual relations were still unacceptable. At least in white society.

Lewis and Clark served in the Army together in the 1790s. Lewis was a lieutenant, Clark a captain. There's nothing to indicate their friendship was especially close. However, when Lewis — neighbor, secretary, and friend of Thomas Jefferson — was given the opportunity to lead the Corps of Discovery, he wrote to Clark and asked him to join as co-commander. His invitation must have been a surprise to Clark, and it was especially warm, even ardent. Lewis wrote, "Believe me there is no man on earth with whom I should feel equal pleasure" as a companion on the trip. He added, "I should be extremely happy in your company," and signed off with, "With sincere and affectionate regard, your friend and humble sevt. Meriwether Lewis." Nothing specific, but "pleasure," "happy in your company," and "affectionate" are all suggestive.[34] At least if you're looking for suggestiveness. (Excerpts from this letter are in Appendix C.)

A 2003 novel, *I Should Be Extremely Happy in Your Company* by Brian Hall, is about a homosexual Lewis attracted to a heterosexual Clark. At least partly because the attraction is not mutual, or at least not mutually sexual, Lewis at age 35 commits suicide.[35] For decades historians argued over whether Meriwether Lewis died from suicide or murder, but today nearly all Lewis and Clark experts agree it was suicide caused by depression.[36] Jefferson, when he learned Lewis killed himself, indicated a lack of surprise because he always knew Lewis to be extraordinarily depressed; Jefferson later wrote, "Lewis had from early life been subject to hypocondriac affections. It was a constitutional disposition in all the nearer branches of the family of his name, & was more immediately inherited by him from his father.... While he lived with me in Washington, I observed at times sensible depressions of mind" (see Jackson, *Letters of Lewis and Clark Expedition*, pp. 591–592.)

If depression was common in the family, as Jefferson, who knew many members of the Lewis family, believed, the Hall thesis that Lewis's suicide was caused by depression because he was homosexual seems less likely.[37] There's no way to know. The historical record simply did not provide evidence of that, one way or the other.

During the winter of 1804–1805, when the Corps stayed with the Mandans, Clark wrote in his journals about a group of men in the neighboring Hidatsa village who dressed and acted as women. They have come to be known as Berdaches.[38] Clark described them as "men dressed in Squaws Clothes" (Clark, *Journals*, December 22, 1804). They performed tasks, like gathering wood and preparing food, normally done by women. There seems to also have been a smaller group of women who dressed and acted as men, including joining hunting parties. Clark simply reported what he observed and did not pass judgment. Is that a sign he might have extended that attitude toward and been tolerant of homosexuality? Certainly if he suspected Lewis of having homosexual urges for him, he was not repulsed, or at least not repulsed enough to not join the expedition. No doubt Clark, regardless of what he suspected or thought of Lewis's sexuality, could not resist what one historian, Donald Jackson, has called "one of the most famous invitations to greatness the nation's archives can provide"[39] (Jackson, *Thomas Jefferson and the Stony Mountains*, p. 138). And if Lewis proposed or hinted at or attempted a sexual relationship with Clark during the Corps's voyage to and from the Pacific, it could not have bothered Clark too much, for in 1808 his 17-year-old wife, Julia, gave birth to the first of five children and they named him Meriwether Lewis Clark.[40]

(*Berdache*, a term first applied to these Indians by French trappers, comes from a French word that refers to the younger man in a male homosexual relationship. Many observers, however, do not consider Berdaches homosexual, but rather as a sort of third gender. Beginning in the 1990s, some observers have used the term *two-spirit* to refer to these men. A very small number of Plains Indian women who adopted male roles were also called berdaches, but almost all people to whom the term was applied were biologically males assuming female gender roles. Starting in the late 19th century, when most Indians were successfully, often against their will, restricted to reservations, Christian missionaries denounced and punished berdaches. They were forced to do work normally expected of males, and publicly scolded and subjected to corporeal punishment. By the mid–20th century Euro-centric views condemning homosexuality made being a berdache socially unacceptable on most reservations. As gays campaigned in white society for more social acceptance in the second half of the 20th century, the gains they made in white society were mirrored on the reservations, and that resulted in the acceptance of two-spirited people, or modern-day berdaches.)

Lewis, once the expedition was concluded, told friends he made attempts to court several women[41]—one he referred to as Miss A—n R—sh, and another as Miss E—B—y; there was also, according to a letter from Clark, a Miss C—and he may have proposed to Lettissia Breckenridge, whom he called "one of the most beautiful women I have ever seen" (Ambrose, p. 440). If he did, she rejected him. And he complained several times he could not find a wife. Was it a ruse, an attempt to hide his homosexuality, perhaps even from himself? He was, after all, famous, a member of a well-off family, widely considered good looking and personable. Surely such a man, if he really wanted to, could find any number of women willing to wed him. Maybe his standards were unreasonably high, as some historians have suggested. A related suggestion is that he had an idealized view of the perfect woman that no flesh-and-blood women could match. Yet, it's not hard to imagine that his own sexual urgings made the idea of having sex with a woman unacceptable, even impossible.

Clearly any speculation Lewis was homosexual is reasonable but far from conclusive. The argument that Clark was homosexual seems, by contrast, far-fetched.[42] Three strong possibilities are that Lewis had homosexual urgings but never acted on them, that Clark sensed Lewis's sexual leanings and tolerated them without ever having to repulse them, and that Lewis's confusion about who he was sexually was easy to ignore while he was busy with the tasks of leading the Corps (Jefferson, among others, believed Lewis' tendency toward depression was probably lessened during the expedition because of those tasks[43]), but that once the expedition was over and he was pursued (as opposed to being the pursuer) by many women, he was forced to confront a sexuality that he knew would be condemned and that led to his suicide.

If, as some historians (and one movie) have suggested, Clark loved Sacagawea, that may have been a defensive reaction to two difficulties he faced on his long journey. Being separated from his future wife, Julia Hancock, he may have transferred his love for her to the young Indian of about the same age. And, being confronted by a man who loved him, he may have felt he could reject any male sexual advances and not lose his friendship with, and perhaps his respect for, that man by affecting a love interest in the only female on the expedition.

Jefferson's interest in ethnology, including his interests in the sex lives of Indians, contributed to his decision to send Meriwether Lewis to explore what is today the American West. Lewis expected the men who accompanied him to contract venereal disease through sex with Indian women and he prepared for that by taking a large supply of mercury pills, which contributed to the early deaths of nearly half the men making the trip. Lewis invited William Clark to join the expedition because of his homosexual interest in him, and Clark developed, or contrived, a love interest in Sacagawea to help ward off any potential advances by Lewis. When the expedition was completed, Lewis, no longer having the work of the trip to occupy him, had to confront his homosexuality, and now living in a society unaccepting of his sexual leanings, was driven deeper and deeper into depression, leading finally to suicide. Sex, thus, dominated the first important and successful American exploration of the West.

2

Mountain Men
Escaping to Sex

After Lewis and Clark, a four-way competition for control of the West continued for four decades. Americans sought to expand ever westward, as far as they could go. The Spanish, and later the Mexicans, tried vainly to control what would become the U.S. Southwest. The British sought control of the Northwest, today's Oregon and Washington. Indian nations already in the West tried to resist all of them. Not until the 1840s would the United States establish actual towns and cities in the West, assuring the area would become American. In the meantime the United States sent military explorers to the West, and a group of rugged men chose to live there free of polite social restraints. Many of these men, explorers and mountain men, had in common an inability to interact with women in a way acceptable to Eastern society.[1]

The Bon Vivant Mountain Man

John C. Frémont was talented at seducing women, something he inherited from his father, and it nearly made him president of the United States. His mother, Anne, was married at her parents' insistence at age 17 to a man 45 years her senior, John Pryor. Pryor was from a well-to-do Richmond, Virginia, family, but he was short, fat, and had the gout. Young Anne found him physically repulsive. Then a man who said his name was Charles Fremon showed up claiming to be a member of French royalty and who said he had been imprisoned by the British in the Caribbean for several years on unspecified charges. Fremon taught French and dancing and painted frescoes. Anne swooned. The fact Fremon lived with a woman he was not married to just made him more romantically interesting. Anne was prettier than the other woman, so Fremon, without difficulty, seduced her. Pryor found out about the seduction and threatened to kill her.

That gave her the excuse she wanted, and the next morning she fled with Fremon. In less than a year she gave birth to the first of three children she would have with him, a boy they named John Charles. The father, historians later learned, although Anne evidently never knew this, was actually from Quebec; his name was Louis-René Frémont. He had run for some elective office in Quebec City, lost, and sailed for Saint-Domingue (now the Dominican Republic), where he had a rich aunt. He was accustomed to living off women. Why not an aunt? He was, instead, imprisoned by the British in the Caribbean, mostly because he was on a French ship that was captured by a British frigate. He either escaped or was given his freedom and made his way to the United States. When his oldest son was five, Fremon disappeared from the pages of history. Most historians think he died of some disease.

When John Charles was born on January 21, 1813, in Savannah, Georgia, his mother and father were not married. They may never have married. John Charles Frémont, who at some point added the "t" that had originally been part of his father's name, was born a bastard at a time being one could be a serious social handicap. But it didn't prevent him, when he grew older, from excelling at the one thing his father excelled at, even exceeding his father's accomplishments: seducing beautiful women.[2]

Frémont's mother moved him and his younger brother and sister around the South, but they ended up in Charleston, South Carolina, where they lived for 13 years. He was admitted, at 16, to the College of Charleston, but had little interest in attending class. His primary interest was a Creole girl named Cecilia, and he spent so much time with her, rather than his studies, that the college expelled him. He then met Joel Poinsett,[3] who had been the first American ambassador to Mexico (Poinsett brought a bright red flower back to the U.S. with him, and it was named after him, the poinsetta) and who helped young Frémont secure a series of interesting jobs, one as a teacher of mathematics on a Navy ship that visited, among other places, Buenos Aries, where had a brief affair with the daughter of the American ambassador to Argentina, Miss Palmer. After that voyage, Poinsett helped him get a job on a surveying expedition in the mountains of South Carolina and North Carolina. One report said he seduced, in Greenville, South Carolina, "a very pretty girl, in moderate circumstances" and "He was engaged to her, and deserted her without cause" (Roberts, *A Newer World*, p. 115).

Poinsett then became secretary of war in the administration of President Martin Van Buren and arranged for Frémont to become a second lieutenant in the Topographical Corps when he was 25. In that position he helped map the upper parts of the Mississippi and Missouri Rivers. Along the way, Frémont had several more affairs with attractive women, both married and unmarried. He was a handsome man, fluent in English and French, and charming. He had little difficulty finding women who were attracted to him. He never spoke or wrote about these relationships, but companions often did, at least briefly. In 1840, when he was 27, Poinsett introduced him to Thomas Hart Benton, senator from Missouri and among the dozen most powerful men in the country. He met Benton's 15-year-old daughter, Jessie, and that almost destroyed his career. Senator Benton was not a man to cross. But, also, Jessie was not a young woman to simply capitulate to a father's wishes.

Frémont first saw Jessie at a concert at Miss English's Female Seminary in Georgetown, the school she attended. A half century later Frémont wrote of that first sighting, "She made the effect that a rose of rare color or a beautiful picture would have done" (Roberts, *A Newer World*, p. 118). No doubt he saw another potential seduction. And Jessie was willing. She was so devoted to her father that she wanted to drop out of school and stay home with him, but when he insisted she remain at Miss English's Seminary, she simply transferred her fidelity to another man, Frémont.

Senator Benton saw in Frémont something of himself, an ambitious man who knew how to use people, and he didn't like what he saw.[4] He made Jessie promise not to marry until she was at least 17. He and his wife hoped young Jessie would find a more suitable suitor. Benton then talked Secretary of War Poinsett into sending Frémont to survey the Des Moines River. That would keep him away from Jessie for more than a month. As much as Senator Benton disliked Frémont, part of Frémont's attraction to Jessie was the help the powerful politician could offer to his career. Frémont was as interested in conquering fame and success as he was in seducing women.

Knowing he would never have Benton's approval to marry his daughter, he and Jessie eloped. They were married in October 1841 by a Catholic priest in Washington.[5] The elopement was the source of more gossip than any other event in Washington for months. When the couple met with Senator Benton, whose nickname in the Senate was "the Thunderer" because of his booming voice, he screamed at Frémont, "Get out of the house and never cross my door again. Jessie shall stay here" (Roberts, *A Newer World*, p. 121). Frémont froze. But not Jessie. She took her husband by the arm, looked him in the face, and quoted, for her father to hear, the Book of Ruth: "Whither thou goest, I will go, and where thou lodgest, I will lodge. Thy people shall be my people, and thy God my God" (Roberts, *A Newer World*, p. 121).

Jessie had a flair for the dramatic. Perhaps she learned that from her ardent reading of the novels of Sir Walter Scott. Or maybe because she had that flair she was attracted to Scott's writing. Whatever the connection, she learned from Scott and what she learned would later be of immense benefit to her husband.[6]

Faced with a daughter who was as obstinate as him, the senator quickly changed his attitude. He would help his son-in-law's career. He would make this young Frémont worthy of his daughter. And, at the same time, he would send the womanizing scoundrel on a long trip. He arranged for the young lieutenant to head a survey of part of the Oregon Trail, and Frémont soon found himself on a steamboat headed up the Missouri River. This was an assignment Frémont privately felt was beyond his capabilities. He was a talented enough surveyor and had been on extended trips before, but he realized he was entering a part of the country few white men had ventured into. He was always conscious of how others would see him. He knew he lacked the instinct to make the quick judgments a dangerous frontier would require.

One evening as he leaned on the railing of the steamboat, he entered into a conversation with a man about the same age, several inches shorter, with much broader shoulders, a man who also seemed depressed. The man was out of work, didn't know where he was going in life. He wasn't even quite certain why he had booked passage on the steamboat. His immediate goal, like his life plans, were undefined. Frémont, who usually found a way to turn any conversation so it focused on him, told the stranger he was going upriver to lead a survey expedition and he wished he knew more about the places he was headed, wished he had more of the skills needed for traveling on the frontier. Frémont did not often admit to shortcomings, but this was just a stranger he was talking to, an uneducated ne'er-do-well. The stranger said that he, in fact, knew the frontier well, that he was a good hunter and tracker and spoke a bunch of Indian languages. He said, "I can guide you to any point you would wish to go" (Roberts, *A Newer World*, p. 102). Frémont was skeptical. The stranger had told him his name, but Frémont hadn't paid close enough attention to recall it, so he asked the man to repeat it and said he would check up on him, see if what he said was true. The man said, "Kit Carson."

Joel Poinsett. Jessie Benton. Now Kit Carson. When it came to chance meetings that make careers, no man in American history was as lucky as John Charles Frémont.[7]

Carson, too, would encounter problems with women, but of a very different kind. Carson did lead Frémont and his men on the trek into Wyoming, and when Frémont returned to the East he tried to translate his notes into a book-length manuscript, but his writing was awkward to the point of being almost unreadable. Jessie rewrote his manuscript. Her writing consisted of long, flowing sentences, easy to grasp metaphors and similes, a sense of anticipation to propel the reader forward, all the elements she had learned from her careful and devoted reading of Sir Walter Scott. The federal government printed a thousand copies of her book, with her husband listed as author. The public bought all 1,000 copies within days. There was reprint after reprint.[8] Among its many fans was Henry Wadsworth Longfellow, who praised both the style and content "What a wild life, and what a fresh kind of existence!" America's most famous poet wrote[9] (Roberts, *A Newer World*, p. 126). The surveying trip was ordinary, but the report was a best seller. Far more than the modest adventure, it was the book written mostly by Jessie that gave Frémont, at age 30, his first national celebrity. The man had, indeed, married well.

There would be more trips, most guided by Carson, more reports, all written primarily by Jessie, and when Frémont happened to be in California when the Mexican War broke out, he saw another opportunity for fame. Navy Commodore Richard Stockton appointed Frémont governor of the newly captured California, but Army General Stephen Kearney was in charge of the military on the West Coast, and when he ordered Frémont to report to him and Frémont didn't, the famed explorer was in serious trouble.

By now, Frémont was a lieutenant colonel, the result of a series of promotions he owed more to his fame and his powerful father-in-law than to any particular military talent. He was court-martialed and convicted of mutiny and insubordination, but President James Polk, who said he found Frémont's behavior appalling, dismissed the sentence. Polk, a popular president, was not about to lessen his popularity by allowing the popular Frémont to be punished. The episode did nothing to damage Frémont's reputation among his millions of fans.

When the Republican Party was formed and ready to run its first candidate for president in 1856, Frémont — outspoken against slavery, in favor of better treatment for Indians, a smooth speaker, and more famous than anyone else the new party could find who was willing to run — was their choice. But the Republicans were not yet a true national party, and they could not manage to get Frémont's name on the ballots in eleven Southern states. Despite that, Frémont won 33 percent of the popular vote to the Democrats' James Buchanan's 45 percent. Ex-president Millard Fillmore, running as a Whig, won eight percent. A better organized and a truly national Republican Party would have made the outcome close.

Despite all his fame and despite the contributions Jessie made to her husband's successes, Frémont continued to be a womanizer. During the 50 days he spent as Commodore Stockton's appointee as governor of the newly captured California, with Jessie living in the East, he kept what some people called a harem of Mexican women. Years later he had a mistress, Margaret Corbett, in Philadelphia, and they traveled around Europe together. He later had another mistress in New York City, and one of Jessie's friends found out about it and told her. But Jessie either did not believe the rumors or chose to ignore them. She remained devoted to her womanizing husband until his death from a burst appendix in a New York City boarding house in 1890.

Jessie devoted the remaining 12 years of her life to writing article after article, giving speech after speech, about what a great man her husband had been.

Frémont was a man of little talent but great ambition, both in seeking fame and women to seduce. His excessive womanizing led him to the beautiful Jessie Benton and that led her powerful father, Senator Thomas Hart Benton, to send him to explore the West, and in that way Frémont's sex drive contributed to making America a continental country.

The Little Mountain Man

Kit Carson, a famous mountain man, was a misfit.[10] He was born in Kentucky in 1809, the son of a father who traveled from Pennsylvania to North Carolina to Kentucky with Daniel Boone. At age one and a half, Kit moved with his parents to Missouri, and at 15 was apprenticed to a saddler. Decades later he recalled the saddler, David Workman, as a kind man but the work as extraordinarily boring. So he ran away to the Rocky Mountains. Workman placed a notice in a newspaper that said in part, "All persons are notified not to harbor, support or assist said boy under the penalty of law. One cent reward will be given to any person who will bring back the said boy" (Roberts, *A Newer World*, p. 56). One cent? Even by 1826 standards this was so little that every reader of the notice must have realized Workman was hoping the boy would not be caught. Not that he didn't like young Kit. Rather he understood the boy did not fit in a town like Boon's Lick, Missouri. Too much civilization.

Carson went to New Mexico. Five years earlier, any American going to New Mexico risked death at the hands of the Spanish, whose dominant policy for their northern frontier was to make certain the Americans didn't steal it from them.[11] But in 1821, Mexico won its independence, and the Mexicans were anxious to encourage trade. Carson settled in Taos, which, despite the lifetime of wandering that lay ahead of him, would be his home, the place to which he always returned, the place where he chose to be buried.

A move to the West early in life is something Carson had in common with most other mountain men. What he did not have in common was his physical appearance. Although he came from a family of large men, many of them over six feet tall and more than 200 pounds, Carson was 5'6" and weighed about 135. And, after he achieved fame, a status that would assure that those who met him would remember him, even write about him, he had three qualities that stood out. His surprising smallness. His extreme shyness. And what surprised people most, his movements sometimes looked like those of a girl.

2. Mountain Men

Carson spent years traveling around the West with other mountain men, mostly trapping beavers and hunting buffalo. He learned to go days in the desert without water, to track animals, to remember the details of landscapes as accurately as if he wrote them down. He never did learn to write beyond an ability to sign his name, and he never learned to read. But he learned to speak Spanish, French, Navajo, Cheyenne, and several other Indian languages. He also learned to kill Indians. He seems to have killed dozens, from half a dozen or more different tribes, over the years.

Unlike some other mountain men, he never made Indian hunting a sport, but he several times joined in ambushes. When a group of Apaches told the white mountain men to stop hunting on their lands, the Apaches were ambushed and a dozen or more of them killed. When a wagon train of white men were found killed by Indians, the next group of Indians the mountain men found were killed. Whether they were the ones who did the first killing was unimportant. Later in life, Carson came to regret these and other killings, but as a young man, he was prone to go along with whatever his comrades did.

Carson achieved his first flirtation with legend when he attended one of the famed mountain men rendezvous, this one in 1835 in southwestern Wyoming.[12] About 200 mountain men attended for more than two weeks of trading, heavy drinking, and competitions in shooting, hatchet throwing, and other sports. Indians also often attended, and beginning in 1834 Christian missionaries showed up, although they seldom converted anyone. This was Carson's second rendezvous, and he was surprised when no one seemed willing to stand up to a large bullying French trapper, whose name may have been Chouinard. The Frenchman particularly delighted in insulting Americans.

Carson's ire was really aroused when Chouinard (or whatever his name was) made some obscene remarks to a pretty Arapaho girl named Waanibe, which is usually translated as Singing Wind. Carson told Chouinard, who was at least half a foot taller and outweighed Carson by at least 50 pounds, to leave the girl alone and to stop saying nasty things about Americans. Chouinard mounted his horse and, holding his rifle ominously, dared Carson to back up his words. Carson mounted his own horse, drew a pistol, approached Chouinard so closely their horses touched, and made it clear he was not a man to back down. From anyone. A few more words were spoken, both men fired their weapons, Carson felt a bullet whiz by his head, and Chouinard was knocked from his horse by the force of the bullet that slammed into his arm. Chouinard then backed down from any further fighting. Waanibe was wooed by the gallant defense of her honor. Or at least that is one version of the story that has passed down to us through the always unreliable history of the mountain men. In any case, Carson and Waanibe did marry.

A year later, maybe two, Waanibe gave birth to a baby girl, Adeline. A year after that a second child was born to Waanibe and Kit, a daughter whose name has escaped the annals of history. It may have been a particularly difficult delivery. Shortly after the birth, evidently suffering from puerperal fever, an ailment common in the 19th century among women who recently delivered a baby, Waanibe died.[13] Carson was away on a trading trip when she died. Carson seldom talked about personal matters, even to his closest friends. The only comment he is known to have made to anyone about Waanibe was, "She was a good wife to me. I never came in from hunting that she did not have the warm water ready for my feet" (Simmons, p. 23).

At some point, Carson had a very brief affair, probably the only one in his life that did not result in marriage, with a woman named Antonia Luna, in Taos. He was not the first famous mountain man she shared a bed with. Jim Beckwourth, often referred to as the best known of the black mountain men (actually he was one-quarter black), had earlier been her lover.[14] Luna was not known for being tactful, and when she told Carson that Beckwourth was better at sex, Carson, his feelings hurt, ended the relationship. (Some biographers have suggested Carson was a bigot and resented in particular the unfavorable comparison to a black man, but that is just speculation; Luna is known to have had a long series of lovers and Carson's reaction probably had more to do with prudishness than bigotry.)

There is no recorded comment about his second Indian wife, and if there was it certainly wouldn't have been positive. Carson, despite his lack of experience in formal society, intuitively understood the 19th century code of chivalry that dictated what a man could say about a woman. It must always be neutral or kind. If a woman, particularly a wife, had anything negative in her appearance or intellect or personality, no polite man would ever comment upon it.

(Another aspect of his code of chivalry borders on the brutal. The Sand Creek Massacre of November 29, 1864, in which the Colorado militia under Colonel John Chivington attacked a peaceful village of Southern Cheyenne and Arapahos in southeastern Colorado, killing more than 200, maybe more than 300 Indians, sickened Carson because more than half of the dead were women and children. When Carson heard about the massacre he said, "I tell ye what. I don't like a hostile Redskin any better than you du. And when they are hostile, I've fit em, fout em, as hard as any man. But I never yit drew a bead on a squaw or papoose, and I loathe and hate the man who would. Taint nateral for brave men to kill little women and little children" [Roberts, *A Newer World*, pp. 282–283]. That is, it's all right to kill Indians as long as it's only grown men who are getting killed.)

After Waanibe's death, Carson moved to Bent's Fort in central Colorado with his two daughters.¹⁵ There he met and married a Cheyenne girl named Making Out Road. Historians disagree on the meaning of her name. It might refer to an ability to follow tracks or an ability to lay out a path. One of her daughters said, however, it referred to a tendency to "lay down the law" (Simmons, pp. 35–36). If so, that matched her personality. Where Waanibe was gentle and accommodating, Making Out Road was stern and demanding.¹⁶ There is no known photograph of her (or of Waanibe), but many men referred to her as beautiful, and that may explain Carson's attraction. She did not like that he had children and that he made weeks-long, sometimes months-long hunting and trapping trips away from their home. Nor did she like any expectation he had that she should perform domestic chores. Carson's lone known comment about Waanibe was contrasted by the fact that Making Out Road never had warm water or anything else ready upon his return.

During one of his trading expeditions back to Taos, he met Maria Josefa Jaramillo, probably 14 years old at the time, and was attracted to her gentle nature and youthful prettiness. He must have known his marriage to Making Out Road was a mistake and would not last. Josefa was not too young for courting by the standards of early 19th century Taos society. She was from a well-to-do Spanish family in a town where Spaniards and Americans often intermarried. But Carson did not act on his attraction to Josefa as long as he was married to Making Out Road. The marriage lasted less than a year. The exact dates of their marriage and divorce are unknown. Among the Cheyenne at the time, no ceremony accompanied a marriage. A couple simply announced they were married and lived together in a teepee. And, although women were clearly treated as servants in a typical Cheyenne marriage, it was the wife, not the husband, who could initiate divorce. That was done by waiting until the husband was away and placing all his belongings outside the teepee. The other men in the village would hang around to make certain the husband never again entered the teepee. That's what happened to Carson. Making Out Road also put Adeline and Carson's other daughter outside the teepee.

Carson understood the rules. He left the village, taking his daughters with him. Making Out Road gave birth to a child who died a month later, but it's unclear if that happened before or after the divorce. Late in life Carson was interviewed many times because of his fame, and not one time is he known to have made any reference to Making Out Road. Details of his brief, unhappy marriage come entirely from other sources. It's likely Josefa, who would become his third wife, never knew he was once married to a Cheyenne woman.

Once back in Taos, Carson decided his four-year-old daughter, Adeline, would be better educated in Missouri, so he took her to the home of one of his sisters, who agreed to see to her education. Either while he was on this trip or just before he left, or perhaps just after he returned, his other daughter, the infant whose name is today unknown, was being cared for by a woman who was boiling soap and the child accidentally fell into the cauldron and was boiled to death. As with so much else in Carson's life, his reaction to the tragedy went unrecorded.

Far more is known about Josefa than about Waanibe or Making Out Road, partly because she and Carson were married so much longer, a quarter of a century. They both died in 1868, Carson just one month after his third wife. She was dignified in appearance and habit, a member of one of the leading families in Taos. From the beginning the marriage was a happy one and never deviated from that state. This despite the fact that she was 14 on her wedding day and he was 18 years older. The most famous description of her comes from a work of fiction but is widely considered accurate. Willa Cather wrote in *Death Comes for the Archbishop*,

> The Bishop went out of his way to make a call at Kit Carson's ranch house. Carson, he knew, was away buying sheep, but Father Latour wished to see the Senora Carson.... The Senora received him with that quiet but unabashed hospitality which is a common grace in Mexican households. She was a tall woman, slender, with drooping shoulders and lustrous black eyes and hair. Though she could not read, both her face and conversation were intelligent. To the Bishop's thinking, she was handsome; her countenance showed that discipline of life which he admired. She had a cheerful disposition, too, and a pleasant sense of humour. It was possible to talk confidentially to her [pp. 153–154].[17]

That Carson's marriage to Josefa was happy is revealing. During their two and half decades together he would leave her in Taos and travel thousands of miles as Frémont's guide. He would see two oceans, meet the most powerful men in Washington, and fight in the Mexican War. But he always returned to Taos. Always returned to Josefa. Like Waanibe, she always welcomed his return. Unlike Making Out Road, she never scolded or disagreed with him on anything important. And he always treated her reverentially.

On one of his trips to Washington he obediently sat and listened while Jessie Frémont read aloud long passages from the novels of Sir Walter Scott. He may have suffered from boredom but remained polite enough to not reveal it. In any event, he was always obedient to the social wishes of women, and Jessie Frémont was one of the few people to whom he was willing to reveal any of his inner emotions. And she was willing to write about them. Among the most revealing comments he made to her was his fear that being what he called a squaw man, that is a white man who had been married to an Indian woman (he probably never told Jessie about Making Out Road), would make him unacceptable in polite society.

Carson — like so many of the mountain men, men of extraordinary courage, men willing to face hostile Indians, grizzly bears, harsh winters, men who fought in wars and against each other, rugged, tough, strong men — suffered from a sense of social inferiority. They went west partly to seek adventure and fortune and partly to revel in a craggy freedom not available in the East. Some Indian cultures were far more accepting of a woman marrying a white man than white culture was of a white man marrying an Indian woman. In their sexual relations, as in so much else, these men felt more comfortable in the West than they did in the East.

Mountain Men and Their Wives

The era of the mountain man lasted less than 20 years, beginning in the early 1820s and ending in the late 1830s.[18] The total number of men who can accurately be called mountain men was about 1,000. Although many of them by the nature of their personalities were loners reluctant to share their deepest feelings, and some of them possessed little talent for conversation, they did not work alone, almost always hunting and trapping in groups of 30 or more. Working in solitude would have been suicide. The Blackfeet Indians in the Northern Rockies in particular fought an unrelenting war against the mountain men. The Blackfeet, like the mountain men, trapped beaver for sale and shipment to the East and then to Europe. They did not want the competition and they killed dozens of mountain men. In fact, mountain men in the Northern Rockies would have become an extinct species if the Blackfeet were not themselves nearly exterminated by a smallpox epidemic.

Fewer than half of the mountain men were Americans. The largest group, by far, were French Canadians. Dozens were Indians from the East, particularly Iroquois from New York, and some Delaware from the mid–Atlantic states. A smaller group, probably less than a dozen, were free blacks, some of whom had escaped from Southern plantations.

Many mountain men married Indian women. Any number for this group would be merely a guess, because not only were records not kept, but what was considered a marriage in many of the Indian cultures in and near the Rockies seemed, by white standards, mere cohabitation. Wedding ceremonies were rare. Sometimes the husband-to-be paid a dowry to the father of the bride, and if the father accepted, that amounted to a marriage license. Kit Carson did not pay a dowry for either Waanibe or Making Out Road. However, Making Out Road's third husband, also a white man, Charles Rath, did.[19] A measure of how Cheyenne society viewed marriage to whites, however, is revealed by an incident that occurred in 1863, when Rath and Making Out Road were operating a trading post in Kansas. A group of Cheyenne warriors showed up one day and told them whites and the Cheyenne were about to go to war. They took Making Out Road with them and told Rath to leave the area, which, fearing for his life, he did. Just as many whites looked down on a white man who married an Indian woman, many Indians, both men and women, looked down on an Indian woman who would lower herself by marrying a white man.

Just as in white society, Indian reaction to interracial marriage varied widely, both by tribe and by individual. The Shoshoni man to whom Sacagawea had been promised rejected her when she returned with Lewis and Clark to her native village not because she had married a white man but because she had a child by any other man. While the Mandan and Clapsop Indian men did not mind sharing their women, some Indian women were killed by relatives for having sexual relations with mountain men. Still, some Indian women preferred white husbands because polygamy was common in many plains and mountain tribes, but rare, until the Mormons arrived in the 1840s, among whites. Also, although many of the white men could be violent with a woman, other white men usually condemned such behavior, although they rarely punished it, while most Indian cultures allowed a husband to do whatever he wanted with a wife. A typical punishment for infidelity by a married Indian woman in the West was for the husband to cut off the tip of her nose. The idea was that her transgression would be visible to everyone, like Hester Prynne's scarlet A.

While generalizations about the Indian women who married mountain men would be unfair and misleading, one generalization about the relationships mountain men had with women is clearly justified: these were men who, at least in their early manhood, avoided lasting ties with women. Maybe the call of adventure, maybe discomfort in even the most rudimentary civilization, maybe one of a thousand things drove these men to become the first long-term resident Americans in the West, but a careful observer cannot help but notice that nearly every one of them had relationships with women that, by the standards of Eastern society, seem at least mildly unconventional. None of them were born in the West. They all went there as young men. And in doing so, they willingly left Eastern society and everything that entails, including the possibility of marriage, settling down, raising children, being conventional members of a community. There is no evidence these men were homosexuals. Quite the contrary, nearly all of them are known to have had sexual relations with women. It was not sex they were avoiding. It was the conventionality of marriage in a white community. Consider some examples.

John Colter was the first mountain man.[20] He was, in fact, a mountain man a decade before the era of the mountain man began. He was a member of the Corps of Discovery, a private who served capably under Lewis and

2. Mountain Men 43

Clark, but on the return trip from the Pacific, the Corps met two Easterners, Forest Hancock and Joseph Dixon, who were headed west to do some trapping. Colter requested, and was granted, an early discharge from the Army so he could join them. The three men canoed up the Missouri and camped the winter of 1806–07 in what is now northwestern Wyoming. That bitter winter was too much for Hancock and Dixon and the following spring they returned to St. Louis, but Colter declined to join them. He had a canoe full of beaver pelts, had not seen anyone in his family for three years, and was overcome with loneliness, so a few months later he too headed down river.

Along the way he met a group of 42 men, including several other veterans of the Corps of Discovery, heading upriver. The group was headed by Manuel Lisa, and they were the first large scale trapping company to enter the West. Colter joined them. His loneliness, clearly, was not for female company. An additional three and a half years passed before Colter would leave the West. In 1807, Lisa sent Colter on a mission to encourage Indian tribes to bring beaver pelts to a fort Lisa established where the Bighorn and Yellowstone Rivers meet, east of present-day Billings, Montana. As he traveled he became the first white man to see the Grand Tetons and the geyser fields of Wyoming shooting streams of water a hundred feet or more into the air. (Colter didn't name the Grand Tetons. That honor goes to French trappers, years later, who thought the mountains look like large breasts. A direct translation captures the mild vulgarity the trappers intended: big tits.)

When Colter returned to Lisa's fort and told everyone there what he had seen, none of the men believed such a thing as water shooting into the air existed. Traveling with Lewis and Clark and being the first man to see Old Faithful would establish any man's fame, but Colter was to experience the first incident that would earn mountain men their reputation for extraordinary toughness. That came in 1808 as Colter and another of Lisa's men, John Potts, were visiting a village of Crow Indians in what is now Montana and the village was attacked by a war party of Blackfeet. Colter helped his Crow hosts defend themselves and killed at least one Blackfeet warrior.

Sometime later, after Colter and Potts left the Crow village, they unexpectedly found themselves surrounded by Blackfeet. Potts was killed, Colter captured. The Blackfeet stripped him naked and indicated with hand gestures he should walk away. They made what were clearly insulting remarks, although Colter could not understand the language. When he was about 400 yards away several dozen warriors began running after him. He had no clothes, no shoes, no weapon. For the Blackfeet, this was great sport. Colter ran. And ran and ran and ran. Arrows rushed past his naked body. His feet bled. Colter, a strong, athletic man propelled by fear, hardly dared turn to look back, but when he did he saw that after perhaps two miles of running, he had left most of the warriors behind, exhausted and unable to keep up with the white man. Colter ran so hard that blood spurted from his nose, coating his chest in red.

Finally he had outrun all but one warrior, a strong, young brave intent on capturing his prey. Colter suddenly stopped, turned around and poised to battle the Indian. The surprised warrior, every bit as exhausted as Colter, tried to stop and throw his spear at the same time, and instead fell, his spear still in his hand. The spear snapped in two. Colter charged at the warrior, grabbed the spear and plunged the pointed end into the young man. Colter then continued running, coming finally to a river, jumped in, floated downstream, being too tired to swim, and hid beneath a logjam as Blackfeet warriors looked for him. When they gave up, and he was a little rested, he swam several miles further downstream. More than a week and more than 150 miles of walking were needed before he reached Lisa's fort and safety.

With that feat Colter wrote the first story in the mythology of the mountain man. But even for a man as tough as Colter, life in the West in the early 19th century could wear one down. In 1810 he was with a group of trappers who were attacked by a much larger group of Blackfeet. Five of the whites in the party were killed and as the battle raged Colter prayed, promising that if his life were spared he would leave the West and return to civilization. He survived and reached Lisa's fort, and the day after that he got in a canoe alone. He paddled nearly 2,000 miles to St. Louis. He married a woman named Nancy Hooker and they lived together in poverty until he died three years later. She couldn't afford a coffin or funeral, so she left his body in their small cabin and went to live with her family in Illinois. For Colter, marrying was the same thing as leaving the West.

Other mountain men would contribute to the reputation the breed enjoyed for incredible toughness. In 1823 near the Black Hills, in what is now western South Dakota, a 16-man hunting and trapping party led by Jedediah Smith[21] encountered a huge grizzly bear. The bear attacked Smith at the head of the caravan of men and pack horses, lifted him in the air, threw him to the ground, and ripped its claws through his scalp. Smith, incredibly, survived. Three or four or five ribs were broken and his scalp and an ear hung loose on one side of his head, which bled heavily. Smith instructed one of the other men, Jim Clyman, to use a needle and thread to sew his scalp into place. Then Smith told him to sew his ear back on, too. Clyman did the job "nice as I could" (Clyman, p. 189), he later said. Although Smith carried noticeable scars the rest of his life, his scalp and ear were saved. Clyman later wrote, "This gave us a lisson on the character of the grissly Baare which we did not forget" (Clyman, p. 190). Or the character of the mountain man, either.

But nothing in the annals of the mountain man — not even the toughness of John Colter fleeing the Blackfeet or Jedediah Smith having his scalp sewn on after the grizzly bear ripped it off—compares to what Hugh Glass did in 1823 in what is now north-central South Dakota.[22] Glass was walking apart from the hunting outfit he had hired on with when he came upon a female grizzly with cubs. In defense of her cubs she attacked Glass, who fired a shot at her, hitting her squarely, but still she came at him. Glass started to climb a tree, but the bear grabbed him, tossed him angrily to the ground, and lashed at him with her sharp claws. Then the bear dropped from its bullet wound, dead, right on top of the badly bleeding Glass. One of Glass's legs, one arm, his back, face, and the top of his head were bleeding, covered with elongated cuts from the grizzly's claws. Other members of the hunting party came running when they heard the shot, and when they found Glass, the dead bear on top of him, he was, one of them later explained, "tore nearly to peases" (Utley, p. 57).

Although they were certain he would die, other members of the party cleaned Glass as best they could, bandaged him here and there, and waited. Waited for him to die. Captain Andrew Henry, leader of the party, decided the next morning if they waited any longer they would be inviting an attack from Arikaras. The Indians had made it clear they did not want white men in their lands. So a litter was constructed and Glass placed on it, and the party set out. For two or three or four days they proceeded that way, but the litter slowed down the company. Henry, convinced Glass would soon die, decided he had no right to risk the lives of the other men in the outfit. He offered money to anyone who would volunteer to wait with Glass until he expired. They could later catch up with the rest of the outfit. Two men volunteered, John S. Fitzgerald and Jim Bridger, who was 19 years old.

A day or two after Henry reached safety in his fort at Three Forks (where the Jefferson, Madison, and Gallatin rivers meet to form the Missouri), Fitzgerald and young Bridger showed up. They carried Glass's rifle and a few of his other possessions. They reported Glass had died shortly after the main party left and that they buried him. It was a lie. When they left him, Glass was still alive, although Fitzgerald and Bridger were certain he would die. They did not want to die, too, so they said goodbye—Bridger apologized to Glass—and left.

Glass could not stand. But he could crawl. He crawled and crawled and crawled. He ate berries. He killed a rattlesnake with a rock and ate the snake. He continued to crawl. And crawled some more. For weeks. Maybe two weeks. Maybe three or four or more. He drank water from the Grand River. At some point he had regained enough strength so he could walk, at first stumbling and barely able to remain upright. Then with more steadiness. Finally, six weeks after Fitzgerald and Bridger in fear for their own lives had abandoned him, he reached Fort Kiowa. He had crawled and stumbled for almost 200 miles. But he was alive. And he burned with vengeance.

He stayed a while at Fort Kiowa to regain his full strength. Then he went looking for Fitzgerald and Bridger. Captain Henry meanwhile moved the location of his fort, but Glass had no trouble finding it. When he entered the new fort, everyone in Henry's outfit was startled. Fitzgerald and Bridger told them Glass had died and they had buried him, but now Glass stood before them. And he wanted to see Fitzgerald and Bridger. Fitzgerald had left. Chances are the two men passed each other as they traveled along the Missouri River in opposite directions. Glass vowed he would find him later. For now he confronted the teenaged Bridger. What was said when the man and boy stood face to face has not been recorded. The other men in the fort were evidently prepared to allow Glass to kill Bridger. This was not a land where grievances went unpunished. Bridger might have begged. Maybe he said nothing. Whatever transpired, however, kept him alive. Maybe the apology the boy had uttered just before leaving Glass to die made the difference. Bridger, who would become, along with Kit Carson, one of the two most famous of the mountain men and who was often interviewed in later years, never mentioned anything about Hugh Glass. What is known is that the older man thought Bridger was too young. It was probably Bridger's youth that saved his life.

Glass would not be so forgiving with Fitzgerald. He set out after him. Sometime during the following Spring, Glass found Fitzgerald. A confrontation took place at Fort Atkinson on the Missouri River (near modern day Council Bluffs, Iowa). But by then Fitzgerald had joined the United States Army. The fort's commander, Colonel Henry Leavenworth, sympathized with Glass, but he would not allow him to kill one of his soldiers. Glass left, his vengeance never fulfilled.

(The 1971 movie, *Man in the Wilderness*, directed by Richard Sarafian and starring Richard Harris and John Huston, is loosely based on Hugh Glass's abandonment. In the movie, Glass's character, played by Harris, is called Zachary Bass.)

Bridger would later become, along with Kit Carson, an important mountain man in helping to make the West American.[23] What he had in common with Carson is revealing. Bridger was born in 1804 in Richmond, Virginia, and when he was a boy his family moved, like Carson's, to Missouri, where at age 14 he was apprenticed to a blacksmith. Unlike Carson, he completed his four-year apprenticeship and then headed west as part of a 100-man beaver trapping company. He differed in size; he was an inch or two over six feet tall. And no one ever reported that he exhibited any of the girl-like mannerisms of Carson. Like Carson he had an extraordinary mind for both languages and topographical details. He learned Spanish and four or five Indian languages, and his memory of the lands he visited — thousands of square miles — was both legendary and encyclopedic, although he never learned to read or write. He also had extraordinary eyesight. Once, when in his 60s and serving as a guide for the U.S. Army, he said he could see smoke about 50 miles away. He said that was likely to be the location of an Indian village. A young Army officer looked through his spyglass but couldn't see smoke. Two days later, traveling in the direction Bridger had seen the smoke, the soldiers came upon an Indian village. The others could not see the smoke until they were only two or three miles away.

Bridger earlier served as a guide or leader for several beaver-trapping expeditions, for several military explorations, for a lavish hunting trip by a rich Englishman, and for groups of settlers moving to the West. He was the chief Army scout during the 1857–58 war between the United States and the Mormons under Brigham Young. Young, in fact, was his principal antagonist, at one point sending a posse to arrest him at his outpost, Fort Bridger, in what is now southwestern Wyoming. Bridger, who believed Young was intent on seeing him killed, escaped. Before that incident, one observer noted that Fort Bridger consisted largely of two or three shabby buildings and about 25 lodges in which lived mountain men with their Indian wives.

Bridger, during the 46 years he spent in the West, from 1822 to 1868, married three times. His first and second wives were Flathead Indians, his third a Ute. He had four children with them, three daughters and one son. He sent his oldest daughter, Mary Ann, to be educated at a Presbyterian mission school in Walla Walla, Oregon Territory, and she was kidnapped by Cayuse Indians and then lost to history. She may have been killed, adopted into the tribe, or sold off. Three of his children were born to his first wife, who died shortly after their third child was born. The fourth child was born to his third wife and was named Virginia Rosalie. In his old age (he lived until age 77), the nearly blind Bridger lived with his daughter on a farm in western Missouri. Sometimes the man who guided armies across the plains and mountains and who prided himself on his great eyesight became lost and his dog had to race home to find someone to lead him back.

Little is known about his three wives — even their names are uncertain — but the pattern of Bridger's marital life was typical of mountain men. The wives were almost always Indian, attempts were made to educate the children in white schools, and late in life the men returned, usually but not always with an Indian wife, to white society.

The exploits of John Colter, Jed Smith, Hugh Glass, and Jim Bridger are the stuff of legends, but they are also representative of the lives led by the fewer than 1,000 men who ventured into the West between Lewis and Clark's Corps of Discovery and the first white settlements in the region. They filled an important gap. Without their time in the West the American claim to the area would have been a little bit weaker. Without the knowledge they provided as guides the many U.S. Army explorations into the area would have been less successful. Without their roles, either the U.S. would not have become a continental country stretching to the Pacific or, more likely, the establishment of American towns and cities in the West would have been delayed for decades, and that might have meant competing powers, especially Britain and Spain (and later Mexico) might have had time to build larger, more lasting communities that could have, and probably would have delayed American expansionism.

But the Colters, Smiths, Jim Bridgers, Kit Carsons, and other American mountain men, although patriotic men with a strong commitment to their native country, did not think of themselves as the vanguards of an expanding nation. Rather they were men looking to make a living while trying to avoid the restraints of conventional society. They were misfits and the United States benefited immensely from their inability to feel comfortable in the world east of the great American plains.

The toughness of these men, a way they are seen not just by history but the way they saw themselves, was part of their anti-domesticity, part of the reason they were misfits in Missouri and Kentucky and Pennsylvania.

They did learn to fit into the world of the Western plains and the mountains beyond them, and the lands beyond the mountains. Part of that fitting in grew out of their relationships with Indian women. In some Indian societies, such as the Shoshoni and Flathead, a woman who married a mountain man, with his hunting and trapping skills, gained some social prominence in her native village. And there were at least a few women in most of the Western Indian nations more than willing to marry these rugged men, for, although by Eastern white standards they were uncouth, even uncivilized, by the standards of the native tribes they often treated women with much respect. Just as the Hidasta kidnapping of Sacagawea and her sale or loss in a gambling match to the Mandans was indicative of the near-slave-status of many women in tribal cultures, few women in the Indian West saw much opportunity for themselves beyond drudgery and inferior social positions.

While a few of the Eastern tribes, including the six nations of New York's Iroquois, gave women some political say in tribal decisions, that was rare, close to non-existent, in the early 19th century West. For Indian women, marriage to a mountain man offered a better life. For the mountain men, it meant sex and the other benefits of marriage without what they considered repressive social constraints. Expected standards of relations between men and women helped drive these men into the West and the differing marital standards they found in the West helped keep them there. As Indian men often sacrificed their lives in vain battles designed to drive the white man away, a few Indian women, with their willingness to bed and marry mountain men, made the West more attractive to whites. And that helped make the West American.

James Beckwourth

The exact relationship between Indian women and the mountain men is difficult to determine because whatever information we have about those unions comes almost entirely from memoirs written or dictated by the men. There are no extant memoirs from any of the women involved, mostly because none of the tribes had a written language in the early 19th century and, as far as we know, none of the Indian women who married mountain men learned to read or write English, although sometimes the children of those unions did. And the memoirs of the mountain men, in many cases, are highly suspect in their accuracy. None is more suspect than the one by James Beckwourth.[24]

Beckwourth, born in Virginia in 1798, was the son of a white father and a mother who was the daughter of a white father and a black slave mother. Therefore, Beckwourth, by the standard used at the time, was one-quarter black. (He often referred to himself as being white.) When he was still a boy, he moved with his father to Missouri, and his father three times signed papers giving him his freedom. In his mid-twenties he became a mountain man, a group that included more than its fair share of men known for telling self-serving tall tales. In these tales the tellers were typically stronger, braver, smarter, and wittier than just about everyone else. Beckwourth differed from others in this tradition only in that his tall tales were written down. *The Life and Adventures of James P. Beckwourth, Mountaineer, Scout, and Pioneer, and Chief of the Crow Nation Indians Written from his Own Dictation* was published in 1856. It was "written from his own dictation to T. D. Bonner" (Beckwourth, title page).[25] It was probably more written by Bonner than dictated by Beckwourth.

For seven years beginning in 1826 Beckwourth lived with several different Indian tribes in the northern plains. He immodestly wrote (or dictated), "I soon rose to be a great man among them and the chief offered me his daughter for a wife.... I accepted his offer, and, without any superfluous ceremony, became son-in-law to As-as-to, the head chief of the Black Feet.... To me the alliance was more offensive than defensive, but thrift was my object more than hymeneal enjoyments" (Beckwourth, p. 114). The wording is awkward, but Beckwourth seems to be saying he didn't enjoy sex with his wife, not that he didn't have sex with her.

Not long after the marriage another more difficult problem came up in his relations with his wife, one that reveals much about his sense of racial identification. Remember, this is a man who was both white and black and who lived for years with Indians: "A party of Indians came into camp one day, bringing with them three white men's scalps.... In accordance with their custom, a scalp-dance was held.... My wife ... wished to join them in the dance. I replied, 'No; these scalps belonged to my people; my heart is crying for their death; you must not rejoice when my heart cries; you must not dance when I mourn" (Beckwourth, p. 114). But his wife joined the dancing anyway. "This was a sting which pierced my very heart. Taking my battle-axe, and forcing myself into the ring, I watched my opportunity, and struck my disobedient wife a heavy blow in the head with the side of my battle-axe, which dropped her as if a ball had pierced her heart. I dragged her through the crowd, and left her; I then went back to my tent" (Beckwourth, p. 117). Many in the tribe shouted out that they should kill Beckwourth for having killed a Blackfeet woman, but his father-in-law, the chief, defended him, saying, "Warriors! I am the loser of a daughter, and her brothers have lost a sister; you have lost nothing. She was the wife of the trader; I gave her to him. When your wives disobey your commands, you kill them; that is your right. That thing disobeyed her husband; he told her not to dance; she disobeyed him; she had no ears; he killed her, and he did right.... Warriors! wait till you meet him in battle, or, perhaps, in his own camp, then kill him; but here his life is sacred" (Beckwourth, pp. 117–118).

Then the chief addressed Beckwourth: "My son, you have done right; that woman I gave you had no sense; her ears were stopped up; she would not hearken to you, and you had a right to kill her. But I have another daughter, who is younger than she was. She is more beautiful; she has good sense and good ears. You may have her in the place of the bad one; she will hearken to all you say to her" (Beckwourth, p. 119). Beckwourth's response? "'Well,' thought I, 'this is getting married again before I have even had time to *mourn*'" (Beckwourth, p. 119). He told his father-in-law, "Very well, my father, I will accept of your kind offer" (Beckwourth, p. 119). Shortly, "My second wife was brought to me. I found her, as her father had represented, far more intelligent and far prettier than her other sister, and I was really proud of the change" (Beckwourth, p. 119). However, that night "while I and my wife were quietly reposing, some person crawled into our couch, sobbing most bitterly. Angry at the intrusion, I asked who was there. 'Me,' answered a voice, which, although well-nigh stifled with bitter sobs, I recognized as that of my other wife, whom every one had supposed dead. After lying outside the lodge senseless for some hours, she had recovered and groped her way to my bed. 'Go away,' I said, 'You have no business here; I have a new wife now, one who has sense.' 'I will not go away,' she replied, 'my ears are open now. I was a fool not to hearken to my husband's words when his heart was crying, but now I have good sense, and will always hearken to your words.'... I thought myself now well supplied with wives, having two more than I cared to have" (Beckwourth, p. 120). Meanwhile, he says, he was really in love with a white woman.

Years later, he was living among the Crow Indians, when a white man, as a joke, convinced the Crows that Beckwourth was really one of them and had been captured by the Cheyenne when he was small. Beckwourth wrote, "Orders were immediately given to summon all the old women taken by the Shi-ans at the time of their captivity so many winters past, who had suffered the loss of a son at the time. The lodge was cleared for the *examining committee*, and the old women, breathless with excitement, their eyes wide and protruding, and their nostrils dilated, arrived in squads.... At length one old woman ... Mrs. Big Bowl" (Beckwourth, p. 145–147), identifies him as her long lost son because he has a mole over his left eye, just as her son did. His new father, "Mr. Big Bowl," then offered to arrange for him to have a wife. "I assented, of course. 'Very well,' said he, 'you shall have a pretty wife and a good one.'... The name of my prospective father-in-law was Black-lodge. He had three very pretty daughters, whose names were Still-water, Blackfish, and Three-roads.... The ensuing day the three daughters were brought to my father's lodge by their father, and I was requested to take my choice" (Beckwourth, pp. 148–149). He chose Still-water, the oldest, because he hoped her name indicated she was obedient. "The acceptance of my wife was the completion of the ceremony, and I was again a married man.... My wife's deportment coincided with her name; she would have reflected honor upon many a civilized household. She was affectionate, obedient, gentle, cheerful, and, apparently, quite happy. No domestic thunder-storms, no curtain-lectures ever disturbed the serenity of our connubial lodge" (Beckwourth, p. 149).

He became a leader in many battles against the enemies of the Crow, and, if he had to say so himself, "I was lionized" (Beckwourth, p. 154). At one point he was invited by a chief to join in a war raid, but "I replied I would rather not go on such an errand. I have women to live for, and defend against the enemies of the Crows. 'Ah!' answered he, 'you a leader of the Dog Soldiers, and refuse to go! There are prettier women in the land of the Great Spirit than any of your squaws.'... I, not wishing to be thought cowardly ... consented to accompany him'" (Beckwourth, pp. 184–185). Eventually, he left the Crow to return to live with whites, whom he considered his own people. "I was well aware that many of my [white] friends knew of the life I was leading, and I almost feared to think of the opinions they must form of my character. But, in justification, it may be urged that the Crows had never shed the blood of the white man during my stay in their camp, and I did not intend they ever should, if I could raise a voice to prevent it.... Crows were uniformly faithful in their obligations to my race" (Beckwourth, p. 198). Clearly Beckwourth considered himself white. Despite having had at least three Indian wives, and living with Indians for years, he never overcame a condescending attitude: "I found the Indian would be Indian still, in spite of my efforts to improve him" (Beckwourth, p. 199).

How much of Beckwourth's stories can be believed? His sense of superiority over a group of people who befriended him suggests an inability to be a generous observer. More tellingly, almost every exploit he wrote of (or dictated), including the sexual ones, were also claimed by other mountain men. In other words, it's possible he didn't lie by making up adventures but rather by stealing them.

Osbourne Russell

In sharp contrast to Beckwourth is the life of Osbourne Russell, who wrote what is widely considered the most trustworthy of the mountain man memoirs. Trustworthy, and notably less interesting. Certainly among the most common reasons for a mountain man, or anyone else, to lie was to make himself more interesting than he really was.

Osbourne Russell, born in Bowdoinham, Maine, in 1814, became a mountain man at age 20, when he joined a beaver-hunting expedition led by Nathaniel Wyeth.[26] When Wyeth's company encountered financial difficulties, and a likelihood it would be unable to pay Russell the $250 it promised him for 18 months of employment, he switched to Jim Bridger's Rocky Mountain Fur Company. Two years later, he became a "free trapper," a man who worked for no one, but instead sold his beaver skins, or whatever else was salable, to whoever would buy them. Russell knew how to read and borrowed whatever books he could. He in particular read the Bible with great care, and it convinced him he was leading a sinful life. Because of that conviction, he gave up the life of the mountain man in 1842 and settled in Oregon, where he led an active political life, at one point gaining appointment to the territory's supreme court. During his years as a mountain man he kept a journal and years later tried unsuccessfully to get it published. He died in 1892 in California, but *Journal of a Trapper* was not published until 1914.

The credibility of Russell's journal is established largely by the details he provides about the land, animals, and minute-to-minute drudgery of everyday life. It sounds true not because it is interesting but because it is detailed. He also noticed, as other observers of 19th century Indian cultures did, the sexual relations of the native's he encountered during his time in the Rockies. Of the Flatheads, a tribe he much admired, he noted, "Larceny, Fornication, and adultery are severely punished" (Russell, *Journal*, p. 33). During the 1836 mountain man rendezvous on the Green River (in what is now Southwestern Wyoming) he met the first two white women to travel by land to the Far West, the wives of Presbyterian missionaries Marcus Whitman and H.H. Spaulding. Russell wrote, "The two ladies were gazed upon with wonder and astonishment, by the rude Savages they being the first white women ever seen by these Indians and the first that had ever penetrated into these wild and rocky regions" (Russell, *Journal*, p. 41).

Russell also peppers small jokes throughout his journal that infuse it with a sense of friendliness absent from the braggadocio of Beckwourth and others. At one point he says, "The men about the Fort [Fort Hall in Idaho] were doing nothing and I was lending them a hand" (Russell, *Journal*, p. 38). At another he refers to the discourses he has with other mountain men as "Rocky Mountain College" (Russell, *Journal*, p. 51). He is consistently self-effacing, and that, too, adds credibility to his narrative.

He also expresses a sensitivity for nature usually missing from the writings of other mountain men. He came upon a scene where a bear had just killed a buffalo calf, and writes, "The Mother was standing about 20 paces distant Moaning very pitifully for the loss of her young" (Russell, *Journal*, p. 84). At another point he reports a similar reaction to elk: "I have often seen the female come about the hunter who has found where her young is secreted uttering the most pitiful and persuasive moans and pleading in the most earnest manner that a dumb brute is capable of for the life of her young — the mode of persuasion would I think excite sympathy in the breast of any human that was not entirely destitute of the passion — the fawn has a peculiar cry after it is able to run which resembles the faint scream of a child by which it answers the Dam who calls it by a note similar to the scream of a woman in distress" (Russell, *Journal*, pp. 137–138).

Just before Russell's company engages in a fight with a group of Blackfeet, he reports, "One of them called to us in the flathead tongue and Said that we were not men but women and had better dress our selves as such for we had bantered them to fight and then crept into the rocks like women. An Old Iroquois trapper who had been an experienced warrior trained on the shores of Lake superior understanding this harangue turned to the Whites about him and made a speech in imperfect english nearly as follows My friend you see dat Ingun talk? He not talk good he talk berry bad He say you me all same like squaw, dat no good, spose you go wid me I make him no talk dat way" (Russell, *Journal*, p. 87). The Old Iroquois trapper's irritation at being compared to a woman is consistent with the way the Iroquois insulted the Delaware Indians, once defeating them in battle and then ordering them to be "like women" and not go to war without the permission of the Iroquois (see Morgan, *League of the Iroquois*, pp. 15, 338n-339n).

Russell also thought, as many mountain men did, that the highest possible praise for an Indian woman was to compare her to white women. Once while visiting a Snake Indian village he met a French trapper with a Flathead wife and wrote that the Frenchman's lodge was "neatly arranged by his wife who was a flathead but the neat manner in which her lodge and furniture was kept would have done honor to a large portion of the 'pale faced' fair sex in the civilized world" (Russell, *Journal*, p. 113). He noted that Indian women and children always did the cleaning after a feast and that when Indian men sat around to talk, the women were expected to leave the lodge or campfire. He notes that some Snake Indians "cannot smoke in the presence of a female or a dog" (Russell, *Journal*, p. 144). He also provides a summation of Snake marital relations: "A plurality of wives is very common among the Snakes and the marriage contract is dissolved only by the consent of the husband by which the wife is at liberty to marry again. Prostitution among the women is very rare and fornication whilst living with the husband is punished with the utmost severity. The women perform all the labor about the lodge except the care of the horses. They are cheerful and affectionate to their husband remarkably fond and careful of their children" (Russell, *Journal*, p. 144).

He offers, also, a summation of the marital customs of the Crow Indians: "Prostitution of their wives is very common but sexual intercours between near relatives is prohibited — when a young man is married he never after speaks to the mother in law nor the wife to the father in law altho they may all live in the same lodge. If the husband wishes to say anything to the mother in law he speaks to the wife who conveys it to the mother and in the same way communications is conveyed between the wife and father in law — the custom is peculiar to the Crows. They never intermarry with other nations but a stranger if he wishes can always be accommodated with a wife while he stops with the Village but cannot take her from it when he leaves" (Russell, *Journal*, pp. 146–147). He also makes a curious comparison between the Crows and Jews: "There exists among them many customs similar to those of the ancient Israelites. A woman after being delivered of a male child cannot approach the lodge of her husband under 40 days and for a female 50 is required — and 7 days separation for every natural menses. The distinction between clean and unclean beasts bears a great degree of similarity to the Jewish law" (Russell, *Journal*, p. 148).

Throughout his journal, Russell reports and seldom passes judgment on Indian customs. In addition there is no indication of his personal relations with Indian women, suggesting he never married one and, if he had sexual relations with any, he did not, unlike Beckwourth, brag about the liaison.

The journal, however, was republished in 1955 by the Oregon Historical Society, and added to it, by the editor, Aubrey L. Haines, were three letters and part of a fourth Russell wrote to his two sisters in Maine. And the partial letter — or, more accurately, the part Haines did not include — reveals a lot about Russell's attitudes towards women.

The first letter, dated April 3, 1848, was mailed from Oregon to his sister Martha in Hallowell, Maine, and gives news of the previous year's massacre of Marcus Whitman and others by Cayuse Indians at Walla Walla. Among other details he writes, "The men were nearly all killed and the women subjected to indignities too horrid to be described, for about twelve days, when their freedom was purchased by the Hudson's Bay Company" (Russell, *Journal*, p. 182). Actually, although several women were held prisoner after the massacre, there is no evidence any were in any way molested. He also refers to a letter from Martha dated January 31 (the letter itself has not survived): "You seemed to be pleased that I was not married.... I have not at present the least inclination to marry in this country" (Russell, *Journal*, p. 184). He later adds, "You thought I had better go to Maine and get a load of Kennebec girls and fetch out to Oregon. Such a cargo would doubtless find a ready market in Oregon, if the policy of insurance upon it were not purchased too dear, and I think no man in his right senses would ship such a cargo without having it insured, not only against the insults of Neptune, but the wantonness of Cupid" (Russell, *Journal*, p. 185). The reference to Neptune reflects the fact that in the mid–19th century many whites from the East who went to the Oregon Territory did so by ship that sailed around the tip of South America and not overland.

The next day he wrote a letter to his other sister, Mrs. Eleanor Read of Lewiston, Maine. He refers to a letter dated January 31, 1847, from Eleanor that he received seven and a half months later, on September 18, 1848. In that letter (which has not survived) she must have informed him she had recently married Lemuel Read. Russell wrote, "It affords me consolation to know that you have a partner suited to your wishes. May your days glide smoothly in uninterrupted happiness and may you continue to dwell in the affections of your husband and favour of your God, and may Lemuel be a faithful discharge of the duties he owes to his family, to society, to his country and his god, continue to merit those affections" (Russell, *Journal*, p. 187).

The third letter is written from California and is dated Nov. 10, 1849. It is addressed to Eleanor and refers to a letter he received from Martha telling him she planned to get married but, evidently, without many details of the planned marriage, because he writes, "Not that I have the least wish to prevent her from uniting with the man of her choice, but I must hear of her being certainly married, and to whom, before I shall know how to direct a letter to her" (Russell, *Journal*, p. 190).

Only a small part of the final letter from Russell is quoted by Haines, who writes that it was "written from Placerville, California, on August 26,

1855 to his sister, Eleanor.... Russell's words appear to be little more than irrational ravings. Since most of the information conveyed — the causes of his estrangement with his family — is of no importance to history, the letter is omitted except for the conclusion of the postscript" (Haines in Russell, *Journal*, p. 191). The portion of the letter Haines quotes says, "I have asked Martha 4 times if she ever received a package entitled a *Rocky Mountain Journal*, or rather *A Trapper's Journal During Nine [Years] Residence in The Rocky Mountains*, by O. Russell, sent her privately by PSUS. Now cannot any of you tell me if she has or has not received it. That one I was offered one thousand dollars for last week but my reply was, 'my youngest sister has the copyright'" (Russell, *Journal*, p. 191). He had sent the only manuscript of his book to Martha by the Postal Service of the United States (PSUS) with instructions that she contact possible publishers.

Parts of the letter[27] omitted by Haines do, indeed, seem to be irrational ravings, but when put in the context — never explicitly mentioned in the letter — of being a response to rumors that Russell had improper relations with a girl, perhaps a teenager, more than 20 years younger than him, much of it makes sense. The rumors were probably contained in a letter written by an acquaintance of Osbourne named Eleanor, and by Martha Ann, perhaps a cousin, in California. (It could be just a coincidence that these two women had the same first names as Russell's sisters, or it might be a result of a confused mind confusing names.) When writing he was suffering from one more in a series of illnesses that had plagued him for a decade. In the letter (which is now at Yale University Library), Russell — referring to himself as judge — writes, "You will probably be astonish'd but it is a fact, that in all my sickness since 1831 I have never had a white woman to attend on me until the present attack in the present case a girl from Ohio seventeen years almost an [illegible] to me, told her Aunt [illegible] (at whose house I now staying) — she requested their permission to attend [illegible] judge [illegible] during his illness do you wish to attend on the judge for he's a stranger to you I know it [illegible] but you know the judge loves [illegible].... I shall leave this place in a few days perhaps never to see this pretty affectionate child Martha Ann R___ again but may God bless her come towards one her father as she calls me" (Russell, letter to his sister Eleanor, August 26, 1855).

The letter clearly suggests Russell had an infatuation, at the least, with a 17-year-old girl when he was 41. Since in his journal, which covers the years 1834 to 1843, he gives no indication of sexual relations with any woman, it's probable he considered any mention of sexual relations with any woman to be improper. That would explain both the absence of any such mention in the journal and becoming upset with any rumors mentioned in any letter sent to Maine by a cousin or anyone else.

The contrast between Osbourne Russell and James Beckwourth is revealing. For Beckwourth, bragging about sexual exploits, real or imagined or wishful thinking, was part of his personae. For Russell, the standard was reserve and modesty. And since hyperbole always attracts less credibility than understatement, Russell is more believable than Beckwourth. Neither Beckwourth's memoirs nor Russell's journal are typical of the writings of the mountain men; Beckwourth's brag too much, Russell's provide convincing if incomplete details. Examining the sex lives of mountain men is just like examining any other historical phenomena.

3

The Missionary
Saving Indians from Sex

The position of Christian missionaries who went to the West in the early decades of the 19th century was that the souls of the Indians they sought to convert could not be saved unless, among other things, they made drastic changes in their sexual habits. The Indian sex lives the men in Lewis and Clark's Corps of Discovery and the mountain men so much enjoyed, that in fact helped those men make the West American, was anathema to the missionaries.[1]

The Whitmans

As the era of the mountain men was coming to an end in the late 1830s, the era of the Western missionaries was beginning. Marcus Whitman, a doctor and Presbyterian minister from New York, first visited Oregon Territory in 1835 with the Rev. Samuel Parker. They decided to establish a mission near what is now Walla Walla, southwestern Washington. The mission would provide for the education and medical needs of both white settlers and the Cayuse Indians. They returned to the East via ship, with the intent that Whitman would return the following year. But Whitman encountered an unexpected problem. The venture needed the approval of the American Board of Commissioners for Foreign Missions, an interdenominational Protestant body, and its members, disturbed by all the reports of mountain men marrying Indian women, decided only married missionaries would be sent into the far West and that they must take their wives with them. Whitman was single but he found in Narcissa Prentiss, a 28-year-old devout Presbyterian, also from western New York, someone who also wanted to help save the souls of Indians by converting them to Christianity. The fact she was beautiful, with long auburn-blonde hair and large bluish grey eyes, simply made Whitman all the more willing to wed her.[2]

3. The Missionary

The church then decided the Whitmans should be accompanied west by another minister, Henry Spalding.[3] Spalding had earlier asked Narcissa to marry him and she said no. Oh, well. Such are the plot twists of television soap operas and history's footnotes. Spalding found another woman, Eliza Hart, to marry him and the two couples set out to bring a Christian God to the Indians. As they traveled overland they engaged mountain man Thomas Fitzpatrick to guide them, but Fitzpatrick, fearing the two women would simply make the party an attractive target for Indians, tried at one point to leave. Whitman rode after him and persuaded him to stay. The Whitmans established their mission at a place called Waiilatpu, or Meadow Where Rye Grass Grows, just north of the Columbia River. They would work with the Cayuse Indians. The Spaldings went farther north, near today's Lewiston, Idaho, to work with the much larger Nez Percé tribe. The Methodist church, meanwhile, had established a mission near present-day Portland, Oregon.

These and other missions were the first long-term settlements by Americans in an area Britain and the United States had agreed in 1827 could be jointly settled, with the expectation that, realistically, one of them would eventually assume sole control of the area, or perhaps split it between them. While the British mostly sent trappers employed by the Hudson Bay Company, the Americans concentrated initially on missionaries. The British primarily concerned themselves with the land north of the Columbia River, what is now the state of Washington, while the Americans wanted all of the Oregon Territory, modern day Washington and Oregon. The Whitmans and other missionaries mailed reports to the East that were printed in newspapers and that painted a picture of a paradise and thereby encouraged Americans to migrate to the Oregon Territory.

Simply by arriving in Oregon Territory, Narcissa Whitman and Eliza Spalding assumed an historically symbolic importance. They became the first two white women to cross the Rockies.

Marcus Whitman was the most visible proponent of annexation of the full Oregon Territory by the United States. James Polk campaigned for president in 1844 with an implied threat to go to war with Britain to gain the full territory.[4] (He also threatened to go to war with Mexico, which he eventually did.) Passions peaked in both the U.S. and Britain over the threat, but the matter was settled with a thud. The Hudson Bay Company, Britain's de facto government in the territory, decided for purely economic reasons to move its regional headquarters to Vancouver Island. It would be easier to supervise their domain from there. With their waning desire to stay and the territory's growing population of Americans enticed by the writings of Whitman and other missionaries, the British decided Oregon Territory, which British Foreign Secretary Lord Aberdeen called "a pine swamp" (Billington, *Westward Expan-*

sion, p. 173), wasn't worth a war. Problems were brewing for the British all around its empire, the empire on which the sun never set — nor did its hot spots ever cool — and war was possible in Ireland and Afghanistan. And with China and France. Oregon hardly seemed as important. In 1846 the U.S. and Great Britain signed a treaty making all of the Oregon Territory American. Certainly worldwide politics played a role, but the final decision was influenced by the Whitmans and other missionaries settling in the area, and they settled there partly because they felt a need to convert the Indians, including convincing them their sex lives needed reigning in.

The Presbyterian church sent hundreds of missionaries into the West over nearly half a century, and much of what they taught the Indians was consistent: polygamy is bad, easy divorce is bad, sex outside of marriage is bad, a woman not covering her breasts is bad, even enjoying sex is bad. Sex was for creating children, not having fun. Whether they actually taught Indians the only proper way for a man and woman to engage in sex was with the women underneath, on her back, with her legs spread, and the man lying between her legs — that is, the missionary position — can not be substantiated by the historical record, but they so consistently wanted to limit the sex lives of Indians that the possibility is at least metaphorically accurate.

The Whitmans became as much a symbol of the role white missionaries played in converting Indians to white morality as Custer later became for killing Indians who left the reservation. It is not a coincidence that Vine Deloria, Jr., titled his angry, 1969 best-selling book about the clash between white and Indian religions *Custer Died for Your Sins*.[5]

The Kindly Priest

The only rival the Whitmans had as the most famous missionary trying to convert Indians in the 19th century West was Pierre-Jean De Smet, a Roman Catholic priest, a Jesuit, who shared their sense of cultural superiority but none of their unlikable personality traits.[6] In his journals he often referred to the various Indians he met as dirty and lazy, but, unlike the Whitmans, he seems to have genuinely liked them.[7] He thought they were friendly, easy going (except when drunk), willing to be helpful, and, what he considered most important, willing to be converted. Where the Whitmans seem to have converted a few hundred Cayuse to Presbyterianism over several decades, De Smet converted thousands of members of a dozen different tribes to Roman Catholicism in a similar period. In fact, the Flatheads sent representatives nearly two thousand miles from the Oregon Territory to present-day Council Bluffs, Iowa, to recruit him. One estimate says he traveled 180,000 miles, including crossing

3. The Missionary

the Atlantic Ocean 17 times, to raise money, recruit other priests, and visit American officials in his efforts to educate and convert the Indians.

He was born to wealthy parents in Belgium and began his missionary work at age 37, in 1838, with the Potawatomi Indians along the Missouri River. He opened a school where Indian children received instruction in reading, writing, good work habits, and how to be good Catholics. Reciting Hail Marys, making the sign of the cross, and memorizing sections of the Bible were part of the curriculum.

Unlike the Whitmans, he did not spend a lot of time telling the Indians how bad they were. He reserved most of his cultural imperialism for his journals. In person, according to the numerous written comments made about him in letters and journals by people who met him, he appears endlessly optimistic and good-natured. He responded to ribald jokes with little more than a disapproving glance. He urged Potawatomi men to give up polygamy by emphasizing what he said were the advantages of monogamy, not by denouncing it as evil. Instead of accusing Indian men and women of living in sin by cohabiting without a marriage ceremony (most Plains tribes recognized a marriage if the couple simply said they were married), he convinced such couples to submit to a Catholic marriage ceremony. Many didn't object, and he performed hundreds of marriages. He also tried to discourage divorce, which was easy to accomplish in most of the Plains tribes. A woman, although clearly in an inferior social position, could typically dissolve a marriage at will.

Among many of the Indian tribes he worked with, he noted that women were little more than slaves. The men went to war or hunting, or else they gambled, drank, slept, played games, or otherwise did things that were not productive, he wrote. But the women tended the children, prepared the meals, did what little cleaning was done (he consistently complained in his journals that Indians did virtually no cleaning, of themselves or their children or their clothes or their homes), and typically worked dawn to dusk. But he never came up with a strategy that successfully addressed the problem.

One of the best known, if minor, incidents involving Father De Smet reflects his own attitude towards women. Being guided from Council Bluffs to the Oregon Territory by the famous mountain man Thomas Fitzpatrick (who had years earlier guided the Whitmans), their party came to a swollen North Platte River, near present-day Casper, Wyoming, and De Smet was understandably reluctant to cross. But when John Gray, one of the Iroquois mountain men, put his wife on a horse, himself on another, and the one-year-old daughter of another woman in the party on a third, lashed them together, and had them swim across the river, De Smet, not wanting to be embarrassed by being afraid to do something a woman did, urged his own mount into the stream and crossed unharmed.

Hurons

De Smet wrote a great deal about the flora and fauna of the West and about the sociology of mountain men and the languages of the Indians, and those writings are a major source of information about the early 19th century West, but he wrote little about the sex habits of the Indians, and that no doubt resulted from his interests residing in other areas. But he was a member of the Society of Jesus, a Jesuit, and we do know how Jesuits reacted to Indian sexual habits elsewhere. For example, Jesuits (and another Catholic religious order, the Recollects, a branch of the Franciscans) left a highly detailed written reaction to Indian sex as early as the 17th century, when they encountered the Hurons in Ontario, Canada.[8]

The Hurons did not consider sex something to be hidden. Mid-teens was a good time to start and both girls and boys were allowed to have as many sexual partners as they wanted. Because Hurons lived in long houses, which typically held eight families each, privacy was obtained by the boy and girl going into the woods. Married couples usually sought the same privacy. Seven families looking on, and listening, was just too much. One result, not surprisingly, is that very few babies were born in the fall, because that meant they would have been conceived, out of doors, in the winter. Because multiple sex partners was the norm, Huron society tended to find jealousy unacceptable. Unmarried couples lived together openly but that did not prevent either partner from having intercourse with other people. Such cohabitation was common and available to all unmarried people, but marriage required more. A man was not deemed an acceptable marriage partner until he had successfully hunted and fished, and — most importantly — displayed courage in war. Most of the wars were against the Iroquois Confederacy to the south, in present-day New York.

One aspect of Huron sexuality the Catholic priests found particularly curious was what happened when an unmarried woman became pregnant. By the European model they were familiar with, they expected most young men to deny any responsibility, but in a culture that measured manhood partly by how many children were produced, it should not have been surprising that every young man the young woman had slept with — sometimes dozens — said he was the father. That left the young woman in a position many young American women today might envy. She could pick out whichever one she wanted and he would feel compelled to marry her. That helps explain why Hurons traced their ancestry through a mother's family. You just couldn't be certain who your father really was.

While the open acceptance of premarital sex dismayed the Recollects and Jesuits, many aspects of Huron marriage met with their approval. For

3. The Missionary

example, a young man usually had a potential wife selected for him by his parents. Mature judgment, the priests felt, was a better guide than youthful love. The young man then approached the girl's parents. If they said no, that was the end of the matter. If they said yes, he then approached the girl. Usually he put on facial paint and jewelry and his finest clothing. This was a serious occasion. He also brought the girl gifts, maybe bracelets or a necklace or a robe made from beaver skins. If she didn't want to be married to the boy, she rejected the presents, and the matter was over. If she did like him, she accepted the presents and he was permitted to spend several nights with her. Without talking. Silence for two or three or four days. If they could get along without conversation, the priests felt, that was a good sign. The priests, however, did not approve of the fact that the boy and the girl during this period had sex. Chances are the two had slept together previously, but part of the purpose seems to have been to see if they were sexually compatible over a slightly more extended period. After this test period all the concerned people — the boy, the girl, the four parents — would make a judgment. Any one of the six could nix the marriage, but the girl's judgment was the most important. Most parents acceded to a daughter's wishes in such matters and, in effect, the boy's parents had already recommended the girl. If everyone was in agreement, the actual marriage ceremony was held. That consisted of the four parents arranging a big feast — roasted dog was a favorite on such occasions — and the father of the bride announced to everyone who came that his daughter was now married.

It was not a religious ceremony and the priests found that their attempts to make it one caused problems. Any young man who converted to Christianity and, by implication, agreed to a religious ceremony found that almost all young Huron women lost interest in him. A big part of the problem was divorce. For Hurons, both men and women, divorce was just common sense. If a man and a woman could not get along, they should part ways. The Catholic concept that a God wanted them to remain married forever was alien, even frightening. Typically, divorce amounted to either partner saying he or she was tired of the other and no shaman, or religious leader, in the culture even had the job of offering marriage counseling. You can't get along? Get divorced. For Hurons, marriage, divorce, premarital sex were all pretty simple affairs in no way tied up with religion or the commands of an unseen God.

Even infidelity in marriage was not a particularly big deal. Or at least not a moral issue. If the husband went away for an extended period, say to fight against the Seneca in Western New York, his wife could, if she wished, have sex with whatever man who remained behind that she wanted to. She could even marry another man. If the first husband was killed in war, her future was already settled. If he came back, he could simply accept that he was no longer married or he could try to claim her again. If that was all right with the new husband, he just moved out. If they both wanted her as a wife, however, the choice was usually made by the woman's father. The father usually did not want to offend the families of either man — Huron villages were small, seldom consisting of more than two or three thousand people, so the old cliché held true, everyone did know everyone else — so he typically devised some competition. A common one was to place a stake in the ground and have the two men race for it. The winner won his wife, the loser lost the same wife. The village, as always, discouraged the loser from saying or acting with any jealousy.

All this changed, however, with the birth of a child. Divorce and extramarital sex became rare after a child was born. In fact, for many married couples, sex became rare once a baby entered their lives (an observation made by many men in many societies). A man who left a wife with a baby was likely to find that his wife's family would no longer feed him. While men procured whatever meat there was through hunting, or fish through fishing, those foods and whatever was gathered or grown belonged to the wife's clan. A man who would abandon the mother of his own child was unworthy of eating. The appeal of eating regularly had a magnetic attraction that helped keep married couples with children together. And while there was no marriage counseling for childless couples, relatives and friends usually tried hard to talk couples with children into staying together regardless of difficulties in their relationship.

The Catholic priests approved of the pressure to keep parents together, but they found odd a social requirement that a surviving spouse of a deceased partner could not remarry for at least three years. If three years did not pass before remarriage, the new husband of a widow was likely to have the late first husband's clan take all of his possessions as payment. The new wife of a widower would almost certainly see her husband become a social outcast. The three-year waiting period could be waived only with the approval of the family of the deceased spouse, and that was seldom given.

But the Huron sexual practice that seems to have confused the Jesuits and Recollects the most was the one where an ill person would ask a man and a woman to have sex in his or her presence. In one case, a half dozen or so unmarried women were in a lodge with an ailing woman, and they were asked by a male chief who they would most like to have sex with. Each named an unmarried man in the village, the chief went out and found them and brought them back. The couples paired off and spread throughout the lodge. At each end of the lodge a male chief chanted something designed to help the ailing woman get better and the couples engaged in sex throughout the night. Sexual intercourse was an activity for the healthy and the idea was that some of that good health would pass off to the ailing woman. On some other occasions the ailing person would simply ask that several members of the opposite sex dance naked in front of him or her. And in what may be the oddest reference in Jesuit reports on the subject, an ailing woman said she had a dream that required her to drink urine directly from the penis of a particular man. He was summoned and he urinated directly into her mouth.

Despite the openness of sexual relationships, the Huron had some strong limitations on what was acceptable. Most notable to the priests was the total absence of hugging, kissing, or petting in front of other people. Physical affection was a private matter and not for public display. And for the two or three years a woman breast-fed a baby, the husband understood there would be no sex. Another group expected to willingly do without sex, but only for short periods, were religious leaders, or shamans. Shamans could be either male or female and their sexual abstinence was usually accompanied by fasting, and the combination was supposed to aid in creating holy visions, which usually involved seeing a spirit who offered some guidance on how to live a life or what the village as a whole should do. If after two or three days of fasting and sexual abstinence the spirit did not appear, well, better luck next time. No one was expected to do without food or sex for very long. Wasn't healthy.

There was one other occasion you had to avoid sex. When a prisoner was taken in war, he was tortured for two, three, or four days, but on the night before he would finally be killed, every one in the village abstained from sex. For Hurons, sex was often a loud and raucous occasion, and the execution of a warrior, especially a brave one, called for dignified quiet.

The Huron often subjected prisoners to sexual depredations, including homosexual rape, sex with animals, sharp objects inserted into the anus, and castration. Often they were urinated on. Sometimes forced to eat excretion. The more easily a prisoner succumbed to these insults, perhaps in the mistaken belief he would be spared something worse, the more painful the torture. The more he resisted, the longer the torture lasted. Sex for the prisoner of the Huron was primarily an act of humiliation.

If much of this seemed odd to the Catholic priests who entered Huron society, the sex lives of the priests seemed just as odd to the Hurons. The priests resisted all attempts by even the most attractive Huron women to seduce them. To the Hurons, this was unnatural. And the refusal of a priest to marry a Huron woman was seen as an affront to the entire clan, a statement the Black Robe, as a Jesuit priest was usually called (Recollects and other Franciscans were Brown Robes), considered Huron society beneath his social standing. The Jesuits and Recollects were almost all Frenchmen, but the Hurons did not blame their behavior on their nationality. They blamed it on their religion. After all, French trappers slept with, sometimes married, and often had children with Huron women. In fact, many French trappers seemed to particularly enjoy the open sexuality of Huron culture. Clearly, it was the religion of these Black Robes that caused the insulting behavior.

But the Black Robes did have some success in winning converts, and that damaged traditional Huron society. A Huron man who converted to Christianity often failed to find a Huron wife, so he often married outside his tribe, decreasing the number of warriors available for war. Huron women seldom converted and with understandable reasons. Becoming a Christian meant surrendering the sexual freedom they enjoyed. Worse, it meant divorce was impossible. And a Christian marriage required obedience to a man. All this was both alien and unappealing to a Huron woman. When a significant number of both men and women in a Huron village were converted, however, they usually formed their own clique apart from others. Those who were not converted sometimes playfully, sometimes mischievously, encouraged a non–Christian Huron woman to seduce a Christian Huron man. One Jesuit recorded an incident in which a Christian Huron man who was the target of a playful non–Christian Huron woman's seductive efforts leaped naked into a pile of snow to cool his passions. The Jesuit commentator called the man's action "a victory" (see Anderson, "As Gentle as Little Lambs"). But for many Hurons, every victory of the Jesuits and Recollects was a defeat for their culture and for their sexual freedom.

Iroquois

Contrasting the Jesuits' view of the Hurons is the view of the Iroquois recorded in the mid–19th century by Lewis Henry Morgan, one of America's first ethnologist.[9] The Hurons and Iroquois had much in common. The Huron during the first contact with whites were located north of Lakes Ontario and Erie and east of Lake Huron, while the five Iroquois tribes were located just a little south, across what is now Northern New York (a sixth tribe would join the Iroquois confederacy in the early 18th century). The Hurons and Iroquois spoke languages that were so close they had little difficulty conversing with each other. Both built long houses (which typically housed about eight families each), cultivated corn and other crops, practiced monotheistic religions, and overall had cultures similar enough to sometimes led white observers to see few differences between them. Despite these similarities, however, the Huron and Iroquois were deadly enemies for centuries. In the early 17th century, the Huron were decimated by smallpox (which they got from whites) and that weakened them so much that two decades later they were nearly obliterated by repeated attacks by the Iroquois.

3. The Missionary

When comparing Morgan's description of Iroquois sexual practices with Jesuit accounts of Huron sexuality, the two cultures seem to have little in common. That reflects the differing approaches of the whites who created the written records. The Jesuits were looking for, and therefore found, proof that the Hurons were in need of their salvation. Morgan, who relied extensively on his friend Ely Parker,[10] a full-blooded Seneca (the largest Iroquois tribe), was less interested in reforming Indians than in studying them. He consequently both reflected Parker's admiration of the Iroquois and concentrated more on cultural observation and less on cultural condemnation (although a modern reader of Morgan's classic 1851 study, *The League of the Ho-De'-No-Sau-Nee, Iroquois*, will be struck my Morgan's frequent references to how the Iroquois can be improved and elevated to be just like whites. In a later book, *Ancient Society*, published in 1877, Morgan developed a theory that human cultures progressed from promiscuity to group marriages to polygamy to, its most advanced state, monogamy. Although that book comes 26 years later, its tone is consistent with his admiration of the mating habits of the Iroquois.[11]

According to Morgan, in the 1600s the Iroquois confederacy engaged almost continually in war, almost always winning, and subduing tribes as far west as today's Illinois and as far south as Tennessee. Some of the tribes they subdued, such as the Delaware, located mostly in Pennsylvania and New Jersey, were "made women" (Morgan, *League of the Iroquois*, pp. 15, 338n–339n). Morgan, in using this term, is reflecting what he said was the Iroquois way of expressing their victory. It means, essentially, that the Delaware agreed they would not go to war against anyone without the permission of the Iroquois. That is, they would engage only in pursuits reserved for women, and war was a man's occupation. When, in 1742, the Delaware sold some land along the Delaware River to the colony of Pennsylvania, an Onondaga chief, speaking for the Iroquois confederacy, visited them and scolded them for the sale, saying, "We conquered you. We made women of you. You know you are women and can no more sell land than women" (Morgan, *League of the Iroquois*, pp. 15, 338n–339n). He then ordered the Delaware tribe to move to a place in Northeastern Pennsylvania where the Iroquois could keep a closer eye on them.

Morgan believed the unity of the league owed its success largely to the fact that a member of one clan (which Morgan calls a tribe, which can create some confusion in a modern reader who uses the term differently) could not marry within the same tribe. Thus, a member of the Bear clan of the Seneca could not marry another member of the Bear clan, but could marry a member of the Heron clan. And intermarriage among what we today call tribes was permitted. So a Seneca could marry a Mohawk, Cayuga, Onondaga, or

Oneida, or, after 1715, when they joined the league, a Tuscarora. Children were considered members of the mother's clan and property was passed down through the mother's line of descent. Therefore, while restricting the Delaware to doing "women's work" was a way of subjugating them, women in the Iroquois six nations had an influence in community affairs found in few other of the estimated 500 tribes that populated what would become the United States.

Most important in the laws of inheritance was the fact that political power in the Iroquois league rested in a group made up of sachems, an inherited position. Each tribe had its own sachems, and the son of a sachem could not inherit the position from his father, because he could inherit something only from his mother, and women were never allowed to be sachems. (A son could not even inherit his father's tomahawk.) Nor could the position of sachem pass from one tribe to another. That is, for example, a Cayuga could never become a Mohawk sachem. Thus, when a sachem died, his position would pass to another male in his pre-marriage family, such as a brother or the son of a sister. To complicate the matter further, if a sachem misbehaved, the men in the tribe could, and often did, vote to remove him from the office and elected someone to replace him. In addition, sachems could not make any decisions individually. They needed to be unanimous in their decisions for them to have the rule of law. The system amounted to the adult men in the tribe electing royalty and giving that royalty legislative powers that became executive powers only when they came to unanimous agreement. The system assured there would be no dictators.

When America's political elite met in Philadelphia after the Revolution with the intent of replacing the nearly unworkable Articles of Confederation with the strong centralized government created by the Constitution, they made many references to the system used by the Iroquois, with its inherent checks and balances. The idea was to create a strong, and therefore effective, central government with limitations that would assure the young country would not end up being run by a despot. The Iroquois confederacy provided a working model. Except, of course, white Americans saw no need for a political role for women.

The role women played in Iroquois society is indicated by the absence of sex in heaven. The conception of an idealized place that omits sex is inconsistent with the role of women in many other Indian cultures and that much of American white culture envisioned. Iroquois women clearly were seen as more than mere sex objects. (And only one white person was granted admission to the Iroquois heaven, George Washington, because, they believed, he dealt fairly with them. Nor were whites sent to hell. Since they were not created by the Great Spirit, or God, they just disappeared when they died.)

3. The Missionary

In the early 1800s, a Seneca religious leader, Handsome Lake, greatly influenced Iroquois religious thought. He preached that drinking alcohol was forbidden by the Great Spirit and that marriage, especially a marriage that produced children, was a blessing. He preached that "parents must also guard their children against improper marriages. They, having much experience, should select a suitable match for their child. When the parents of both parties have agreed, then bring the young pair together, and let them know what good their parents have designed for them. If at any time they so far disagree that they cannot possibly live contented and happy with each other, they may separate in mutual good feeling; and in this there is no wrong" (Morgan, *League of the Iroquois*, p. 238). Marriages should be arranged and divorce should be easy. But "to abandon a wife or children is a great wrong, and produces many evils" (Morgan, *League of the Iroquois*, p. 239).

His preaching placed much of the blame for whites encroaching on Indian territory on Indian leaders: "Your chiefs have violated and betrayed your trust by selling lands. Nothing is now left of our once large possessions, save a few small reservations.... Whoever sells lands offends the Great Spirit and must expect a great punishment after death" (Morgan, *League of the Iroquois*, pp. 239–240). While the three topics mentioned here—marriage, alcohol, and selling land—seem distinct, Handsome Lake intermingled a discussion of each so thoroughly in a standard long speech (it takes up 26 pages in Morgan's book) that he made an emotional, if not obviously intellectual, connection among them. He condemned the common Iroquois practice (common, also, among the Huron) of a wife whose husband has gone on a long hunting expedition, perhaps lasting months, taking on a new lover. "It sometimes happens," Handsome Lake said, "that a man goes out for the hunt, leaving his wife with her friends. After a long absence he returns, and finds that his wife has taken another husband. The Great Spirit says that this is a great sin, and must be put from among us" (Morgan, *League of the Iroquois*, p. 241). He gave detailed instructions on how to punish a child who misbehaves: the child must never be whipped, but it is OK to put his or head under water for a moment. However, the instant a child promises to do better the punishment must cease. He preached that although there clearly are differences among people (example: "The Great Spirit ... has given [some people] a pretty face, to others an ugly one" [Morgan, *League of the Iroquois*, p. 247]), all are equal in the eyes of God: "it is wrong for one man to exalt himself above another" (Morgan, *League of the Iroquois*, p. 247). He warned Indians that while they could copy some things that whites do, such as raising cattle, they must remain Indians. The Great Spirit, he said, "has made us, as a race, separate and distinct from the paleface. It is a great sin to intermarry, and intermingle the blood of the two races. Let none be guilty of this transgression"

(Morgan, *League of the Iroquois*, p. 251–252). He warned that a husband and wife who argue all the time spend eternity in hell arguing all the time. While on earth, everyone was to be kind to the poor and elderly. Adopting orphans pleased the Great Spirit.

Despite the higher role assigned to women in Iroquois culture, they were seen as distinctly, in some ways, inferior to men. Morgan cites one translation of a war dance song this way: "I am brave and intrepid. I do not fear death, nor any kind of torture. Those who fear them are cowards. They are less than women" (Morgan, *League of the Iroquois*, p. 270n). The sense of women being inferior is largely relegated to hunting and war activities. For example, in most Iroquois dances, the woman, not the man, selected a dancing partner. Contrast that with the fact that at some musical concerts women were not allowed to be present. Morgan includes a chart on which he lists 32 distinct dances (Great Feather Dance, Great Thanksgiving Dance, etc.), and notes that 14 of them involved both sexes, seven were for females only, and 11 for males only. The role of women in Iroquois society was complicated, even inconsistent. Which, of course, is much like the role of women in most societies.

But the key role women played in shaping Iroquois society was as mothers empowered to select marriage partners for their children. Love between a young man and a young woman was not considered a practical basis for marriage. Mothers consulted with older men and women in a village, and a common bit of advice in what Morgan calls "ancient times," by which he meant the 16th and 17th centuries, called for young men to be paired with women at least several years older than they were, "on the supposition that he needed a companion experienced in the affairs of life" (Morgan, *League of the Iroquois*, p. 320). A man was seldom deemed ready for marriage until about the age of 25. Prior to that he was expected to be both a warrior and a hunter, and after marriage "his freedom was curtailed and his responsibilities were increased by the cares of a family" (Morgan, *League of the Iroquois*, p. 320). It was not unusual that a man of 25 would be married to a woman of 40, often a widow. Conversely, a man of 60 often married a woman of 20. By the mid–19th century, however, the marriageable age of both men and women was reduced to about 20 and the age discrepancies all but disappeared.

In both "ancient times" and mid-19th century, a mother who decided it was time for her son or daughter to marry typically consulted with the elderly members of the tribe, both males and females. But the consultation was advisory only. The mother made the final decision. Or, more accurately, the two concerned mothers made the decision. A mother with a son would talk with the mother of a daughter, and if they didn't agree that their children should marry each other, the mothers looked for other matches. When two mothers

3. The Missionary

agreed on the match, however, the decision was final. The elderly in the tribes concerned could not overrule them. Nor could the children. In fact, the children were often not even aware the mothers were looking to marry them off. As Morgan wrote, "The intimation they received being the announcement of their marriage, without, perhaps, ever having known or seen each other" (Morgan, *League of the Iroquois*, p. 321).

They never objected. Iroquois social pressure insisted they accept their lot in life. "They received each other as the gift of their parents" (Morgan, *League of the Iroquois*, p. 321). The fathers, like the children, played no role in the marriage negotiations. They, like the children, were simply informed once the decision was made. The day following the announcement, the young woman was escorted by her mother, and perhaps by some young female friends, to the home of the young man. The young woman took some cakes with her, usually corn bread, to give to her mother-in-law. The gift symbolized the ability of the newest member of the household to be useful. Then the mother of the groom gave some venison, or other meat, to the mother of the bride. This symbolized the ability of the new son-in-law to provide food. That exchange of food, from young in-laws to new mothers-in-law, constituted the entire marriage ceremony.

Both before and after marriage, the sexes led separate lives. Men hunted and went to war. Women cultivated crops and raised children. There was little interaction between the sexes. Prior to marriage, anything resembling courting was unlikely. Thus, arranged marriages seldom interfered with hopes and aspirations of young men and women. Affection between a husband and wife was expected to develop, not be the basis of the marriage. And it usually did. The arranged marriages of the Iroquois were not like the arranged marriages of, say, European royalty. There was no thought of establishing or strengthening political alliances or accumulating family wealth. The mothers had as their primary concern the happiness of their children. And if they chose poorly, that could be rectified. If, after marriage, the couple was incompatible, sexually or in temperament or in any other way, the mothers would attempt a reconciliation. If that failed, the couple might agree to separate and the mothers would make no attempt to prolong a bad marriage. If one partner wanted to continue the marriage and the other did not, that too usually ended the relationship. In the 17th and 18th centuries, community pressure was usually enough to keep all but the most quarrelsome couples together, but by the 19th century, the Iroquois had what amounted to easy divorce. After a divorce, any children produced by the marriage remained with the mother and the father had neither any rights or obligations to them. Whatever property either owned before the marriage they continued to own after the divorce. The lone exception was any gift the husband gave to the wife during marriage. That was her property to keep. Unlike what often happened in white society, a divorced Iroquois wife was not left destitute.

There was one way, however, in which a married woman was treated differently, and far worse, than a married man. Although adultery was forbidden for all, only the woman was punished. The punishment was determined by a special community council gathered for that purpose. If the council found her guilty, someone, not the husband, would be appointed to publicly whip the woman. Morgan wrote that "such transgressions were exceedingly rare" (Morgan, *League of the Iroquois*, p. 331).

Morgan's view of Iroquois marriage is consistent with a mid–19th century white ideal, and that, no doubt, was greatly influenced by the fact his principle source of information on Iroquois culture was Ely Parker, who, culturally, was as much white as he was Seneca.[12] Parker would later befriend an Illinois store clerk, once joining him in a fist fight against a gang of bullies. Parker later served as a military aide to his friend during the Civil War, and when the man, Ulysses S. Grant, became president, he was appointed the first Indian to head the Commission on Indian Affairs (today's Bureau of Indian Affairs). In Morgan's Parker-influenced analysis of Iroquois culture, the Iroquois were admirable and not a lot different in intellect, potential, and morality than Christian whites. Neither Parker nor Morgan saw the Iroquois — or Indians in general — as being in need of the moral salvation that religious missionaries saw. Unfortunately for Indians, missionaries, not ethnologists or their friends, were the first whites from the East to settle in the West.

Prejudices

Narcissa Whitman wrote letters to relatives in New York that reflected attitudes and prejudices towards Indians that were typical of most white missionaries.

One letter written while the Whitmans were traveling west reflects the related facts that Narcissa Whitman was one of the first two white women to cross the continent by land, and that she knew she was a curiosity to the Indians (all letters are from *The Letters of Narcissa Whitman* and are presented in that volume, and here, chronologically):

PLATTE RIVER, SOUTH SIDE
SIX DAYS ABOVE THE FORT LARAMIE FORK
NEAR THE FOOT OF THE ROCKY MOUNTAINS
June 27, 1836

Dear Brother and Sister Whitman....

In the morning, we met a large party of Pawnees going to the fort to receive their annuities. They seemed to be very much surprised and pleased to see white females; many of them had never seen any before. They are a noble Indian — large, athletic forms, dignified countenances, bespeaking an immortal existence within....

The next day we passed all their villages. We, especially, were visited by them both at noon and at night; we ladies were such a curiosity to them. They would come and stand around our tent, peep in, and grin in their astonishment to see such looking objects.

An 1840 letter from Narcissa Whitman, now in Oregon Territory, to her mother in New York, reflects her conflicting views about saving a people from a culture she looks down upon:

Rev. Mrs. H.K.W. Perkins, Wascopum
WIELETPOO
May 2, 1840

My Dear Mother....

We feel that we cannot do our work too fast to save the Indian — the hunted, despised and unprotected Indian — from entire extinction.

A tide of immigration appears to be moving this way rapidly. What a few years will bring forth we know not....

The greatest trial to a woman's feelings is to have her cooking and eating room always filled with four or five or more Indians — men — especially at meal time, but we hope this trial is nearly done, for when we get into our other house we have a room there we devote to them especially, and shall not permit them to go into the other part of the house at all. They are so filthy they make a great deal of cleaning wherever they go, and this wears out a woman very fast. We must clean after them, for we have come to elevate them and not to suffer ourselves to sink down to their standard.... As a specimen I will relate a circumstance that occurred this spring. When the people began to return from their winter quarters, we told them it would be good for them to build a large house (which they often do by putting several lodges together) where it would be convenient for all to attend worship and not meet in the open air. They said they should not do it, but would worship in our new house and asked us if there were not houses in heaven to worship in. We told them our house was to live in and we could not have them worship there for they would make it so dirty and fill it so full of fleas that we could not live in it. We said to them further, that they did not help us build it and that people in other places build their houses of worship and did not let one man do it all alone, and urged them to join together by and by and build one for themselves of adobe. But it was of no avail to them; they murmured still and said we must pay them for their land we lived on. Something of this kind is occurring almost all the time when certain individuals are here; such as complaining because we do not feed them more, or that we will not let them run all over the house, etc., etc.

They are an exceedingly proud, haughty and insolent people, and keep us constantly upon the stretch after patience and forbearance. We feed them far more than any of our associates do their people, yet they will not be satisfied. Notwithstanding all this, there are many redeeming qualities in them, else we should have been discouraged long ago. We are more and more encouraged the longer we stay among them.

They are becoming quite independent in cultivation and make all their ground look as clean and mellow as a garden. Great numbers of them cultivate, and with but a single horse will take any plow we have, however large, and do their own ploughing. They have a great thirst for hogs, hens and cattle, and several of them have obtained them already....

Dear father, I will relate one more anecdote and then must close. Te-lou-ki-ke said to my husband this morning: "Why do you take your wife with you to Mr. Walker's? Why do you not go alone? You see I am here without my wife; why do you always want to take your wife with you when you go from home? What do you make so much of her for?" He told him it was good for me to go with him; that we were one, and that wives were given as companions. He replied "that it was so with Adam because a rib was taken from him to make his wife, but it was not so now; it was different with us." This has often been brought up by them; the way I am treated, and contrasted with themselves; they do not like to have it so; their consciences are troubled about it. May they be more and more so until a reformation is made among them.

In a letter to her sister and brother-in-law dated March 1, 1842 (but with sections written on other dates), Narcissa reflects clear cultural prejudices even as she lovingly writes about Indian children she has adopted.

Mr. Dear Jane and Edward:

[March] 2d–

After attending to the duties of the morning, and as I was nearly done hearing my children read, two native women came in bringing a miserable looking child, a boy between three and four years old, and wished me to take him. He is nearly naked, and they said his mother had thrown him away and gone off with another Indian. His father is a Spaniard and is in the mountains. It has been living with its grandmother the winter past, who is an old and adulterous woman and has no compassion for it. Its mother has several others by different white men, and one by an Indian, who are treated miserably and scarcely subsist. My feelings were greatly excited for the poor child and felt a great disposition to take him. Soon after the old grandmother came in and said she would take him to Walla Walla and dispose of him, there and accordingly took him away. Some of the women who were in, compassionated his case and followed after her and would not let her take him away, and returned with him again this eve to see what I would do about him. I told her I could not tell because my husband was gone. What I fear most is that after I have kept him awhile some of his relatives will come and take him away and my labour will be lost or worse than lost. I, however, told them they might take him away and bring him again in the morning, and in the meantime I would think about it. The care of such a child is very great at first — dirty, covered with body and head lice and starved — his clothing is a part of a skin dress that does not half cover his nakedness, and a small bit of skin over his shoulders. Helen was in the same condition when I took her, and it was a long and tedious task to change her habits, young as she was, but little more than two years old.

3. The Missionary

She was so stubborn and fretful and wanted to cry all the time if she could not have her own way. We have so subdued her that now she is a comfort to us, although she requires tight reins constantly.

Mary Ann is of a mild disposition and easily governed and makes but little trouble. She came here last August. Helen has been here nearly a year and a half. The Lord has taken our own dear child away so that we may care for the poor outcasts of the country and suffering children [the child Narcissa gave birth to died by drowning in the river]. We confine them altogether to English and do not allow them to speak a word of Nez Percés.

Read a portion of the Scriptures to the women who were in today, and talked awhile with them. Baked bread and crackers today, and made two rag babies for my little girls. I keep them in the house most of the time to keep them away from the natives, and find it difficult to employ their time when I wish to be engaged with the women. They have a great disposition to take a piece of board or a stick and carry it around on their backs, if I would let them, for a baby, so I thought I would make them something that would change their taste a little. You wonder, I suppose, what looking objects Narcissa would make. No matter how they look, so long as it is a piece of cloth rolled up with eyes, nose and mouth marked on it with a pen, it answers every purpose. They caress them and carry them about the room at a great rate, and are as happy as need be. So much for my children.

[March] 3d.-....

This evening an Indian has been in who has been away all winter. I have been reading to him the fifth chapter of Matthew. Every word of it seemed to sink deep into his heart; and O may it prove a savour of life to his soul. He thinks he is a Christian, but we fear to the contrary. His mind is somewhat waked up about his living with two wives. I would not eas[e] him any, but urged him to do his duty. Others are feeling upon the subject, particularly the women; and why should they not feel?—they are the sufferers.

The little boy was brought to me again this morning and I could not shut my heart against him. I washed him, oiled and bound up his wounds, and dressed him and cleaned his head of lice. Before he came his hair was cut close to his head and a strip as wide as your finger was shaved from ear to ear, and also from his forehead to his neck, crossing the other at right angles. This the boys had done to make him look ridiculous. He had a burn on his foot where they said he had been pushed into the fire for the purpose of gratifying their malicious feelings, and because he was friendless. He feels, however, as if he had got into a strange place, and has tried to run away once or twice. He will soon get accustomed, I think, and be happy, if I can keep him away from the native children. So much about the boy Marshall....

[March] 9th.-

Attended maternal meeting this afternoon. Sister G. and I make all the effort our time and means will permit to edify and instruct ourselves in our responsible maternal duties. Read this P.M. the report of the New York City Association for 1840, and what a feast it was to us! It is a comforting thought to us in a desert land to know that we are so kindly remembered by sister Associations in our beloved land. But the constant watch and care and anxiety of a missionary mother cannot be known by them except by experience. Sister G. has two of her own and I have three half-breeds. I believe I feel all the care and watchfulness over them that I should if they were my own. I am sure they are a double tax upon my patience and perseverance, particularly Helen; she wants to rule every one she sees. She keeps me on guard continually lest she should get the upper hand of me. The little boy appears to be of a pretty good disposition, and I think will be easy to govern. He proves to be younger than I first thought he was; he is not yet three years old — probably he is the same age Helen was when she came here. His old grandmother has been in to see him today, but appears to have no disposition to take him. She wanted I should give her something to eat every now and then, because I had got the child to live with me and take care of, also old clothes and shoes. So it is with them; the moment you do them a favour you place yourself under lasting obligations to them and must continue to give to keep their love strong towards you. I make such bungling work of writing this eve I believe I will stop, for I can scarcely keep my head up and eyes open. So good night, J., for you do not come to sleep with me, and I must content myself with Mary Ann.

An undated letter (but probably written between October 1844 and April 1846) expresses fear of the Indians:

My Dear Parents....

We have had some serious trials this spring with the Indians. Two important Indians have died and they have ventured to say and intimate that the doctor [i.e., Marcus Whitman] has killed them by his magical power, in the same way they accuse their own sorcerers and kill them for it. Also an important young man has been killed in California by Americans; he was the son of the Walla Walla chief and went there to get cattle, with a few others. This has produced much excitement also. We are in the midst of excitement and prejudice on all sides, both from Indians and passing immigrants, but the Lord has preserved us hitherto and will continue to, if we trust Him....

Your affectionate daughter,
Narcissa

One of the last letters she wrote points to one of the major sources of conflict between whites and Indians as Manifest Destiny came closer and closer to being achieved: there were just too many whites for the Indians to accommodate.

WAIILATPU, OREGON TERRITORY.
July 4th, 1847 [written Aug. 23]
My Dear Mother....

The poor Indians are amazed at the overwhelming numbers of Americans coming into the country. They seem not to know what to make of it. Very many of the principal ones are dying, and some have been killed by other Indians, in going south into the region of California. The remaining ones seem attached to us, and cling to us the closer; cultivate their farms quite extensively, and do not wish to see any Sniapus [whites] settle among them here; they are willing to have them spend the winter here, but in the spring they must all go on. They would be willing to have more missionaries stop and those devoted to their good. They expect that eventually this country will be settled by them, but they wish to see the Willamette filled up first....

From your ever affectionate daughter,
Narcissa.

Metis

The French trappers who married Huron women dismayed the Jesuit and Recollect priests, who thought they were setting an immoral example for the Indians. The trappers' behavior would impact Canadian history and help explain why Canada's westward expansion was so different from their southern neighbor's. In what would become the U.S. West, children of Indian women and white men often faced discrimination and a lack of acceptance in both Indian and white cultures, although many found little difficulty fitting into one or the other. For all these children, once they became adults, the choice was figuring out which culture to live in. In Canada, a third choice was offered. Many of these children, as adults, formed their own culture. They were called Metis,[13] a French word meaning mixed, and created their own communities in Western Canada. A few of these communities were also started near the Missouri River in United States territory, but these tended to be shorter-lived, and their residents either moved to similar towns in Canada or did the best they could to become assimilated into Indian or white communities in the U.S.

Many of the original Metis in Canada moved from Ontario to what is now Manitoba or other western provinces as employees of the Hudson Bay Company.[14] While most western exploration in the United States was government sponsored, such as the military treks of Lewis and Clark and, later, John C. Frémont, much of the exploration of western Canada was a business enterprise. The Hudson Bay Company was a near-monopoly created in the 17th century by the English crown for the benefit of family members. The company was given, in effect, governmental powers and acted as police, army, navy, tax collector, and all-around bureaucrat in an area that came to stretch from Ontario's western edge to the Pacific Ocean, from the United States' northern border to the Arctic Ocean. It was a company town bigger than most of the world's countries.

The first expedition from the eastern half of the North American continent to the Pacific Ocean was in 1792–1793 across southern Canada, a full decade before Lewis and Clark completed their trek hundreds of miles farther south. That expedition, led by Alexander Mackenzie, a Scotsman employed by the North West Fur Company,[15] the only significant rival the Hudson Bay Company faced, was a business venture designed to locate a trade route to the Pacific. Although Mackenzie and nine men under his leadership made a successful trip, it was such a difficult journey that it failed to open the Canadian West to more trade or settlement. Among the most avid readers of the book Mackenzie wrote about his adventure, however, was Thomas Jefferson, who insisted Meriwether Lewis also read it.

For those intent on avoiding Euro-centrism, we should recognize it's very possible some Indians traversed the North American continent before Mackenzie or Lewis and Clark, and at least one, a member of the Yazoo tribe from central Mississippi, made a strong claim that he did just that. Moncache-ape, whose name means Killer of Pain and Fatigue, in 1729, when he was an old man, told Le Page Du Pratz, a French historian, that when he was a young man his wife and children died and, in despair and loneliness, he took a long trip, by canoe and foot.[16] He went north and northeast and saw the Atlantic Ocean and Niagara Falls and met with the Iroquois Indians. When he returned home, years later, his desire to travel remained inflamed, so he next went west. This trip lasted five years. He reached the Pacific Ocean, met Russians at their settlement near San Francisco, went north to the Oregon coast, and returned home. At least that is how the Frenchman recorded the old man's story.

Many historians dismiss the story as either unlikely or not provable, but Moncache-ape (sometimes spelled Moncacht-ape or Moncachtape) could speak a dozen or more Indian languages, some of them from tribes hundreds of miles from his own village, and his details about the sights he saw were unlikely to have been available to him any other way. And, of course, other Native Americans may have made similar trips, but since none of the approximately 500 native cultures, or nations, that were in what would later become the United States when Columbus arrived had a written language, and since we tend to give more credence to written records than to oral traditions, it's easy to dismiss the possibility and the story told by Moncache-ape. But, a sense of adventure and a desire to see new lands and meet new cultures was never a purely European trait. Moncache-ape's story just might be true.

The struggle between the Hudson Bay and North West companies was so intense that it included several battles, the bloodiest of which was fought at Seven Oaks, near present day Winnipeg.[17] In that battle, on June 19, 1816, a Hudson Bay Company force foolishly attacked a much larger North West Company force and was overwhelmed. Twenty-one Hudson Bay men were killed. Only one man on the North West Company side died. Most of the North West men were Metis. The two companies engaged in a half-century of trade and bloody warfare that ended in 1821 when the much richer Hudson Bay Company bought out its smaller competitor.

Even after that merger, the Metis were in a constant struggle against Canadian authorities. Not until 1869 did the Hudson Bay Company sign its lands over to the Canadian government, and then the Metis, under the leadership of Louis Riel,[18] rebelled. The Metis wanted their own government and in effect would soon get it. The Manitoba Act of 1870 assured the Metis a controlling interest in whatever local government was created. That included allowing the Catholic Church to run local schools, since most Metis, although not all, were Catholic. Riel, fearing he would be executed for his part in the rebellion, fled to the United States. Meanwhile, the Metis in the newly created province of Manitoba kept electing him to the national Parliament in Ottawa, but the House of Commons never let him take his seat. He then started to see visions. He had as a young man studied for the priesthood and was always very religious. But, since he already had powerful enemies, these visions were seen as proof that he was crazy, and when he did return to Canada he was locked up for a couple of years in an insane asylum in Quebec. When he was released, he moved to Montana, married an American Meti, and taught at a Catholic school. To help assure he could not be deported to Canada, he became an American citizen. But some Metis, not satisfied with their status in Manitoba, decided to rebel a second time and invited Riel to lead them. He accepted, returned to Canada, set up a separate Meti government, and raised a Meti army, which was promptly defeated by the Canadian army. Riel was tried for treason, found guilty, and on November 16, 1885, executed by hanging in Regina, Saskatchewan. Today, Riel is a national hero to the tens of thousands of people who call themselves Metis, considered a traitor by an even larger number of non–Meti Canadians, and, according to one poll, remains unknown to most 21st century Canadians.

Never Smiling

While most of the proselytizing of Indians in Canada was done by Catholic priests, particularly by Jesuits, most attempts to convert Indians to Christianity in the western territories of the United States in the first half of the 19th century was done by Methodists and Presbyterians, with Jesuits coming in number three.[19] But prior to the efforts of American clergymen to save, from their perspective, the souls of heathens, the dominant non-native religious force in the area, before it became owned by the United States, were the Franciscans, or, to use a term that distinguishes them from their rival Jesuits, the Brown Robes. (In Canada, French Franciscans were often called Recollects.)

The Spanish crown, whoever was on the throne at the time, generally insisted that conquest of the Americas not be separated from attempts at conversion. The argument was, in its simplest form, that if Indians refused to become Catholic then it was all right to kill or enslave them. And most of the Indians refused. They already had their own religions, thank you, and the widespread evil, including indiscriminate murder and rape, drawing and quartering, done by the Spaniards, hardly seemed a ringing endorsement of the religious beliefs they represented. Many of Indian conversions to Christianity in Spanish America in the three centuries following the arrival of Columbus were achieved by force and fear, not by logic or gentle persuasion.

With a New World capital in Mexico City, the missions established a thousand miles to the north, in present-day New Mexico and Arizona, were both isolated and beyond the legal and social pressures of European norms. The Spanish established missions that were more than religious centers. They were also governmental and military posts and exercised oppressive control over the Indian villages, or pueblos. The few Spanish women who moved to the missions and pueblos found they were powerless to keep their husbands from cheating on them with pueblo women. But they did try, often using the same powders, herbs and potions Indian women used to seduce men. One paste, made from crushed worms, was spread over the body of a man to increase his sexual pleasure. The Franciscan priests found the pueblo women as enticing as the Spanish soldiers did.

In many of the pueblo cultures, sex with a holy man or holy woman was seen as a way to obtain some of the special powers he or she was assumed to possess. The Franciscans quickly discovered this and some of them used that belief to have sex with the Indian women. They also told Spanish women that as long as their husbands were cheating on them with Indian women, and they no doubt wanted to therefore cheat on their husbands, it was best to cheat with a man of the cloth. The brown cloth. Still, they found time to condemn the Indians for not having sex according to church-approved standards. In the Taos Pueblo in 1638, one priest, Fray Nicolas Hidalgo, twisted off the penis of an Indian man who disagreed with him. Priests grabbing and squeezing the testicles of men who refused to convert was so common that many men tried to avoid contact with the Franciscans. Both men and women were whipped for engaging in dances that were part of their culture but considered too suggestive by the priests. The priests who had sex with pueblo women were often the same ones who punished them for improper, by European standards, behavior.

In some pueblos, young unmarried women routinely went around naked. When the priests denounced this practice, they were told that it made sense because if a young woman did anything she wasn't supposed to, everyone would see it and know. The logic did not convince the priests. Whippings and other punishments were so frequent, as was the repression of Indian religious practices, that several times the pueblos rebelled. A half dozen times the rebellions were suppressed and the leaders executed or sold into slavery. But in 1675, the 30,000 Indians in the 70-plus pueblos the Spanish controlled, rose up against the 2,300 Spaniards who had caused them so much misery.[20] They killed 400 Spaniards, including 21 Franciscan priests (out of 33 assigned to the pueblos), and the survivors fled to Mexico City. The Spanish were unable to return for 12 years. Four years after that, they reconquered the pueblos. And they were as repressive as ever.

Farther west, in California, Franciscans voiced their same sex-is-bad attitudes, with similar punishments for non-conforming Indians, but with far less of the sexual interaction between Indian women and priests that marked their reign in what would become Arizona and New Mexico. That was largely because of the severe personality of Junipero Serra, a Franciscan who founded a series of missions in California beginning in 1767.[21] He was as humorless as any man who ever lived. Everyone who met him and wrote about the meeting noted that he never laughed. Never. Or smiled. Or enjoyed the food he ate. He just ate it without complaint or compliment. He had, as a young man, renounced all physical pleasures, and he spent the rest of his life — he lived until age 73 — perfecting the promise. He refused to read poetry or look at works of art. And, unlike his Franciscan brothers a thousand miles to the east, he never had sexual relations with anyone. He died a virgin. Living such a life, you might think, he would view himself as fully pure. But no, not for someone as permanently solemn as Junipero Serra. He whipped himself with ropes, beat his breast with rocks, burned himself with torches to punish himself for his sins. Presumably God knew what they were.

And he expected everyone associated with his missions to have as little fun. Both the Spanish soldiers who guarded the missions and the Indians the missions were intended to serve — that is, to convert to Christianity — were constantly subjected to his harangues about the evils of physical pleasures. While many of the soldiers managed to sleep with Indian women anyway, and while Indian men and women did several times rebel, Serra ran the California missions as a dictatorial theocracy. When Mexico City, as capital of New Spain, sent civilian governors to administer California, Serra constantly feuded with them, and although they technically had authority over government, few important decisions were made without Serra's approval. In fact, critics at the time, and even more of them today, charged Serra's missions were really feudal forts in which Indians were serfs, forced to perform farming and other tasks that Serra insisted was labor necessary for saving their souls. He envisioned, and strove constantly to create, his version of an earthly paradise in which everyone was obedient to church authority and no one had fun. Sex outside marriage was typically punished by flogging. As was dancing.

A year after Serra died 1784, Dona Eulalia Callis, wife of the civilian governor of California, Pedro Fages, filed for divorce, charging, "I found my husband physically on top of one of his servants, a Yuma Indian girl" (Beebe, p. 237).[22] Serra would have disapproved of any divorce, but if he ever found joy in anything, it might very well have been in the sexual infidelity of Governor Pedro Fages. But he wouldn't have smiled.

Dying for Their Sins

By the time Marcus and Narcissa Whitman arrived at the Walla Walla River in 1836 Oregon Territory, Christian missionaries had spent more than two centuries trying to suppress Indian lifestyles, including sexual habits and religious beliefs. By 1847, when they had been there 11 years, the Whitmans were convinced, as so many missionaries in so many places were convinced, that the Indians respected, even loved them.[23] How could they not? Had they not brought Jesus Christ into their lives? Did not many of them learn Christian prayers and attend Christian church? Did not they come to Dr. Whitman, Christ's representative, to be cured of diseases? And, besides, wasn't Narcissa both beautiful and a paragon of Christian virtue? Oh, yes, she constantly told the Cayuse their way of living was wrong, that God didn't approve of polygamy or easy divorce and young women dressing so immodestly, but certainly the Cayuse understood she wanted only to save their souls. Oh, certainly an obdurate Indian now and then complained about this or that. But the Whitmans believed in the deepest reaches of their hearts that they were loved by the Cayuse. Sure, that Joe Lewis, that newly arrived Canadian, was constantly complaining about not being treated fairly and certainly some of the Cayuse spent time listening to him. But he was just a loudmouth who, they expected, would be leaving the mission soon enough. The problem with the measles, that was the only real problem.

The previous year, a wagon train passing through included several passengers with measles. The disease spread quickly. Whites and Indians both suffered. But what a few misguided Cayuse said, that wasn't true, was it? That the white people always recovered from the disease and the Indians always died? No. Well, maybe it seemed that way. There had never been more than a few thousand Cayuse. They were a rich but small tribe. They were probably the first Indians in North America to master the bronco, the small, highly stable horse that later would sometimes be called the Cayuse. Nearly every

3. *The Missionary*

man in the tribe owned at least a half dozen. A few of the chiefs seemed to own more than a thousand. They traded them to whites and other Indian tribes, and the Cayuse never seemed to be hungry, were usually at peace with neighboring tribes, prospered visibly beyond tribes that were once their enemies. But there were so few of them that they could barely keep their language alive. Most Cayuse, in fact, spoke the language of the much larger neighboring tribe to the north, the Nez Percé. If it wasn't for the measles, all would be well. Dr. Whitman gave what medicines he could to both whites and Cayuse, and, yes, what some Cayuse said seemed to be true. The whites suffered, but none of them died. One report put the Cayuse dead at 30. Another at several hundred.

Later, scientists would say whites had developed an immunity to measles. Measles did not exist in the New World when Columbus arrived. Like smallpox and other deadly diseases the Europeans brought, Native Americans had no immunity to it. On the East Coast, tribes had several hundred years to develop an immunity. Many died, but those who survived gave birth to children who were also likely to survive. And the children of those children fared even better. It's how evolution works, how a species survives. But for West Coast Indians, measles was much newer. And for those inland from the West Coast, like the Cayuse in 1847, measles was a first-generation terror. Immunity was non-existent.

When the Whitmans first arrived they arranged for some Cayuse men to help them build the mission buildings. They helped but felt strange. In their culture, women put up the lodges, not men. This was women's work. The whites were insulting them by having them do this labor. And, an additional insult, Narcissa Whitman just stood by. She did not help in erecting the buildings. She did not do women's work. Nor did she plant seeds or cut meat from killed animals. For the Cayuse, that was work for a woman, but for the whites, it was work for a man. Not just different, insulting. And the chiefs and other wealthy Cayuse men could not understand why Marcus Whitman had only one wife. Having three or four or five wives meant more work was done. It also showed ones status in the village. What status was there for a man with only one woman? And when the men looked in the windows of the buildings, the buildings they had helped to erect, Mrs. Whitman chased them away. A woman giving them orders? And they were only looking, not an act to bring a scolding.

In the fall of 1847, a son of Tilaukait, one of the Cayuse chiefs, died. Two, maybe three, of his other children had died months earlier. Tilaukait and Tomahas went to the mission, went to Whitman's home, talked to Narcissa. They wanted to see the doctor. It was about two in the afternoon. Narcissa was frightened. She knew Tilaukait and Tomahas were angry. And there were other Indians inside the mission. Dr. Whitman was upstairs seeing to a young white man recovering from measles. When he came down the narrow, steep steps, Narcissa told him the chiefs were insisting he see them. He went into the kitchen, and Tilaukait confronted him. He accused Whitman of killing his son. Not just not saving him, but killing him. Whitman was tired of these allegations. The Indians didn't understand disease. He started to explain, with exasperation. But Tilaukait was angry. And then the blade of a tomahawk slammed into Whitman's skull. Tomahas would listen to no more lies, no more white explanations. One of the Indians placed the barrel of Whitman's own rifle against the top of his chest, where it meets his neck, and pulled the trigger.

Narcissa had gone outside, and when she heard the argument, she looked through a window just in time to see her husband tomahawked and shot. The Indians ran outside and shot her, but she didn't immediately die. The Cayuse dragged her away from the building and sliced her with hatchets and knives, especially her face. Even after she bled to death, they continued slicing at her face.

Seventeen-year-old John Sager saw Marcus Whitman murdered, and he tried to stop it and was shot to death. Fifteen-year-old Frank Sager ran out of his loft when he heard the shooting, and he too was shot to death. L.W. Saunders, a school teacher, ran from the school room towards his home to protect his wife, and was stabbed to death. Walter Marsh was working at the grist mill when he heard the shooting and ran to see what was wrong and, while running, was shot and killed. Isaac Gilliland was sewing a suit for Marcus Whitman when he was stabbed to death. Andrew Rodgers was at the river when several Indians attacked him and stabbed him repeatedly. He lay in the mud for two or three or four hours before he died. The next day, Crockett Bewley and Amos Sales, both so sick with measles they could not leave their beds, were beaten to death with slats from those beds. An hour or so before the slaughter at the mission, two men slaughtering a cow a half mile away were killed by the Indians. Sixteen men and one woman, Narcissa, were killed. Several men escaped. Fifty-four women and children were unharmed but held captive.

When Five Crows, a Cayuse chief who did not take part in the killings, heard about what happened and heard that except for the arrogant Mrs. Whitman, all the women were unharmed, he sent several of his men to talk to Tilaukait. He wanted Lorinda Bewley. Months earlier he had offered the whites dozens of horses for her. The offer was a token of his esteem for the family of the woman he wanted as a wife. He already had four or five, but he thought Lorinda more beautiful than any of them. When the whites told him — with arrogance, he thought — that they do not sell their women, he left in anger.

3. The Missionary

But now he did not have to deal with the white men. Tilaukait was far more reasonable.

When Lorinda realized what was happening, she begged Tilaukait to let her remain with the other women, but he had no sympathy for her. Did she think that as a white woman she was too good to be the wife of an Indian? A chief? "You will be safer at the camp of the chief," he explained. "All the Indians will be glad to protect the squaw of Five Crows, but here you will become the common property of all and I can not help you. You will do well to marry with the great chief who wants a yellow haired wife" (Flora, "Aftermath"). Simply having to explain the obvious annoyed Tilaukait. Besides, he had a more serious problem. He had just orchestrated the murder of more than a dozen whites, and other whites would be angry. Sending one hostage to a safe place seemed wise. It would show he meant no harm to any of the hostages.

The group sent by Five Crows took Lorinda about five miles to the Catholic mission. It was smaller and with even less protection than the Whitmans' Presbyterian mission. Bishop Magloire Blanchet understood the fear Lorinda felt. And he understood the danger he and others in his mission faced. Father Rousseau fed Lorinda some meat and bread and gave her tea to drink. Father Brouillet tried to comfort her. He had gone to Waiilatpu two days earlier. The Cayuse let him preside over a Christian burial for the dead. Surely these men would save her. They were men of the cloth. But Bishop Blanchet told her, with great sadness in his voice, "We are but a handful of white men among a nation of savages on the warpath. Five Crows is a much finer character than most. I will do what I can to reason with him and delay as long as possible. We are all caught in this trap and are helpless. But do not weep daughter. This great trouble is not your fault" (Flora, "Aftermath").

Her brother was dead. The wonderful Doctor and Mrs. Whitman were dead. So many good Christians were dead. And now she would become the concubine of a savage. What had she done to earn God's wrath?

While Lorinda was waiting to discover her fate, so too were the other 53 women and children held hostage by the Cayuse. And the white authorities in Oregon Territory were determined to rescue them. While a militia was being organized for possible military action, Territorial Governor George Abernethy sent Peter Skene Ogden, the top official of the Hudson Bay Company in the territory, to try to negotiate the release of the hostages. Ogden, a Canadian, had traveled over much of the American West looking for opportunities for his company to make money. He met with the Cayuse chiefs in January of 1848 and spoke to them in harsh terms, with stern warnings, but carefully allowed them an honorable way to end the hostilities. "We are traders and a different nation to the Americans," he said, "but recollect we supply you with ammunition not to kill the Americans" (*Oregon Spectator*, January 20, 1848).

He referred to the massacre at Walla Walla in unforgiving terms: "this revolting butchery" (*Oregon Spectator*, January 20, 1848). He asked, "Have not the Indians pillaged, ill-treated the Americans and insulted their women when peaceably making their way to the Willamette?" (*Oregon Spectator*, January 20, 1848 [the Willamette River flows through modern-day Portland]). Remarks made to Indian women were acceptable, but Ogden revealed more than a little cultural arrogance by criticizing Indian men for similar remarks to white women. Next, he added an odd criticism, one the Cayuse probably had difficulty fully understanding with its reference to classical mythology. "Why do we call you Chiefs," he asked rhetorically, "if you have no control over your young men, if you allow them to govern you? You are a set of Hermaphrodites and unworthy of the appellation of men or Chiefs" (*Oregon Spectator*, January 20, 1848).

Could the Cayuse have known that a hermaphrodite was someone who had both male and female sex organs, just like the unfortunate son of Hermes and Aphrodite in Greek myths who had to share a body with a nymph? Whether or not the Cayuse understood the details of Ogden's insult, they certainly understood they were being insulted. Accusing men of acting like or even being women was one of the most common insults whites directed at Indian men and that Indians directed at white men. Despite all their cultural differences, Indians and whites had that in common: a belief that a man acting like a woman was an inferior man. Then he added another insult, a reference to the Indians' belief that Marcus Whitman had either deliberately given measles to the Indians or at least refused to cure them.

"It is not Doctor Whitman that has poisoned [the Indians]," he said, "but God has commanded they should die" (*Oregon Spectator*, January 20, 1848). God, in Ogden's view, was on the side of the whites. But Ogden repeated an offer he had made before, and that, far more than the insults, allowed the Cayuse chiefs a way to return the hostages without shaming themselves in front of others in their tribe. Ogden was willing to pay a ransom. Just as important, perhaps more important, was the realization by the chiefs that they and every Cayuse not killed by measles faced slaughter by revenge-seeking whites. *The Oregon Spectator*, the major newspaper in the territory, had editorialized, "Let them be hunted as beasts of prey; let their name and race be blotted from the face of the earth, and the places that once knew them, know them no more forever. Oh how terrible should be the retribution" (*Oregon Spectator*, January 20, 1848).

The chiefs may have been told about the editorial, but even if they hadn't, they understood that the whites were capable of slaughtering the entire tribe

3. *The Missionary*

just as a few Cayuse had slaughtered the Whitmans and more than a dozen others in the mission. So the Hudson Bay Company donated, according to the *Oregon Spectator*, 62 blankets, 63 cotton shirts, 12 rifles, 600 loads of ammunition, 12 flints for the rifles, and 37 pounds of tobacco. The women and children were released and the merchandise was delivered to the Indians the next day. A ransom from a Canadian company freed the American women and children.

Meanwhile Lorinda Bewley was waiting at the Catholic mission in Walla Walla when Five Crows showed up. The priests spoke to him. He spoke to Lorinda. The priests must have convinced him of something, for he did not simply take her away. He reasoned with her. Told her how much she would enjoy being his wife, that he was a rich man with much influence in his village. She said nothing. She only shook her head. He told her how his other wives enjoyed each other's company and that they would like her and she would like them. She shook her head. Repeatedly. He said his people were not like some in the other villages, that they liked whites, appreciated what whites had done for them, and reminded her that even Marcus and Narcissa Whitman had explained that Indians and whites were children of the same God. She shook her head. Then Five Crows spoke to the priests. Then he thanked Lorinda for listening to him and he left. Lorinda looked at the priests. They smiled. She was free, they said, to rejoin the other women.

The aftermath for the Cayuse was predictable. Territorial Governor George Abernethy ordered a militia raised, and Cornelius Gilliam, one of the least admirable men in the territory, was put in charge. Gilliam, before moving to Oregon Territory earlier in the year, had lived in Missouri, where he had been a bounty hunter who specialized in capturing escaped slaves and commander of a company of volunteers who tried to carry out the 1838 executive order of Missouri Governor Lilburn Boggs to exterminate all Mormons in the state. He was also a county sheriff and a member of the state legislature. He was elected "general" of a wagon train that went to Oregon Territory in 1844 but resigned in a fit when he threatened to shoot a young man who wouldn't obey one of his commands and everyone watching ridiculed him. The members of the wagon train considered him incompetent and were happy to replace him. He fought against Seminole Indians in Florida and Sac and Fox Indians in the Black Hawk War in Illinois and often called for the extermination of all Indians. He was also a part-time ordained Baptist minister who denounced Mormon polygamy, Indian sexual practices, and anyone whose views on sex differed from his. When he was put in charge of the Oregon Territory's retaliatory militia of more than 500 volunteers, mostly young men in their mid and late teens and early 20s he attacked a group of Cayuse who had nothing to do with the Whitman massacre and killed about 30 of them. That encouraged hundreds of Indians — Cayuse, Nez Percé, and others — who had condemned the Whitman massacre to join in fighting against whites. While planning another attack on an Indian village, Gilliam was pulling a rope from the back of a wagon and the rope caught the hammer of a rifle that had a cleaning rod in its barrel, and the rifle fired, sending the rod through Gilliam's forehead and into his brain, killing him instantly. With their bigoted leader dead, the members of the militia lost interest in killing Indians and went home.

The Cayuse leaders of the massacre went into hiding and were hunted for two years by white soldiers and lawmen, who several times came close to catching them. Tired of running and hiding and believing that if they were not caught many more Cayuse might die, they finally surrendered in 1846. Tilaukait, Tomahas, and three others were tried by a court that lacked legal authority to try them, found guilty, and sentenced to death by hanging. They were offered last rites by a Presbyterian minister. Not surprisingly, they refused anything from a Presbyterian. A Catholic priest then offered to administer last rites and they accepted. Then they were hung.

The Whitmans, the Franciscans in the Southwest, the Jesuits among the Hurons, and even the kindly Father De Smet, all approached their work with a strong sense of cultural superiority, even arrogance. They believed the values they represented — religion-based values — were superior to those of the cultures they encountered. Which is why they devoted their lives to converting members of those cultures. This was most clearly revealed in their attitudes towards the sex lives of the Indians. Polygamy, easy divorce, pre-marital sex, so much of what the Indians accepted as natural, the missionaries saw as evil. When they could not talk the Indians into changing their ways, they often beat them into submission. Marcus and Narcissa Whitman died for their sins.

4

Presidential Sex

Making the West American resulted from, among other factors, men like Lewis and Clark exploring the West partly because of their interest in sex; the mountain men moving to the West because their sexual proclivities contributed to making them uncomfortable in what passed for civilization in more eastern communities, and missionaries establishing settlements in the West and their belief they needed to save native populations from their un-Christian lives, evidenced partly by the Indians' sexual habits.

Most of the men and women involved in these events were ordinary people with ordinary dreams who found themselves swimming in the currents of history. They — John Colter, Father De Smet, and thousands of others — made the West American. But there is another aspect of how these ordinary folk came to assure the West would be American rather than French or Spanish or British or remain the property of Indians, and that is the American leaders who made decisions that moved these ordinary people — people who often possessed an extraordinary courage, an extraordinary determination, an extraordinary right to our admiration — to push the western boundary of the United States closer and closer to the Pacific.

It's tempting to give too much credit to leaders, perhaps too easy to fall victim to Thomas Carlyle's dictum that "the history of the world is but the biography of great men."[1] Yet, men and women history tend to label as great — presidents and generals, rather than farmers and foot soldiers — do often play a role beyond that of other individuals in shaping our world, for good or bad.

We've already briefly examined how one of these men, Thomas Jefferson, made decisions that propelled the United States westward. The sex lives of two other leaders exalted, properly or improperly, in our history books and history movies, helped drive the United States farther west: Sam Houston and Andrew Jackson.

The War Wound

Sam Houston's marriage ended on his wedding night.[2]

Houston was born in Virginia in 1793, the fifth of nine children. Although he had little schooling—less than six months—he loved to read and claimed he memorized almost all of Homer's *Iliad*. When Sam was a teenager his father went bankrupt and then died. His mother used the proceeds of the bankruptcy sale to move the family to Maryville, Tennessee, a bit south of Knoxville. Sam found a job in a Maryville store, but often, instead of going to work, he went to a nearby Cherokee village where he was unofficially adopted by an Indian named Oolooteka (which translates into He Puts the Drum Away). His adoptive father named him Co-lon-neh, or Raven. At age 19 (according to historians [he wrote later that he was 18 at the time]) he opened a school. The income from his teaching helped him pay off some debts, but he had another reason for remembering the profession with fondness. The man who would become the governor of two states (Tennessee and Texas), a U.S. congressman, a U.S. senator, and president of the Republic of Texas, wrote that as a teacher, "I experienced a higher feeling of dignity and self-satisfaction than from any office or honor which I have held since" (Haley, p. 11).

But he also felt called to a mixed sense of adventure and honor. In March 1813, military recruiters passed through Maryville looking for volunteers to fight in the War of 1812. Because he was not yet 21, he needed his mother's permission to join. She gave the permission, along with a gold ring, a musket, and a creed to live by as a soldier: "I had rather all my sons should fill one honorable grave than that one of them should turn his back to save his life. Go, and remember, too, that while the door of my cottage is open to brave men, it is eternally shut against cowards" (Haley, p. 12).

He enlisted as a private but within a year gained promotion first to sergeant and then ensign. He fought in a battle at To-ho-pe-ka, or Horseshoe Bend, in eastern Alabama against the Creek Indians, who had been outfitted by the British. In the battle a barbed arrow hit him in the leg. It entered his inner, upper thigh. He insisted to a reluctant lieutenant that the arrow be pulled out. When the lieutenant hesitated, Houston drew a sword on him, and the lieutenant grabbed the arrow and pulled it hard. The arrow came out and so did several cubic inches of flesh and a great deal of blood. An Army surgeon plugged the wound with rags and Houston returned to the battle. This time bullets entered his right shoulder and arm and he was carried again to the surgeon. One bullet was removed, but the other, buried in bone, remained inside of him the rest of his life. For decades, both bullet wounds occasionally produced bone fragments. The thigh wound left a nasty scar that sometimes oozed pus for nearly half a century.³ Houston's bravery in returning to battle while wounded was noted by the American commander, and a lifelong friendship developed between the two. The commander, Andrew Jackson, would be immensely useful to the young Houston's future political career.

Houston became part of a cadre of personal friends of Jackson who sought and won elective office. Houston twice won election to the U.S. House of Representatives from Tennessee and in 1827 won election as governor of the state. He was 34 with a very bright future when on January 22, 1829, he married Eliza Allen, a 19-year-old member of one of the most powerful families in the state.⁴ Her father was one of the wealthiest men in the state, her brother a U.S. congressman. But something happened on their wedding night. Neither ever talked about the specifics of what happened that night. To anyone. Eleven weeks later they separated. The only comment Eliza is known to have made about her husband came the day after their wedding, when she saw Sam playfully exchanging snowballs with the daughters of a friend. She said, "I wish with all my heart they would kill him" (Haley, p. 57).

They rode together to the state capital, Nashville, where, since there was no official residence for the governor, they stayed in the Nashville Inn. Eliza clearly hated Sam, but she attended some official functions as the wife of the governor. On April 9, at her request, her father arrived in Nashville and took her home. Houston wrote a rambling, nearly incoherent letter to Colonel Allen, the father, saying he didn't blame Eliza for anything, suggesting, some historians think, that he might have accused her of not being a virgin on their wedding night. After begging her father that he be allowed to see Eliza again, the two met in the parlor of the Allen home. Houston knelt in front of her and begged her to return to him. He returned to the Nashville Inn alone. There, on April 16, a whisky bottle in one hand, a pen in the other, he wrote a letter resigning as governor of Tennessee. His friend, Tennessee Congressman Davy Crockett, said Houston told him he intended to leave white society and live with the Cherokees.

He did take a steamboat up the Arkansas River, and at one stop, two of Eliza's brothers boarded and confronted Houston. They were heavily armed. They demanded he do something to assure their sister's reputation was not sullied. He told them they should arrange that Nashville newspapers publish a statement to the effect "that if any wretch ever dares to utter a word against the purity of Mrs. Houston, I will come back and write the libel in his heart's blood" (Haley, p. 63). Instead, they arranged for the newspapers to publish the nearly incoherent letter Houston had written to their father and an announcement that they would form a committee to investigate what had happened. That committee issued a report the following April in which Houston was blamed entirely for the breakup of the marriage. The committee called him a "deluded man" (Haley, p. 74) and said, interestingly, that his allegations of Eliza's "coldness" (Haley, p. 74) were unfounded. About a month after he resigned as governor, Houston wrote to his friend President Jackson calling himself "the most unhappy man now living" (Haley, p. 66).

What happened on the wedding night? For nearly two centuries speculation has dominated the historical record. One theory is that Colonel Allen pressured his daughter into marrying Houston because of his own ambitions. Another is that Eliza loved someone else, perhaps William Tyree, a lawyer who died of tuberculosis before they could wed, or Dr. Elmore Douglass, who, in fact, she would later marry.

Houston settled near Fort Gibson in what is now eastern Oklahoma, where the Neosho River flows into the Arkansas. His adoptive Cherokee father, Oolooteka, had moved there with his family years earlier under pressure from the U.S. government (this was a few years before the infamous Trail of Tears in which President Jackson forced all Cherokees to move out of the South to Indian Territory, today's Oklahoma). Houston lived with a half-white, half-Cherokee woman, a widow named Tiana Rogers Gentry.[5] (One of her descendants would be humorist Will Rogers.) They may have married, but no official record exists. He continued to do one of the things he did a great deal of in Tennessee and that he would continue to do for decades more: drink. The Cherokees nicknamed him *Ootsets Ardeetahskee*, or Big Drunk. He acted as ambassador for the Cherokee nation, making regular visits to Congress and the White House, usually wearing Indian clothing, including shirts with metal ornaments that jingled and a turban-like hat.

On one trip to Washington, feeling that Congressman William Stanberry of Ohio had insulted him by accusing him, on the floor of the House of Representatives, of using improper methods to win some government contracts for the Cherokees, he found the congressman on Pennsylvania Avenue and beat him with a hickory cane. Stanberry brought charges before the House and Houston hired a lawyer, Francis Scott Key, author of the lyrics to "The Star Spangled Banner," to defend him. The trial, held in the House, as publicized in its day as the O.J. Simpson trial would be more than a century and a half later, included testimony from a witness, Missouri Senator Alexander Buckner, that Houston at one point lifted the congressman by the feet and struck him "elsewhere" (Haley, p. 82).

Houston was found guilty, ordered to accept a reprimand from the Speaker of the House and to pay a $500 fine. Next, a congressional committee, chaired by Stanberry, held hearings on the charge of fraud in the Indian contracts, and Houston was found innocent. Whatever Houston thought of Stanberry's character in making the remarks, the Ohio congressman certainly chaired the committee's hearing honorably.

Next, after six years with the Cherokees, Houston moved to Texas, then still part of Mexico, and established a successful law practice. Thousands of Americans, mostly from the South, had moved into Texas, often bringing slaves with them. Slavery was illegal in Mexico, so most slave owners technically gave their slaves papers saying they were free but forced them to sign other papers in which they agree to work for the ex-owner forever, usually for no or infinitesimally little pay. With the major population of Mexico more than a thousand miles away from the major concentration of Americans in eastern Texas, the Americans thought breaking away from Mexico was feasible. There were only a few small Mexican military outposts in Texas.

When the Americans decided to rebel with the intent of joining the United States, Sam Houston, because of his military experience in the War of 1812 and his fame, was put in charge of the haphazard gathering of poorly trained, if enthusiastic, volunteers. The Mexican dictator General Antonio Lopez de Santa Anna countered the rebellion by leading an army of 7,000 soldiers to Texas. They were better trained, better equipped, and better disciplined than the Americans. Putting down the rebellion should have been quick. However, Santa Anna was a terrible general, and although Houston had never previously commanded a whole army, his strategic and tactical skills greatly exceeded Santa Anna's, despite a stupid mistake by one of his highest ranking officers.

Houston ordered Lt. Colonel William Travis to abandon the town of Bexar (now San Antonio), to destroy the Alamo before leaving, and to take all cannon with him. Travis let bravado override military orders, occupied the Alamo with only 182 men, and on March 6, 1836, engaged Santa Anna in battle. Travis, Davy Crockett, Jim Bowie, and the other 179 men in the Alamo died because of Travis's bravado. Forty-six days later, Houston, telling his men to remember the Alamo, surprised a relaxing Mexican army at San Jacinto, just south of Galveston. Santa Anna could not rally his superior forces and his incompetence resulted in disaster: 630 dead, 230 wounded, 730 taken prisoner. Among the prisoners: the general himself. The Americans lost six dead. Twenty-five were wounded, Houston among them. His horse was shot and fell on his ankle, crushing it.

Houston was the great hero of Texas, and when the Texans found the North would not agree to admit them as a slave state, they started their own country, elected Houston as their first president, in 1836, for a two-year term, established a new town to serve as the state capital and named it after him. The Texas constitution did not allow a president to serve consecutive terms, but Houston was elected again in 1841. Mexico never recognized Texas as an independent country (it still hasn't), and becoming part of the United States was the only feasible way of avoiding recapture by Mexico. When James Polk, a slave owner, became U.S. president, he was able to convince Congress to accept Texas as a state. A slave state. Houston was then elected U.S. senator from Texas.

Talk of secession from the Union put him in a difficult position. He spoke often and vigorously against breaking up the union, so much so that the state legislature stripped him of his senate seat. So he ran for governor and was elected. He was the governor in 1861 when the legislature voted to join the Confederacy. He refused to take an oath of allegiance to the Confederacy and the greatest hero in Texas history was once again removed by legislative decree from the political office he held. He also turned down an offer from Abraham Lincoln to send Union troops to Texas to assist Houston if he decided to fight for control of the state.

While history unfolded around Sam Houston, his love life took new turns. In 1837 he and Eliza finally officially divorced. His Cherokee wife, Tiana, died. That is, she almost certainly died. He may have abandoned her. They may never have actually married. The historical record is unclear, as it so often is with Indian nations. So in May of 1840 the 47-year-old Houston was free to marry Margaret Moffette Lea, 21, pretty, and the daughter of a Baptist minister from Alabama. She had two conditions before the marriage, however. He agreed to both. He became a Baptist. And he stopped drinking. No doubt the second was harder to do. She and Sam Houston had four children and remained married the rest of their lives.

So, what happened on the night of his wedding to Eliza? No one can ever know with certainty, but there's one intriguing possibility, that with the objectivity possible a century and three-quarters later, makes sense. Eliza, typical of young, socially prominent ladies of her day, had never seen a naked man prior to her wedding night. But she would have been told things, by her mother and by other young women. And much of what she would have been told would have been incomplete or misleading or wrong. When she saw his war wound, so close to his penis and testicles, perhaps on that night with pus oozing out of it, she might have been repulsed. (In fact, members of her family said exactly that years later.) She may have mistaken the wound and the pus for a venereal disease. In addition to repulsing her, that may have led her to feel (1) endangered and (2) that her husband had slept with other women. The combination of the three would have been difficult for her to talk about, so she didn't. If she accused Houston of not being virginal, he, a man of quick temper, may have responded with doubts about her virginity. And the combination would have been an argument from which their marriage never recovered.

It's thus very possible that Sam Houston's war wound, no doubt ugly and repulsive, resulted in him fleeing Tennessee, settling in what is now Oklahoma, then in Texas, leading the Texan army to victory over the Mexicans, and eventually making Texas part of the United States. Whatever happened on the night Sam and Eliza Houston should have had sex for the first time, and it certainly involved the wound, is what drove him west. That is, the wound that prevented his first wife from having sex with him helped make the West American.

Killing for Love

Andrew Jackson killed for love.[6]

Jackson fought four duels in his life (and challenged a man to still another) to assuage what he considered insults to both himself and his wife, Rachel.[7] He fought the first one in 1788 against Waightstill Avery in Nashville (then in South Carolina, now in Tennessee). Jackson was the solicitor, or prosecutor, and Avery the defense lawyer in a civil suit, when Avery, by far the better attorney, bested Jackson on a legal point to the extent of making Jackson feel humiliated. Avery's son later recalled, "The cause was going against him, and he became irritable. My father rather exultingly ridiculed some legal position taken by Jackson, using, as he afterwards admitted, language more sarcastic than was called for. It stung Jackson, who snatched up a pen, and on the blank leaf of a law book wrote a peremptory challenge, which he delivered there and then" (Brands, p. 53).

Avery ignored the challenge, so the next day Jackson wrote a second note: "When a man's feelings and character are injured he ought to seek a speedy redress. You received a few lines from me yesterday, and undoubtedly you understand me. My character you have injured, and further you have insulted me in the presence of a court and a large audience. I therefore call upon you as a gentleman to give me satisfaction" (Brands, p. 53). They met at an appointed time and place, but by then the 21-year-old Jackson had cooled, so, as sometimes happened in such duels, the two men paced off the agreed upon distance, turned, and each aimed his pistol away from his opponent, and fired. Neither man was hurt, and, as Avery's son said, "They shook hands, and were friendly ever after" (Brands, p. 54).

About the same time Jackson met Rachel Robards. That's *Mrs.* Rachel Robards. At least one person who knew her described her as extremely attractive, saying she had a "beautifully molded form, lustrous black eyes, dark glossy hair, full red lips, brunette complexion, though of brilliant coloring, a sweet oval face, rippling with smiles and dimples" (Brands, p. 57). She had just turned 17 when she married Lewis Robards, but, probably within months, he abandoned her. She moved back in with her widowed mother in Tennessee.

Jackson for a while rented a room in the same house and dined frequently with the family. He became as attracted to Rachel as at least a dozen other men had.

Meanwhile, her father-in-law attempted a reconciliation between Rachel and Lewis, and as a result Lewis also moved into the house. Rachel may have considered a divorce, but at the time that was very difficult for a woman to obtain. Going to a judge wasn't enough. Only the state legislature could grant one. The couple had wed in Kentucky, which was not yet a state, but still a part of Virginia, which meant she would have to travel to Richmond, or hire a lawyer to make the trip, and she just couldn't afford that. The reconciliation must have seemed like a reasonable alternative. A friend of Jackson's, John Overton, later noted that "not many months elapsed before Robards became jealous of Jackson" (Brands, p. 58). Overton suggested Jackson move out of the house, and Jackson agreed, but not before he talked to Robards. The talk escalated into accusations, Jackson challenged Robards to a duel, Robards turned him down, Robards moved out of the house, going back to Kentucky, and Jackson kept his word and also moved out. That is, out of the house, not out of Rachel's life.

Robards now engaged openly in affairs with several women but soon decided to return to Tennessee to reclaim Rachel. Her mother decided to protect her daughter from further heartbreak and took her to Natchez to stay with friends. To protect them on the trip, she asked a Colonel Stark to accompany them, and Stark in turn asked Jackson to join them. When Robards learned Rachel had left, he petitioned the Virginia legislature for a divorce, saying, according to legal papers filed in the case, "the defendant hath deserted the plaintiff, and that she hath lived in adultery with another man since such desertion" (Brands, p. 63). The claim was true, most historians agree, although documentation is hard to find. Jackson seems to have encouraged his friends to say he and Rachel were formally married in Natchez, but no marriage license or any other record of a marriage by the two exists. Probably because the marriage didn't take place. They did, however, live together in Natchez and about the time of the alleged marriage he started to refer to Rachel as Mrs. Jackson.

A year or so later Jackson learned, to his surprise and dismay, that the divorce decree was not issued until at least a year after his claimed marriage to Rachel. She was a bigamist. By now they were living in Nashville, and Overton, as quietly as he could, suggested to his friend that he marry Rachel again. Jackson replied that they were already married. Overton, however, convinced his friend that just to make sure there were no legal problems in the future, a fully documented marriage should exist. Jackson agreed, and in the first month of 1794, he and Rachel were married, or remarried if you accept Jackson's version, by a justice of the peace in Nashville.

Eight years later the questions surrounding when Jackson first married Rachel would lead to his second duel. Jackson, who found disliking some men easy, disliked few as intensely as John Sevier, a two-time governor of Tennessee. Sevier's second (non-consecutive) term came after he lost an election to head the state militia, at the time, in most states, an elective office. He lost to Jackson. Sevier had considerable military experience. Jackson's military experience at the time was limited to serving briefly, at age 14, in the Continental army during the Revolution. His major engagement was a refusal to clean mud from the boots of a British officer, who responded by slashing his sword at the boy, leaving him with lifelong scars on his head and a hand quickly raised to ward off the blow.

At one point, Sevier and Jackson met on a street in Knoxville and exchanged insults, something both men were accustomed to, an activity many politicians of the time engaged in. Anyone who thinks American politics in the early 21st century reached some low in civility is unfamiliar with the tenor of politics in the early 19th century. Their tempers led Sevier to challenge Jackson to, on the spot, draw a weapon. Sevier carried a sword and Jackson only a cane, so Jackson wisely declined the offer. But Jackson defended his record of military service, to which Sevier replied, "Services? I know of no great service you rendered the country, except taking a trip to Natchez with another man's wife" (Brands, p. 106).

Silence gripped the dozens of people who had gathered to witness the argument. Nearly everyone in Tennessee knew of the circumstances under which Andrew and Rachel married, but propriety kept anyone from mentioning them in Jackson's presence. Propriety and Jackson's well known temper. When Sevier made his remark, Jackson maintained silence for a few moments. Then he said, "Great God, do you mention her sacred name?" (Brands, p. 107). Someone — history hasn't recorded who — fired a shot, but no one was hit and the men left each other's presence. Jackson went home to fume. The next day he wrote a letter to Sevier saying, "I request an interview" (Brands, p. 107). In the language of the day, "interview" was widely understood to mean a duel. "You cannot mistake me or my meaning" (Brands, p. 107).

Sevier, as governor, felt dueling the much younger man beneath him. And a Tennessee law, enacted the previous year, made dueling illegal. But, to maintain his sense of dignity, he could not ignore the challenge, so he wrote back to Jackson, saying, "I shall wait on you with pleasure at any time and place not within the State of Tennessee" (Brands, p. 108). He added, perhaps mocking Jackson, "You cannot mistake me and my meaning" (Brands, p. 108).

Jackson wouldn't accept Sevier's terms. He wrote back to the governor: "Your attack was in the town of Knoxville. In the town of Knoxville did you take the name of a lady into your polluted lips. In the town of Knoxville did you challenge me to draw, when you were armed with a cutlass and I with a cane. And now, sir, in the town of Knoxville you shall atone for it or I will publish you as a coward and a poltroon" (Brands, p. 108). *Poltroon* was a favorite word of Jackson's; it refers to a particularly loathsome coward.

Jackson did make a concession. He offered to fight the duel in Indian country, thus evading Tennessee law and whatever laws neighboring states might seek to enforce. Sevier accepted, but insisted his schedule required that the duel be delayed by five days. Perhaps he was hoping Jackson's temper would cool or some stratagem would develop allowing him to evade the confrontation. Jackson didn't intend for either to occur. He published a notice in a local newspaper: "To all who shall see these presents greeting — Know ye that I, Andrew Jackson, do pronounce, publish, and declare to the world that his Excellency John Sevier, Esqr., Governor, Captain General and commander in chief of the land and naval forces of the State of Tennessee, is a base coward and poltroon. He will basely insult, but has not the courage to repair the wound" (Brands, p. 108).

Fate was sealed. The men agreed to meet at Southwest Point, Virginia. Jackson arrived first and waited for Sevier. He was accompanied by his second, Thomas Vandyke, an Army surgeon's assistant. They waited. And waited. Two full days. Then they started back for Knoxville. They had just crossed back into Tennessee when they spotted Sevier, with his second, his son James, riding towards them. Jackson dismounted, took two pistols, and approached Sevier on foot. Sevier also got off his horse. They exchanged several insults. Jackson demanded they duel on the spot. Sevier said he would not and if Jackson fired, it would be an assassination. Vandyke chimed in, insisting it would not be an assassination. He asked the two men to give him their pistols in preparation for the duel. Jackson handed his pistols to Vandyke, but Sevier refused to do the same. Jackson and Sevier exchanged some more insults. Vandyke said the two men should put their pistols in their holsters and get back on their horses. The intent, evidently, was that the two enemies would then ride off in different directions, ending the possibility of a duel. Jackson did put his pistol in his holster and did get back on his horse, but then he drew both a pistol and a sword and rode up to Sevier, who dismounted and drew a sword, allowing his horse to walk away. Two horsemen passing by stopped to watch the proceedings.

James Sevier the son may at that point have drawn his own pistol. Vandyke may have drawn his. Vandyke, in any case, warned the younger Sevier not to interfere. One of the passing horsemen later told a slightly different version. He said that when Sevier drew his sword, his horse was frightened and ran away, taking the governor's pistol with him. Without a pistol (if that version is correct), Sevier ran behind a tree and cursed Jackson. After more mutual cursing, both men remounted their horses and rode off, in different directions. For months afterwards, Sevier partisans told how the governor acted with bravery and the cowardly Jackson backed down, while Jackson partisans had a version of the story that was exactly the opposite. One primary difference between the deliberately aborted duel with Avery and the awkwardly aborted duel with Sevier is that Jackson forgave Avery and developed a friendship with him, while he hated Sevier the rest of his life. That difference was based on the fact that Avery's perceived insult was aimed at only Jackson, while Sevier's was aimed at both Jackson and his wife Rachel.

In the fall of 1805, Jackson was challenged to a duel in a complicated exchange of insults on which history is not completely clear. It began when a Joseph Erwin and Jackson agreed to have their fastest horses race against each other for a $2,000 bet. Erwin, after his horse did poorly in trial runs, decided to not race, thus forfeiting an $800 bond. That would at least save him $1,200. Instead of cash, Jackson agreed to accept promissories, or IOUs, signed by Erwin and his son-in-law, Charles Dickinson. A young man named Thomas Swann told Erwin and Dickinson that Jackson said something negative about the notes, perhaps that Jackson didn't trust the two men would actually pay them off. Some historians believe that in some heated exchange among these four men, Dickinson might have made an insulting remark about Rachel, or a remark Jackson considered insulting, which of course wasn't unusual for Jackson. Jackson accused Swann of lying, Swann challenged Jackson to a duel, Jackson brushed him off as being unworthy of dueling (Jackson was now in his late 40s and, while as hot-headed as ever, in possession of enough common sense to realize the dangers of dueling).

A friend, James Robertson, reminded him that Aaron Burr had both ruined his political career and burdened himself with a guilty conscience by killing Alexander Hamilton in a duel in New Jersey just a year and a half earlier. Instead of dueling, when Jackson and Swann met in a Nashville tavern, Jackson beat the younger man with his cane. Jackson was criticized for the beating by some of Nashville's social elite, and he responded by again making insulting comments about Swann and Dickinson. This time, he also insulted some of their friends, including one named Nathaniel McNairy, who promptly challenged Jackson to a duel. Jackson accepted, and the two men met in a field outside of Nashville. Their seconds, however, talked the two men out of dueling. A few days or weeks after that, however, McNairy did duel with a Jackson supporter, wounding but not killing him. So far, Jackson's dueling record was three duels, no one dead.

The aborted horse race that led to the duel was unaborted and run the following April 3. A newspaper announcing the upcoming race said, "All persons are requested not to bring their dogs to the field, as they will be shot"

(Brands, p. 135). Jackson's horse, Truxton, beat Erwin's horse, Ploughboy. Jackson estimated that the combined winnings of those who bet on his horse totaled about $10,000.

When Dickinson returned to Nashville from a trip to New Orleans, he published an article in a local newspaper calling Jackson "a worthless scoundrel, a poltroon and a coward" (Brands, p. 135). Jackson had thought the matter was over, but he was unwilling to tolerate the published insults, so he challenged Dickinson to a duel. The two men agreed to meet near the town of Harrison's Mill in Kentucky, since dueling was illegal in Tennessee. That would allow the winner, if he killed the loser, to escape prosecution (although Aaron Burr was indicted for murder in New York when he killed Alexander Hamilton in New Jersey). Thomas Overton, acting as Jackson's second, and Hanson Catlet, Dickinson's, spelled out the terms of the duel: "It is agreed that the distance shall be 24 feet, the parties to stand facing each other with their pistols down perpendicularly. When they are ready, the single word fire to be given, at which they are to fire as soon as they please. Should either fire before the word given, we pledge ourselves to shoot him down instantly" (Brands p. 136).

Dickinson was the better shot. He had once shot four bullets into a space no larger than a dollar coin. At 24 feet. Jackson was, according to one historian, at best an "adequate" shot (Brands, p. 136). Jackson knew he was not as good a shot, so he decided to let his opponent shoot first. That way, he could, assuming he was not killed, aim with greater deliberation.

They met on May 30, 1806, a Friday, about 7 A.M., when there was plenty of light but when the sun had not yet risen above surrounding trees. Someone paced off eight steps, three feet per step, and the two duelists took their spots, 24 feet apart. By a draw of straws, the obligation to call "fire" was assigned to Overton, Jackson's second. Overton called, "Fire," and Dickinson raised his pistol, aimed carefully, squeezed the trigger, and following the mini-explosion of the discharge and the mild wind blowing the smoke away, looked in horror to see Jackson still standing. Dickinson's bullet had, in fact, hit Jackson, missing his heart by less than two inches. But Jackson absorbed the shot, stood stoic, raised his pistol, and aimed at Dickinson. Aimed carefully, knowing he needed time to make certain he hit his target. He squeezed the trigger, and watched Dickinson bend over. The bullet hit Dickinson below his lowest ribs. He slumped to the ground.

Jackson mounted his horse and rode with Overton to a nearby tavern. At the time he could not have known Dickinson's fate, but he must have been satisfied that he had redeemed his honor, had avenged the insults. Dickinson's friends realized the young man had received a serious wound. They were not doctors and could do nothing to stop the internal bleeding. Someone was sent to Nashville to ask Dickinson's wife to come. Dickinson was taken to a nearby house. By the time his wife arrived, a few hours later, he was dead.

In 1813, in the spring, Jackson was involved in one more altercation that might be classified as a duel, although technically it lacked the seconds, pacing off, and other details usually associated with dueling. William Carroll, a brigade major under Jackson in the Tennessee militia, dueled with a man named Jesse Benton over some trivial matter that history never recorded. Jackson, evidently with some reluctance, acted as Carroll's second. Carroll was shot in the hand, Benton in the ass, a wound that produced more embarrassment than pain. Benton's brother, Thomas Hart Benton, later to become the powerful U.S. senator from Missouri, blamed Jackson for the wound. He argued that Jackson in some way rigged the duel in favor of Carroll. (Benton's point seemed to be that Jackson suggested the two men pace off and "wheel" and fire, one method of dueling, but not the most common; more common was that both men would turn, pause, and aim before firing; presumably the "wheeling" resulted in his brother's embarrassing wound).

Jackson confronted the Benton brothers about six months later in front of the City Hotel in Nashville. Jackson attempted to whip Thomas Hart Benton with his riding whip, and Benton drew his pistol in self-defense. Jackson drew his own pistol. Benton partisans would later claim Jackson fired first, while Jackson's said Benton fired first. In any case, Jackson was hit twice, one shot severing an artery, while Jackson's lone shot missed Benton. Several friends of each then engaged in a knife fight. Stockley Hays, Rachel's nephew, stabbed Jesse Benton, who pressed his pistol against Hays's heart and pulled the trigger, but the gun misfired. Alexander Donelson, still another in-law of Jackson, fired at Thomas Hart Benton, who fell down some stairs, but was not hit. Others nearby then intervened and made the combatants stop the shooting and stabbing.

Jackson was the only one seriously wounded, and he was taken to the Nashville Inn, bleeding badly. Doctors told him his arm needed to be amputated, but he refused to consent. The doctors expected him to die without the amputation, but they were wrong. Jackson survived. The Benton brothers left town in a hurry. Left, in fact, Tennessee in a hurry. By now Jackson was among the best known and maybe the most respected man in the state. Jesse Benton would hate Jackson the rest of his life. Thomas Hart Benton, however, would meet Jackson again about a decade later and the two became, first, political allies and, later, personal friends. The fracas did not involve an insult to Rachel, so Jackson was willing to forgive whatever sins he thought Benton committed.

A sidelight to the gunfight between Jackson and the Bentons provides one of those minor but strange quirks of history that delights admirers of trivia. Inside the City Hotel, while Jackson and Thomas Hart Benton were trying to kill each other outside, was Charles Fremon and his wife, Anne, whom he had stolen away from another man. With the couple was their infant son, John Charles, who would grow up to add a "t" to the end of his name, marry Jessie Benton, the daughter of Thomas Hart Benton, and become one of the most important explorers of the American West. His earliest explorations of the West came about because his father-in-law wanted to get him away from his daughter. Senator Benton and John Charles Frémont, however, shared one important trait with Andrew Jackson: all three wanted the U.S. to expand as far westward as possible.

The passion that drove Andrew Jackson to engage in duels was inseparable from the passion he brought to military combat, the combat that made him a national hero, first for his victory over the Creek Indians, then his victory over the British at the Battle of New Orleans, and then in wrestling Florida away from the Spanish. And it was the same passion he held for Rachel. When he first met Rachel she was 17 and beautiful, but the beauty alone does not explain the passion. He still possessed the passion later in life when she was decidedly unattractive. One woman who saw her when she was in her late 50s, just before she died, described her as "a coarse-looking, stout, little old woman, whom you might easily mistake for his [Jackson's] washerwoman.... Her face is rather broad, her features plain; her complexion so dark as almost to suggest a mingling of races in that climate where such things sometimes occur.... Her figure is rather full but loosely and carelessly dressed, so that when she is seated she seems to settle into herself in a manner that is neither graceful nor elegant.... [She is] without any culture, and out of the way of refining influences.... Mrs. Jackson, as was her favorite custom, lighted her pipe" (Brands, pp. 403–404).

To understand that Andrew Jackson's passion for his wife Rachel was not an inevitable reaction to her beauty but rather something from inside Jackson himself helps to explain his actions as president. He was the first "western" president; that is, he was the first president who was not from a state that touched the Atlantic Ocean. He was also the first non-patrician president, the first one born into a family that was neither economically or politically privileged. He was born into abject poverty and with his election to the presidency in 1828 began the national myth that anyone can grow up to be president. His support of his friend Sam Houston helped eventually bring Texas into the Union. His insistence that the Cherokees be moved from Georgia and other Eastern states to Indian Country, what would later become the state of Oklahoma, was based on, among other assumptions, a belief that the land the Cherokees were being sent to was land that belonged to the United States, not to the Spanish or Mexicans or British or various Indian nations, all of whom also made some claim to the land. When the U.S. Supreme Court ruled that he had no legal right to require the Cherokees to be expelled from their traditional homelands, he is reputed to have said that Chief Justice John Marshall "has made his decision; now let him enforce it." (Actually, Jackson never said that, but rather the words were written by Horace Greeley to sum up Jackson's attitude towards the high court; the fact that Jackson had a strong personal dislike for Marshall enhanced the tone of the sentiment. Greeley's summation, however, accurately captured Jackson's heart. See Brands, p. 493).

Andrew Jackson's intense passion, a passion most famously demonstrated in his willingness to kill a man for insulting his wife, contributed to the westward expansion of the United States.

5

Saving White Women from Indians

About 800 Comanches approached Fort Parker on May 19, 1836. It was a small, private fort, home to about a half dozen families who had established farms near present-day Franklin, Texas, less than 100 miles northeast of what is now Austin. Most of the men had walked or ridden horses a mile or so from the fort to work on the farms. Only six men, plus the women and children, were inside the fort. Two Comanche warriors approached the fort carrying a white flag. Benjamin Parker went out to talk to the warriors, although he realized he was helpless against such a large force. They talked for a few minutes and then other Indians surrounded Parker and suddenly several of them stuck their spears into him. Inside the fort there was panic. Some tried to run, some tried to prepare for an attack, but nothing anyone could do would help.

Rachel Plummer, 17 years old and four months pregnant, grabbed her year-and-half-old son, James Pratt Plummer, and tried to run, but an Indian chasing her picked up a hoe and slammed it into her head and then grabbed her son out of her arms. She fell to the ground and into unconsciousness. When she woke, two Indians were dragging her along the ground by her hair. She tried to stand but they pulled her down again. Finally she managed to stand and run while they still pulled on her hair. They took her to a large group of Comanches, where she saw her son with two Indian women. She cried for her son, and one of the women ran to her and repeatedly hit her with a whip. Before the Indians were done, they killed five men and took two women and three children captive.[1]

One of the women, Elizabeth Kellogg, was sold to a group of Delaware Indians, and she was later ransomed, six months after she was captured, for $150. Sam Houston put up the ransom money. A young boy, John Parker, grew up as a Comanche and became a warrior, living the rest of his life with the tribe. A young girl, Cynthia Ann Parker, nine at the time she was captured, also grew up among the Comanches.[2] She married a Comanche chief, Peta

5. Saving White Women from Indians

Nacona, and had two sons and a daughter with him. Twenty-five years later a company of Texas Rangers raided a Comanche camp and killed Peta Nacona and took Cynthia Ann Parker and her daughter, Prairie Flower, back to white society. But she didn't want to go, refused to eat, and soon died, as did her young daughter. Both of her sons escaped the attack by the Texas Rangers, and one of them, Quanah Parker, became a famous Comanche chief. Years later, when the Comanches were forced to live on a reservation, whites gave him more authority than they did the tribal elders because of his white ancestry. The other two captives were Rachel Plummer and her son, James Pratt.

Rachel Plummer would later write about her captivity, and the tale she told was one of extreme abuse, of melodramatic horrors. "Narrative of the Capture and Subsequent Sufferings of Mrs. Rachel Plummer, Written By Herself" is only about 13,000 words, but it is typical of a genre of literature unique to America and very popular from the late 17th to the late 19th century and almost forgotten today. Collectively the more than 2,000 works in the genre, ranging from newspaper and magazine articles to books, are known as *captivity narratives*.[3] Each tells the story of a white person captured by Indians and living with them for a few days, a few weeks, a few years, or the rest of their lives. At least two-thirds of them are written by women (or, frequently, dictated by a woman to someone else, often a minister). Few of them were written by men because male captives were usually tortured for a few days and then killed.

Just as mystery stories, science fiction novels, and other genres today have conventions that most of the practitioners follow, most captivity narratives adhered to something approaching a formula. The style was sensationalistic and suggested luridness, although explicit sexual details were almost never mentioned. For example, Rachel Plummer wrote, "To undertake to narrate their barbarous treatment would only add to my present distress, for it is with feelings of the deepest mortification that I think of it, much less to speak or write of it, for while I record this painful part of my narrative, I can almost feel the same heart-rending pains of body and mind that I then endured and my very soul becomes sick at the dreadful thought" (Plummer, pp. 337–338). Later she writes, "I have withheld stating many things, that are facts, because I well know that you will doubt whether any person could survive what I have undergone" (Plummer, p. 348). Although not stated, what she cannot bear to tell and what she has withheld were well understood by her readers. They understood she was raped and probably in other ways sexually abused. Usually, although not always, Indians were depicted as savages and white women as paragons of virtue (this later point was often assumed and did not have to be stated). Collectively, captivity narratives helped justify white westward expansion as needed to protect the purity of white women.[4]

As the Comanches moved west towards New Mexico they would not allow Mrs. Plummer to see her son, James Pratt, but they would allow her to hear him, and what she heard so pained her she prayed he would die to end his suffering. At one point they tied her hands behind her, tied her ankles and pushed her to the ground and beat her with bows. She bled so much she almost drowned in her own blood. She heard James Pratt, a year and a half old, calling for her and crying, and she heard Indians beating him every time he did either. Then some of them jumped on her with their feet. For five days they gave her nothing to eat. Days later, maybe weeks — her narrative isn't clear on the passage of time because she had difficulty keeping track of how many days passed — James Pratt was brought to her and she described his body as "mutilated" (Plummer, p. 340), although she didn't describe in what way. The Indians evidently wanted her to breastfeed him, but once they realized he had been weaned, they took him away. He cried, "Mother, Mother, Mother" (Plummer, p. 340). She never saw him again.

She was given to an elderly man who had a wife and daughter and had to do whatever work any of the three demanded. She was required most often to tend horses and dress buffalo skins. She learned the Comanche language and talked to members of the tribe, although no one befriended her.

In October her baby was born, a son. She named him Luther, after her husband. One day, when he was six or seven weeks old, while she was breastfeeding him, five or six Comanche men approached in a manner that frightened her so much she trembled. One of them grabbed her baby by the throat and pulled him away from her breast and with one hand choked him until he was certain the tiny boy was dead. Then he threw the baby's body into the air and it fell to the ground and another Indian picked him up and handed him to Mrs. Plummer. She cleaned his face and embraced him. He started to breathe again, and one of the Indians snatched him away again, tied a rope around his neck, and dragged him on the ground, through a field of cactus. Another one mounted a horse, took the rope attached to the baby's neck, and rode the horse in circles, dragging the baby behind him. When he was done, another one of the Indians picked up the now dead baby by a leg, walked over to Mrs. Plummer, and threw the child at her.

Even by the standards of the typical captivity narrative, in which torture, brutality, and random killings are the norm, the scene of the baby's murder is probably the single most horrifying one in the entire genre. It may be exaggerated, it certainly is melodramatized, but assuming it is based on an actual incident Mrs. Plummer endured, the impact on readers in the early 19th century could not be anything other than insidious proof Indians were unworthy of occupying the lands whites desired to move onto, that co-existence was impossible, that anything less than extermination, if not of Indian peoples, at least of Indian cultures — cultures that would permit such barbarity — was justified, more than justified, required.

Typical also of the genre was the refusal of the surviving victim to lose her faith in her Christian values. So when Mrs. Plummer was beaten on her first day of captivity, she prayed that God would allow her to forgive the Indians. And when she tells of witnessing the brutal murder of her baby boy, she writes, "But in praise to the Indians, I must say, that they gave me time to dig a hole in the earth and bury it" (Plummer, p. 342). The white woman heroine in the typical captivity narrative is, above all else, a virtuous Christian forced to live among heathens. And as a good Christian she is forgiving of those who commit the most heinous crimes.

Mrs. Plummer relates other episodes. She was allowed to explore a huge cave and walked in it for several days. This was probably part of the Carlsbad Caverns in southeastern New Mexico. She eavesdropped on a parley of Comanche chiefs with representatives of — maybe — a dozen or more tribes. They plotted the overthrow of the white government in Texas (when Mrs. Plummer was captured, Texas had just been granted its independence by General Santa Anna, dictator of Mexico, although the Mexican Congress never ratified the treaty), after which they planned to overthrow the government of Mexico, and then the government of the United States. She had a fight with the daughter of the man who owned her, and she nearly beat the young woman to death with a piece of wood, but allowed her to live. She later had a similar fight with the mother and nearly beat her to death with a buffalo bone, but, again, allowed the woman to live. One of the chiefs then spoke to her and noted that a Comanche would likely have killed the old woman. The woman, however, ordered Mrs. Plummer to gather some straw, and Mrs. Plummer soon realized she intended to burn her to death. Instead, Mrs. Plummer threw burning straw at the old woman. Both were badly burned. The Indian chiefs then held a council to see if Mrs. Plummer should be punished and decided that since the fights were not her fault, her only punishment should be to replace a lodge pole that was broken during the second fight. A defiant Mrs. Plummer said the young woman should have to help her, and the chiefs amended their order to require the two women to do the job together.

While she lived with the Comanches, Mrs. Plummer wrote, she made observations of the way Indian women were treated. She said women did all the work other than hunting and that they had no say in tribal decisions. She wrote, "I knew one young man [who had] his mother hung for refusing to get him feathers for his arrows. He appeared to rejoice at her death" (Plummer, p. 356). If a husband owed a debt to another man and did not pay, his wife was socially ostracized. She also wrote that the Comanches "have no language to express gratitude, only to say I am glad" (Plummer, p. 356). She added,

"They are strangers to any thing like mercy or sympathy, unless it is in war" (Plummer, p. 359). And the mercy and sympathy in war she describes is more like revenge, feeling bad that a comrade has been killed and a need to punish those who did the killing. Such observations were typical of captivity narratives: Indian women were not as well treated by Indian men as white women were treated by white men, and Indian cultures lacked basic Christian virtues, like gratitude, mercy, and sympathy.

Sometime in 1838 a group of Mexican traders visited the Comanches, and when they saw Mrs. Plummer they asked to see her master. "They asked if he would sell me," she wrote. "The trader made an offer for me. My owner refused. He offered more, but my owner still refused" (Plummer, p. 360). She had earlier — when is uncertain because of her understandable confusion about the time frame of her captivity — asked another visiting Mexican trader to buy her and he said he would but never made an offer. This time, however, "the [first] trader made another offer for me, which my owner agreed to take" (Plummer, p. 361). She had been a slave of the Comanches for 13 months. The Mexican traders took her to Santa Fe, where she learned that William Donoho, an American who ran a hotel on the plaza of the then Mexican city, had heard about her captivity and sent the Mexican traders to purchase and free her.[5] She wrote, "Being an American, indeed, his manly and magnanimous bosom heaved with sympathy characteristic of a Christian, [and] devised a plan for our release" (Plummer, p. 362). The "our" refers to the fact that Donoho and his wife Mary (she was the first white woman to travel the full length of the Santa Fe Trail, from Missouri to New Mexico) had also arranged for the release of two other white women held by the Comanches.

Shortly after Mrs. Plummer arrived in Santa Fe, some of the citizens of the city rebelled against the repressive government there and the Donohos thought it wise to return to Missouri, taking Mrs. Plummer with them. On the way, William Donoho accompanied her to Texas and reunited her with her husband, Luther Thomas Martin Plummer. She gave birth to a third child on January 4, 1839; the child may have been named Wison.

The frequent beatings she endured took their toll. The scars from the beating given to her on the first day of her captivity never fully healed. None of the many wounds she received were properly treated. She knew she was dying and wrote, "I am compelled, by my fast declining physical strength, to stop short of what I had intended to write" (Plummer, p. 364). Her final paragraph contains an anguished plea for her son: "I hoped and believed that God has cut short his sufferings, by the intervention of the hand of death" (Plummer, p. 365). Her narrative was published in Houston in January 1838, and she died two months later, on March 19. She was 19 years old. She did not live long enough to learn that her son, James Pratt Plummer, would be purchased from the Comanches four years later and raised by her father. Her new born baby, Wison, died two days after she did.

Hall Sisters

While the cruelty Rachel Plummer endured was not unique, it was not the only type of treatment received by captive whites, although nearly all (there were exceptions) viewed their time in captivity with horror. An incident during the Black Hawk War in 1832 is typical of both an alternate treatment and the horror with which whites viewed the capture of white women by Indians.

Black Hawk was a chief of the Sak (sometimes spelled Sauk) Indians who had signed over all their lands east of the Mississippi River to the United States in 1804. The allied Fox tribe signed the same agreement. They would receive a payment of $1,000 per year. Black Hawk rightly thought the Sak and Fox tribes were cheated and convinced the two tribes to side with the British in the War of 1812. The Americans agreed to renegotiate the treaty in 1815 and again in 1816, but Black Hawk was still dissatisfied. The two tribes did move west of the Mississippi in 1823, but the lands they settled on were far less fertile than the ones they had abandoned and the two tribes suffered from starvation. Black Hawk led part of the tribes back across the Mississippi in 1832 to plant crops on their former lands. An emissary to the whites from Black Hawk was shot and killed for reasons that remain unclear, and that was enough, amid the existing air of hostility, to lead to what is now known as the Black Hawk War. There were two major battles in the war, and the Indians lost both, bringing the war to an end about two months after it started.

Very early in the war, in May of 1832, in southern Illinois, the Indians attacked a white village and killed several dozen men, women, and children. Two sisters, Almira and Frances Hall, aged 18 and 16, were taken captive.[6] A writer named William P. Edwards interviewed them after their release and in the same year published a captivity narrative about their experiences. He used the melodramatic language typical of the genre. Of the original attack on the village, rather than seeing it as a battle in a war, he wrote, "No language can express the cruelties that were committed; in less than half an hour more than one half of the inhabitants were inhumanly butchered — they horribly mutilated both young and old, male and female, without distinction of age or sex!" (Edwards, "Narrative").

The two girls were put on horses and tied up, and as the Indians left the battle site a warrior walked on each side of each horse. The Hall sisters expected the worst, rape and murder. Edwards wrote, "They could not but believe that they were here destined to become the victims of savage outrage and abuse; and that their sufferings would soon terminate, as they would not (as they imagined) be permitted to live to see the light of another day!" (Edwards, "Narrative"). At night, however, they slept guarded only by Indian women sleeping near them. They were given food to eat and water to drink.

When they reached a Sak village the next day they found out why they were treated well: "It was here that it was first communicated to them why their lives had been spared, and why they had been protected from insult, to wit: for the reason that they were to become the adopted wives of the two young chiefs by whom they were first seized! If there was any thing calculated to add more horror to their feelings, it was this, which was indeed calculated to produce a greater shock than the intelligence that they were doomed to become the victims of the most savage torture! (Edwards, "Narrative"). Even though Edwards added that the girls "received none other but kind and civil treatment" (Edwards, "Narrative"), his view — and probably theirs — was that torture and death would be better than being married to an Indian.

Whites organized a militia to seek their rescue. In Kentucky a handbill was distributed calling for volunteers to rescue them. It said, "Two highly respectable young women of 16 and 18 years of age, are in the hands of the Indians, and if not already murdered, are perhaps reserved for a more cruel and savage fate" (Edwards, "Narrative"). The 10th day after they were captured, before the militia located them, several Winnebago Indians showed up with an offer to purchase the girls. They had been sent by whites as intermediaries. A ransom of 40 horses plus "a specified quantity of wampum and trinkets" (Edwards, "Narrative") was paid and the girls were taken by the Winnebagoes to Galena, in the northwest corner of Illinois.

Tellingly, despite the very different fates of the Hall sisters and Rachel Plummer, their captivity narratives have much in common: melodramatic tone, white women depicted as symbols of Christian purity and Indians as heartless savages, an unstated but clear implication that for a white women nothing could be worse than sex with an Indian man, and an undertone that all this justified extermination of Indians.

Just as Rachel Plummer had reported that Comanche women treated her cruelly, William Edwards, although he noted the Hall girls were not tortured, wrote that when prisoners of the Sak and Fox tribes were tortured, the torturing was done as much by women as by men. In writing about Philip Brigdon,[7] a 24-year-old Kentuckian captured by the same group that captured the Hall girls, but a few days later, he said Brigdon "was conducted by the savages to one of their settlements still further west; where on his arrival, he was beset by a throng of the natives, of both sexes and of all ages, armed with sticks and bludgeons, and who commenced beating him to a degree almost to deprive him of life!" (Edwards, "Narrative"). Brigdon was held captive 22 days and repeatedly beaten, but when a white militia approached the village, the Indians fled, evidently forgetting about him, and he escaped.

Edwards, in a separate article, wrote that prisoners of the Sak and Fox were often tortured by burning[8] and "the whole village, men, women and children, assemble round him, every one torturing him in what manner they please, each striving to exceed the other in cruelty, as long as he has life" (Edwards, "Narrative"). The depiction of Indian women participating in the torture of prisoners — white and Indian — was a standard part of most captivity narratives, and more generally of most contemporaneous reports on Indian customs. It was consistent with the way whites viewed Indians: if even their women would engage in barbaric acts, the logic insisted, the culture was not worthy of preservation. It was one more justification for continued westward expansion by the American nation.

More generally, the role of women in Western tribes was seen as proof the cultures were not worthy of respect. Most whites who wrote about visiting Indian villages noted the very heavy workloads of women. Reports written by George Catlin,[9] the first artist to paint American Indians extensively — he completed hundreds of portraits of Indians, many in colorful costumes — usually praised what he saw as nobility in Indian men, but he often noted that Indian women worked long, hard hours. The women, he and others noted, were almost never allowed to go on hunts but provided most of the food either by gathering or growing crops. They also prepared most of the meat the men brought back to the village.

Catlin moved from his home in Wilkes-Barre, Pennsylvania, to St. Louis in 1830 to be closer to Indian cultures not yet distorted by contact with white society. Over a four-year period beginning in 1832 he traveled repeatedly to Indian villages, painting portraits of men, women, and children, and writing extensively about their religions, lifestyles, habits, and everything else he noticed. He was usually sympathetic to Indian lifestyles, even defending the polygamy of Mandans in North Dakota. Noting that Mandan men often died at a young age because of the dangers of hunting and war, activities in which women seldom participated, he wrote that there were not enough men to assure a 50/50 ratio among the sexes. He didn't notice or overlooked the fact that women in most Midwestern and Western tribes had a very high death rate from childbirth complications.[10] Several studies have shown that the average lifespan of Indian women well into the 19th century was the mid-20s, while men on the average lived a decade longer. Polygamy is more likely explained by the inferior social status of women in many Indian cultures, not by battle and hunting deaths of young men. But Catlin's observations are revealing.

While others would be far less kind in their evaluations of Indian cultures than Catlin, his observation of the heavy workload of Indian women reflects a Euro-centric view of what a woman's role should be.[11] Of course, white women in poor families worked every bit as hard as Indian women, but 19th century white Americans had an idealized view of a woman's social status that was based on lives lived by very few white women. That view came from wealthy families, like Catlin's. In this view women supervised servants, who did most of the manual labor. The view conveniently ignored the reality that at least half of the servants were women. Rather than compare Indian cultures to, say, upper middle-class white society, a fairer comparison is with lower middle-class white society in which women and men, and usually children, would have to labor — on farms, in factories, in stores, wherever work could be found — to contribute to the financial maintenance of the entire family. Wages, prices for produce from small farms, all sources of income for the lower-middle class were just too low to allow for the survival of the family without every single one of its members contributing something more substantial than the supervision of non-existent servants.

Ironically, many anthropologists today believe Indian women probably had a lighter workload before whites intruded into their cultures.[12] Because whites were willing to pay for beaver skins, buffalo robes, and other items that, while obtained through hunting by men, were, according to the cultures of most Indian tribes, "dressed" by women, the work women had to perform increased in proportion to the amount of trade a tribe did with whites. Similarly, because whites were far better at killing Indian men than were other Indians, the proportion of men in a tribe did, in fact, often decrease once contact with whites was made. That is, while hunting and wars against other Indians cannot explain polygamy prior to large numbers of whites moving onto Indian lands, wars against whites, once they moved into the neighborhood, do help to explain a shortage of men to perform labor in the village, and the gap was filled by extra work being done by women.

Sometimes the misunderstandings of gender roles between the cultures could be amusing, at least from a 21st century perspective. John Minto was a young man who fled the low wages of the coal mines near Pittsburgh to seek a better life in the West.[13] On a wagon train headed to Oregon Territory in 1844 his youthful good looks and pleasant personality attracted the attention of several older women who sought out his company without any intent of establishing anything beyond friendship. But when the wagon train stopped near a Lakota Sioux village west of Fort Laramie, in what is now Wyoming, three young Sioux maidens saw the same qualities in Minto the older white women did. So they approached one of the women with whom he spent a lot of time, Mrs. Morrison, and offered to buy him. Mrs. Morrison explained he wasn't a slave and couldn't be sold. Instead of being flattered by the attention of the three girls, Minto spent a very nervous week or two worrying that Sioux warriors would try to capture him as a gift for the girls. They didn't.

Dickewamis

Minto's experience attests to the variety and complexity of relations between the sexes when one is Indian, the other white. A more complicated relationship between whites and Indians, and one certainly lacking any humorous undertone, involves Mary Jemison, known widely when she lived and today as the White Woman of the Genesee.[14] Mary was born in the autumn of 1743 aboard the *William and Mary*, a ship crossing the Atlantic Ocean from England to America. Her parents, Thomas and Jane Jemison, bought land along Marsh Creek, near today's Gettysburg, Pennsylvania. Life there, she would recall when she was an old woman, was "a little paradise" filled with "childish, happy days" (Seaver, Chapter I). When she was a teenager, the French and English were fighting for control of the North American continent, a war American history books now call the French and Indian War.[15] That is, since the English won, they named it after the enemy, a combination of French soldiers and warriors from several Indian tribes. (The war started in 1754 when a Virginia militia under the command of 22-year-old George Washington sent by the British governor of Virginia to reconnoiter French forces, foolishly and in contradiction of orders, attacked a small French force in western Pennsylvania.) Of course, other tribes sided with the English. Staying neutral was not an option either side permitted the Indians. A neutral tribe was an enemy tribe.

On April 5, 1758, a group of French soldiers aided by Shawnee warriors, attacked the Marsh Creek area, taking Mary Jemison, her parents, several of her young siblings, and one or more neighboring children captive. Her two oldest brothers escaped. Mary was 15 at the time. The captives were taken west to Fort Duquesne, the site of present-day Pittsburgh (since the English won the war, they got to rename it). Along the way the Shawnee whipped the youngest children for moving too slowly, and when the children pleaded for water forced them to drink urine. Mary's mother realized the Indians intended to kill most of them but intended to let her daughter live. She told Mary it would have been better for her to have died as a baby than to have to live with the Indians. "My dear!," the mother told Mary, "my heart bleeds at the thoughts of what awaits you; but if you leave us, remember my child your own name, and the name of your father and mother. Be careful and not forget your English tongue. If you shall have an opportunity to get away from the

Indians, don't try to escape; for if you do they will find and destroy you" (Seaver, Chapter II).

The Shawnee decided they had too many prisoners and that that was slowing them down, and perhaps that would allow a rescue party, which they assumed would be sent in pursuit, to catch up with them. So Mary and a neighbor boy were taken away. Later Mary would see Shawnees with the scalps of her parents and siblings.

At Fort Duquesne, Mary was placed in a room where "two pleasant looking squaws of the Seneca tribe ... came and examined me attentively for a short time" (Seaver, Chapter III). Then the Shawnee warriors gave her to the Seneca women. (The French often allowed their Indian allies to do what they wanted with white captives; it was a major part of the payment the Indians received for their military support.) The Seneca took her by canoe west to a village along the Ohio River. It was one of the farthest western outposts of the Seneca, who were centered mostly in the western-most Finger Lakes region of New York. The Seneca wanted Jemison to stop being white. She learned their language and customs, dressed as they did, and was required even to shed her white name. She was called Dickewamis, which she said meant "pretty girl, a handsome girl, or a pleasant, good thing" (Seaver, Chapter III).

Unlike the Comanches and Rachel Plummer more than a half century later, the Seneca treated Mary Jemison well, but she was not happy. "The recollection of my parents," she said, "my brothers and sisters, my home, and my own captivity, destroyed my happiness, and made me constantly solitary, lonesome and gloomy" (Seaver, Chapter III). After she had been in the village for more than a year, she was taken on a trip to what had become Fort Pitt. The Seneca, she said, were negotiating a treaty with the English, and she met English-speaking white people. Seneca women who had adopted her as a sister worried the whites would take her away and rushed her to a canoe and paddled quickly down the Ohio. "Although I had then been with the Indians something over a year," she said, "and had become considerably habituated to their mode of living, and attached to my sisters, the sight of white people who could speak English inspired me with an unspeakable anxiety to go home with them, and share in the blessings of civilization" (Seaver, Chapter III). The way the Indian women rushed her away from the fort, she said, "seemed like a second captivity" (Seaver, Chapter III).

She then was moved to another Seneca village farther down the Ohio, and some Delaware Indians later moved into the village. "My sisters told me that I must go and live with one of them" (Seaver, Chapter III), Jemison said. His name was Sheninjee. "Not daring to cross them, or disobey their commands, with a great degree of reluctance I went; and Sheninjee and I were married according to Indian custom" (Seaver, Chapter III). At age 18 she gave

5. Saving White Women from Indians

birth to a baby girl who died two days later. During the fourth year she lived with the Indians, she gave birth to a boy, whom she named Thomas Jemison, after her murdered father. Mary Jemison, Dickewamis, would live 72 more years, always torn between the Seneca world she had unwillingly become part of and the white world that gave her birth, shaped her perceptions, and dominated a large part of her memory.

In 1759, Sheninjee accepted an invitation from relatives to move his family to Genishau (near present-day Geneseo, a variation of the spelling) a village in the heart of Seneca country in western New York. Sheninjee, however, went on an extended hunting and trapping excursion while other Seneca accompanied Mary Jemison to her new home. The following summer she learned her husband became ill from some disease and died shortly after she left. She considered him a "kind husband" (Seaver, Chapter V). A year or two later — she was uncertain of the passage of time — the king of England offered a ransom for anyone rescuing white captives from Indians. A Dutchman, John Van Sice, told Jemison he would take her to Fort Niagara, but she did not want to leave. "I was fully determined not to be redeemed at that time," she said, "especially with his assistance" (Seaver, Chapter V).

Once while she was working in a cornfield, Van Sice came after her and she ran away and hid for three days. When she returned to the village, the Seneca chiefs held a council and ordered that she should not be taken anywhere without her consent. However, in what may have been a political power struggle within the village, "the old king of our tribe" (Seaver, Chapter V) told her he would personally take her to Fort Niagara. One of her "Indian brothers" (Seaver, Chapter V) — evidently the brothers of the Seneca women who adopted her years earlier — argued with the "king" and said he would kill Jemison before he would allow her to be returned to white society. She again went into hiding for several days, but when her brother found her and she realized he did not actually intend to kill her, she returned to the Seneca village. A year or so after that, she married a second time, to a much older Seneca named Hiokatoo. He was often called Gardow, but that was a nickname he disliked. They had six children. Significantly, she named all of them after white relatives: Jane, Nancy, Betsey, Polly, John, and Jesse.

Jemison consistently praised the honesty of the Seneca and acknowledged many kindnesses that members of her adoptive family showed to her. Except for several times she saw Indians, the Delaware once, the Seneca other times, torturing white prisoners, she felt them to be kind, forgiving, and admirable. "The moral character of the Indians was uncontaminated. Their fidelity was perfect ... they were strictly honest; they despised deception and falsehood; and chastity was held in high veneration, and a violation of it was considered sacrilege" (Seaver, Chapter VI).

She lived near today's Geneseo, New York, most of the rest of her life, in a village called Little Beard's Town. Her life was, as are the lives of all of us, shaped by the great issues of her time. The defeat of the French convinced the American colonists they no longer needed British protection and thus helped lead to the American Revolution. Mary Jemison would for the rest of her life seek to remain a Seneca. She had moved from being a young English colonist to being a prisoner of a French ally to fleeing possible repatriation with her English world.

For 12 or 15 years — again she was uncertain of how much time passed — the Seneca lived in peace. Then the American colonies decided to rebel against Great Britain. At first, the Seneca and the other five tribes of the Iroquois Confederacy vowed to remain neutral.[16] A year or so after that vow, however, the Iroquois made the mistake of siding with the British and participated in several attacks on American communities, including, in early July 1778, one that would become known as the Wyoming Massacre, in Pennsylvania's Wyoming Valley.[17] Dozens of whites were killed in the attack. Some were killed after capture by having their heads bashed in with a club and then thrown, still alive, into a raging fire.

George Washington ordered General John Sullivan to punish the Seneca to assure they would withdraw from the war.[18] Sullivan, with an army of 5,000, swept southward through Western New York, destroying one Seneca village after another. Most were deserted because the Seneca knew they were no match for Sullivan's army. Only at Newtown, near today's Elmira, New York, did the Seneca and some loyalists try to engage Sullivan in an actual battle, and Sullivan quickly and decisively defeated them, ending Seneca support of the British forever. One of the villages Sullivan's men burned was Little Beard's Town. Mary Jemison fled with her six children to Gardow Flats, along the Genesee River, where she found and hid with two escaped black slaves. The blacks had planted fields of corn and hired Jemison to help them harvest it. "I have laughed a thousand times to myself," she said, "when I have thought of the good old negro, who hired me, who fearing that I should get taken or injured by the Indians, stood by me constantly when I was husking, with a loaded gun in his hand, in order to keep off the enemy, and thereby lost as much labor of his own as he received from me, by paying good wages" (Seaver, Chapter VII). She was paid 25 bushels of corn.

Somewhere around this time another white hostage was given an opportunity to return to white society with very different results than Jemison experienced. Cornplanter, the best known of all Seneca chiefs, conducted a raid along the Mohawk River in eastern New York and took captive a man called Old John O'Bail.[19] O'Bail's capture was not happenstance. Cornplanter sought him out. After taking the prisoner ten or 12 miles away from the point of capture, Cornplanter told O'Bail that his name, too, was John O'Bail and that he was the man's son. The older O'Bail had had a child, a son, with an Indian woman. Cornplanter gave his father a choice: he could live with the Seneca with an assurance he would always have plenty to eat and would live in comfort, or he could return unharmed to white society. Old John O'Bail chose to return to white society.

When Sullivan's army was gone, Jemison's husband, Hiokatoo, found her and they tried, as best they could, to resume their former lives. But the westward expansion of whites never stopped interfering with their lives. A white man named Ebenezer Allen moved into the area and eventually married three women, one Indian and two whites, and had at least two mistresses.[20] At one point Allen was living with his three wives at the same time. At another point he was living with Jemison and Hiokatoo when he started to beat one of his wives and stopped only when Hiokatoo, hatchet in hand, ordered him to. Allen eventually moved to Canada, taking his two white wives with him but abandoning his Indian wife. She tried to follow him, but he threatened to beat her if she did.

Two decades passed with Jemison and her family living lives free of major disruptions, doing the best they could to feed their children, get along with their Seneca neighbors, and enjoy the small pleasures of life. But in the late 18th century, white land speculators moved into the area.[21] The national government was determined to encourage Americans to move westward, to populate as much land west of the seaboard colonies as possible. The Americans, British, French, and Spanish were all competing for control of the lands. The fact that tens of thousands of Indians already lived there was more of a nuisance than a serious impediment to any of the four white governments. The Americans gave huge tracts of lands, often millions of acres at pennies an acre, to land speculators. The idea was that they would resell the land in small parcels to settlers, who in turn would create communities. Because of that land speculation, Rochester, New York, became America's first frontier city. The westward spread of communities, more than anything else, would provide the political framework for an ever-expanding American nation. The Seneca reluctantly accepted a settlement. They would get 12 scattered reservations and small annual payments, and in return whites would move in unimpeded. The Seneca, like the other five nations of the Iroquois Confederacy, were by now well aware that even their collective armies were no match for the military might of the whites.

Eastern tribes knew how numerous the whites were because they lived in such close proximity to them. Decades later, whites often invited Western Indian leaders to visit the president in Washington, and got them there by a circuitous route that included train stops in Boston, New York, Philadelphia, and other large cities.[22] It was not unusual for a Sioux chief, as an example, to see more people on one block in New York than he had seen in his entire life. Nor was it unusual for him to say, weeks later when he returned to his village of, perhaps, 1,500 people, that the whites cannot be fought, that they are more numerous than ants, that no Indian can imagine how many of them there are. The intent of the presidential visits was to discourage resistance to westward expansion as futile, and it often had the impact whites wanted. The more Western Indians who visited the East, the fewer of their followers who were willing to fight against the whites.

As more whites moved into Western New York, Jemison's oldest son, Thomas, said that if she wanted to return to white society, he would help her, even offering to make the move with her. She wanted to go but considered the move impractical. First, the Seneca chiefs said they would not allow Thomas to accompany her. The young man, they said, had the makings of a fine warrior. "To go myself, and leave him," she said, "was more than I felt able to do" (Seaver, Chapter IX). In addition, she had younger children to care for: "If I should be so fortunate as to find my relatives, they would despise them, if not myself; and treat us as enemies; or, at least with a degree of cold indifference, which I thought I could not endure" (Seaver, Chapter IX).

So, with great reluctance, she stayed. But she and her Seneca family were having more and more contact with the whites who moved to the area and her children were more and more influenced by white culture. The worst part of that influence was alcohol.

Thomas, her oldest son, from when he was a young boy called his brother, John, a witch. That led to frequent fights when they were growing up. As an adult, John married two women. Jemison said, "Although polygamy was tolerated in our tribe, Thomas considered it a violation of good and wholesome rules in society" (Seaver, Chapter X). So in addition to the charge that John was a witch, Thomas now frequently berated his younger brother for having more than one wife. (Thomas had four wives, but never more than one at a time.) "John always resented such reprimand, and reproof," Jemison said. "They never quarreled, unless Thomas was intoxicated" (Seaver, Chapter X). Also, Thomas "often threatened to take my life for having raised a witch and has gone so far as to raise his tomahawk to split my head. He, however, never struck me" (Seaver, Chapter X). But he did once strike Hiokatoo, although Jemison didn't explain the circumstances of that incident. In July 1811, Thomas went to his mother's house when she wasn't home — "somewhat intoxicated" (Seaver, Chapter X), Jemison said — and got into an argument with John, who grabbed Thomas by the hair, dragged him outside, and slammed a tomahawk into his head.

Jemison asked the Seneca chiefs to convene a council to decide what punishment, if any, John should receive for the murder. The chiefs decided Thomas was responsible for what happened and allowed John to go unpunished. At the time of the killing, Thomas was 52 years old, John 48.

In November of 1811 her husband, Hiokatoo, died. She estimated his age at 103, and noted that "Hiokatoo was an old man when I first saw him" (Seaver, Chapter XI). She said he told her that as a boy he practiced cruelty against animals and prisoners to help him prepare to be a warrior. Although she consistently praised the kindness of Seneca towards her, she also consistently noted they were capable of great cruelty. Children, she said, were encouraged to participate in the torturing of prisoners, who were typically killed slowly, over days, with cuts and beatings, to inflict as much pain as possible. Adult male prisoners were almost always tortured. White male prisoners who did manage to escape often reported that they prayed to God for a quick death. Children prisoners, male and female, might be adopted into the tribe, and women, especially young women, were often married to Seneca men. Hiokatoo, she said, once told her about participating in a battle against the Cherokee in the South and taking two Indian women prisoners "whom he sold on his way home for money to defray the expense of his journey" (Seaver, Chapter XI). If her estimate of the age of her husband is accurate, Hiokatoo was either 75 or 76 when their youngest son, Jesse, was born.

Just as John, the second oldest son, killed her oldest child, Thomas, so too would he kill Jesse. One day in 1812, Jesse went to the nearby white town of Mount Morris and while there ran into John. The older brother suggested they return to the reservation together, but Jesse, mindful of the fact John had already killed one brother, declined the invitation. That infuriated John, but at the time he did nothing. A few months later, both Jesse and John were hired, along with some other Indians and some white men, to help a white man in Castile, another nearby town. Jemison admonished her sons not to drink on the job, but they did, and that led to an argument, and John stabbed Jesse. Eighteen times. Jemison said she loved all her children but that she loved Jesse most of all.

"It is the custom amongst the Indians," she said, "for the women to perform all the labor in, and out of doors, and I had the whole to do, with the help of my daughters, till Jesse arrived to a sufficient age to assist us. He was disposed to labor in the cornfield, to chop my wood, milk my cows, and attend to any kind of business that would make my task lighter" (Seaver, Chapter XII). She added, "I am sensible that I loved him better than I did either of my other children. After he began to understand my situation, and the means of rendering it more easy, I never wanted for anything that was in his power to bestow" (Seaver, Chapter XII). Jesse was 27 or 28 years old when he was killed.

Five years later, John, who had murdered his two brothers, would himself become a murder victim. He argued with two Seneca men and they bashed in his head with a rock. "I could not mourn for him as I had my other sons, because I knew that his death was just, and what he had deserved for a long time, from the hand of justice" (Seaver, Chapter XIV). And, "I have nothing to say in his favor" (Seaver, Chapter XIV). John was 54 when he died.

The two Seneca who killed him, known as Doctor and Jack, were scorned by the rest of the tribe. Some suggested they leave the area, not just to avoid punishment but because they were not wanted. A few even suggested they commit suicide. The wife and children of Jack left for a reservation near Buffalo to avoid the scorn. Jack, under societal pressure, ate muskrat root and died from the poison about 10 hours later. When his wife learned of his death, she returned to their home.

In 1816 and 1817, Jemison discussed the possibility of becoming a naturalized American. Some white men she talked to, not all, wanted some of her land in return for their help with the naturalization process. One indicated he had influence with the New York State legislature and could thus secure her naturalization. Another suggested that only the U.S. Congress could grant her naturalization. Jemison discussed these conversations in the context of protecting her ownership rights to at least several square miles of land along the Genesee River. She did not discuss the background to her naturalization. But since both of her parents were born overseas, probably in Ireland, although she wasn't certain, and she was born at sea, she was not a United States citizen. (The large majority of American Indians were not granted U.S. citizenship until 1924.)[23] She said the New York state legislature passed a law on April 19 "for my naturalization, and ratifying and confirming the title of my land" (Seaver, Chapter XV). Legally, only Congress could give her citizenship, but Jemison seemed unaware or uncertain of that and she considered her citizenship, legal or not, very important.

Among the hundreds of whites who moved into the area where she lived, she became something of a celebrity, and she often visited the town of Mount Morris and was invited into white homes for hot tea and dessert. She had many opportunities to return to white society, and she made it clear she considered herself as much white as Seneca, but she feared her children would never be accepted anywhere other than among the Seneca. While she had friends among the Seneca, she often preferred in her later years, when relations between Senecas and whites were usually cordial, the company of whites, especially white women.

In November of 1823 James Seaver, a local doctor, interviewed her and wrote a book about her experiences, *The Life and Times of Mrs. Mary Jemison*. It quickly became the most successful captivity narrative ever written, selling more than 100,000 copies within a year, at a time when a book that sold 5,000 copies was a best seller. She was 81 years old, and Seaver's title reflected her preference for her name. (Seaver says in his introduction that if there are any mistakes in the book it is because the elderly Mary Jemison's memory was fading, which is an unusual claim for a non-fiction book; the standard — then and now — is for the author to thank whoever was interviewed and to take responsibility for errors.) Mary Jemison moved to another Seneca reservation, near Buffalo, where she died in 1833 at the age of 90.

Seaver wrote the book in the first person, as if Jemison was writing it, but it is clearly his work. It's available for free on the Internet, at several different sites, and it prints out, single spaced, to 64 pages, not counting the 10 or more pages of an appendix in Seaver's third-person writing. On any page you can read sentences that seem highly unlikely to have been spoken by a woman who could neither read nor write (example: "The next summer after Sullivan's campaign, our Indians, highly incensed at the whites for the treatment they had received, and the sufferings which they had consequently endured, determined to obtain some redress by destroying their frontier settlements" (Seaver, Chapter VII). Seaver interviewed her over three days and, of course, had no tape recorder. The undertone of the narrative is that the Indians were both noble and savage, capable of great courage and kindness but also of great cruelty. That view reflects one widely held attitude among the most educated and best-read Americans and Europeans of the day, and Dr. Seaver was a member of that class. That is, the narrative reflects Seaver's world view as much as it does Mary Jemison's life.

Still, the narrative is peppered with phrases, sentences, and words that sing with authenticity. Among these, in the book's final chapter, are passages where Jemison speaks of "my reduction from a civilized to a savage state" (Seaver, Chapter XVI), her constant "hope of release, the devising of means of escaping" (Seaver, Chapter XVI), and referring to her life among the Senecas as one of "slavery" (Seaver, Chapter XVI). Mary Jemison became a symbol of white women who adapted well to an Indian culture. The reality is that she entered that culture unwillingly, remembered her youthful years in white society as the happiest of her life, and refused for the more than seven decades she lived among the Seneca to fully surrender everything in her that was white. Mary Jemison never became Dickewamis. She was, until the day she died, a white woman among the Seneca.

Small Streetcars

Of course, one important aspect of how whites viewed the relationship between white women and Indian men was simple racism. That might be more clearly seen by examining a case involving whites and blacks. In 1863, the Omnibus Railroad Company of San Francisco ordered Charlotte Brown, a black woman, off one of its streetcars.[24] Brown sued and the company argued it had an obligation to protect whites, especially white women, from disreputable persons, the implication being that if black women were permitted to ride on streetcars, in fairness black men must be permitted to ride on them also, and that might endanger white women. The streetcars were horse drawn and therefore fairly small, usually about six feet wide and 15 feet long. That meant they were too small to have separate sections for blacks and whites, as was the norm in Eastern and Southern cities. The state legislature had not previously considered the matter, so the case was decided under common law, which, in effect, said no one could be excluded from using a "common carrier." That same year a black man sued for also being forced off a San Francisco street car owned by the city's other transit company, the North Beach and Mission Railroad.

And three years later, two more black women brought similar suits, both against North Beach and Mission. In each case, white lawyers argued the case in front of white judges and white juries. In each case the companies argued that white women in particular needed to be protected from black men and suggested that allowing black women on the streetcars would mean they would also have to let black men on. In each case, the black plaintiff won. Neither company had a stated or written policy barring blacks from using the streetcars, and after Brown won her case, Omnibus simply started to allow blacks to ride. North Beach and Mission, after losing the 1863 case, still barred blacks, which is why the two suits were brought in 1866. After that, North Beach and Mission, without announcing a change, accepted black passengers.

The cases, after being lost in trial court, were appealed by the companies to the California Supreme Court, which overturned punitive damages awarded to the plaintiffs, but upheld the common law principle that blacks could not be excluded from use of common carriers. The reasoning of the companies reflected the same attitude that drove so much of the westward expansion of white America: white women needed to be protected from men who belonged to a different race.

The Tattooed Girls

Perhaps no incident of white women forced to live with Indians reflected the essential racism of white reaction more than the capture of Olive and Mary Ann Oatman by southwestern Indians, probably Tolkepayas, in 1851.

The parents of the Oatman girls were devout, even passionate,

5. Saving White Women from Indians 123

Methodists when, probably in 1840 or 1841, they converted to Mormonism. They participated in their new religion with the same zeal. And after Joseph Smith, founder of the Mormon church, was murdered in Carthage, Illinois, in 1844, and most Mormons in the next few years followed Brigham Young to what is now Utah, Roys Oatman followed, instead, a young man named James Colin Brewster, who had his own vision of what Mormonism should be.[25] Brewster said God told him he, not Young, should head the church. He also said God told him he and his small group of followers would find their Eden at the point where the Colorado and Gila Rivers meet, at present-day Yuma, Arizona, right on the California line. At the time, however, the confluence of the rivers was in northwestern Mexico.

In 1850 a train of more than 25 wagons, with 15 or 16 families, totaling somewhere between 85 and 93 men, women, and children (counts are inconsistent), headed across southern New Mexico Territory towards their Eden. Dissension split the group, so on October 9, 1850, Brewster and about 35 others headed north for Santa Fe and the Oatmans and seven other families continued west. The winter of 1850–51 was the driest ever recorded in what is now the American Southwest, and that resulted in famine conditions for Indians living there. Most of the families traveling with the Oatmans dropped out of the wagon train to stay in Indian villages or other locations that offered some food. By late winter 1851, the Oatman family was alone on their journey.[26]

A group of 17 Indians approached the Oatmans on February 18 and indicated they wanted some food. Olive Oatman later said the Indians were Apaches, but modern scholars believe they were Tolkepayas, also known as Western Yavapais. One reason they are believed to not be Apaches is that Apaches at the time had rifles, and the group that approached the Oatmans had no firearms. Roys Oatman did not display the guns he had, and if he had, the Indians might have acted differently. Oatman probably intended to appear friendly. But suddenly one of the Indians swung a club that smashed into the head of 14-year-old Lorenzo Oatman. Then he was hit a second time and collapsed to the ground. Other Indians attacked other members of the Oatman family.

Within a minute or two, Roys Oatman, his wife Mary Ann, their daughters Lucy and Charity Ann, and their sons, Roys Jr. and Roland, all lay dead on the ground, their heads bashed in with clubs. Thirteen-year-old Olive may have also been hit with a club, or she may have fainted, fallen and hit her head. But when the Indians had gone through the Oatmans' wagon and taken all the food they could find and much of the goods, and were ready to leave, they took Olive and her eight-year-old sister, Mary Ann (named after their mother), with them. Six Oatmans lay beaten and dead behind them. Lorenzo, 14, unknown to the Indians and to his sisters, was still alive.

Olive and Mary Ann were taken to an Indian village and put under the supervision of women and children, who treated them as slaves, ordering them to gather food and wood and to carry heavy burdens. If they did not do what they were told, they were beaten. They were seldom given food and survived only by gathering what little they could for themselves. About a year later, a group of Mohave Indians visited the village. The group included a Mohave woman who expressed sympathy for the two white girls. The Mohave offered to purchase the girls. The captors asked the girls if they would rather go with the Mohave or stay in the village, and Olive and Mary Ann, probably wisely, refused to indicate their preference. If they said they wanted to go and the sale was not completed, they might be beaten for wanting to leave. The Mohave gave the captors two horses, three blankets, and some beads and vegetables in exchange for the girls. The white girls did not know what to expect from the Mohave, but they believed nothing could be worse than staying in the village they were in.

The story of the Oatman girls up to this point was typical of a large group of captivity narratives. Their parents were brutally killed and they were harshly treated. But when they were sold and moved to a Mohave village their lives changed. The village was on the Colorado River, near where the states of Arizona, California, and Nevada now meet. Most of the people treated them so well that what Olive saw as their "sale" might in fact have been more like a payment for an adoption. A woman named Aespaneo, whom Olive identified as the wife of a chief, was particularly kind.

(The term "chief" is easy to misunderstand. Most Native American tribes used some honorary title to show respect to a warrior who had displayed courage in war or to an older man who seemed wise or for someone who was generous with his possessions. Indian villages, particularly in the West, tended to be small, sometimes consisting of only a few hundred people, seldom going above a few thousand [although there were some that reached up to 20,000], small enough to operate on the basis of a community consensus. One reason the U.S. military tended to win almost all — certainly not all — the major battles with Western Indians is that the whites actually had something approaching field discipline; that is, soldiers followed orders, so a battle plan could be executed. The Indians, by contrast, while often displaying great courage, usually acted individually, doing what they wanted, when they wanted. It's no way to run an army. [Of course, superior weaponry and greater numbers also helped the white soldiers]. The concept of a chief who could speak for the whole tribe was something whites assumed was recognized by Indians, and that's one reason there was so much distrust of treaties. In fact, whites often bribed "chiefs" into signing treaties, unaware or ignoring the fact that the chiefs had no political or other authority to speak for the whole tribe.)

5. Saving White Women from Indians

Aespaneo gave the Oatman girls a small piece of land for their own vegetable garden, and Topeka, her daughter, became a friend and allowed them to share her blankets and food. "They seemed really to feel for us" (McGinty, p. 93), Olive said. She and Mary Ann felt like family members. Then they were tattooed.

They were each tattooed on the chin, five vertical lines stretching from the lower lip to the bottom of the chin, with two horizontal lines on each side attached to the two outermost vertical lines. They also each received one long tattooed line on each arm. The tattooing was done by pricking the skin with a long, sharp stick and then dipping the sticks into a blue dye made from the juice of river weeds and ground up river rocks, and placing the dye into the small, bloody holes. Olive called them slave marks, but almost all Mohave were tattooed, some far more elaborately than her or her sister. The Mohave believed that without the tattoos, when you died you would not gain admission to Sil'aid, or Mohave heaven. Each of the Oatman girls would wear their tattoos, unwillingly, until the day she died.

In February of 1854, three years after the Oatman girls were captured and two years after they were sold to the Mohave, a party of more than 100 white men passed through the area. They included civilians but were under the command of Lt. A.W. Whipple of the U.S. Army. They were surveying the area for a possible railroad route across the desert and into California. Whipple and others met with Mohave leaders several times. The Mohave agreed that a railroad could pass through their lands. In his journal, and in one kept by Balduin Mollhausen, a German artist with the party, not a single mention is made of the Oatman girls. And years later, Olive would not mention the Whipple party. Undoubtedly they did not know of each other's presence, suggesting the Mohave kept them hidden or sent them away while the whites visited the area. Although the white girls seemed to fit well into the Mohave culture, the Mohave would not want to take a chance that the Army insist the girls be returned to white society.

Not long after that, Mary Ann, now 11 years old, became seriously ill. The Mohave Valley frequently experienced food shortages. It was, after all, desert and the Mohave, unlike some other desert tribes, had not developed an irrigation system. They were dependent on their major water source, the Colorado River, overflowing its banks, and that did not happen every year. Mary Ann's illness most likely was malnutrition. She was too weak even to help the village gather food. Aespaneo and Topeka provided some, but they didn't have enough for themselves. Mary Ann was placed on bedding outside the chief's lodge, and Olive sat at her side and begged passersby for food. Hundreds of Mohave at the time also suffered from malnutrition and dozens, at least, died. Mary Ann died from starvation.

Olive later provided conflicting information on what year her little sister died. As was common for whites held captive by Indians, she lost track of time. The lack of newspapers, calendars, or writing of any kind made keeping accurate records, and memories, of the passage of time difficult, even impossible. Depending on which version of Olive's stories is believed, Mary Ann died as early as 1852 at age nine or as late as 1855 at age 12. Aespaneo, always kind, took pity on Olive, and after Mary Ann's death provided her with enough to eat, enough to survive the famine.

Meanwhile, her brother Lorenzo was determined to find her. He had survived the attack with a very bad gash in his head. He crawled for a day before he was discovered by two Pima Indians who gave him water and food. They then went to investigate the massacre site he told them about. Before they returned, two wagons with whites who had been part of the original Brewster party appeared. They were on their way to Yuma, but when Lorenzo told them of the massacre, they turned back, taking the 14-year-old boy with them. Lorenzo and others were unsuccessful in getting the Army to mount a search for his sisters. The Army commander at Yuma said he didn't have enough men to spare or the right kinds of animals. He had more mules than horses. Over the years, Lorenzo wrote to politicians, joined prospecting parties in Southern California, and did whatever else he could to learn something about the fate of Olive and Mary Ann. Many people learned of Lorenzo's efforts, and in January of 1856 he received a letter from Duff Weaver, a California farmer, who said he had heard from a man who had passed through the area where his sisters were captured and learned that one or two white girls were being held captive by a desert tribe, although he didn't know which tribe. The letter was published in the *Los Angeles Star* on January 5, 1856, and a charge that Weaver made to the effect that the U.S. Army commander in charge of the fort at Yuma refused to investigate the information created a stir. The commander of the Army's Department of the Pacific ordered an investigation.

A public demand that the state of California organize a rescue party was rebuffed when Governor J. Neely Johnson claimed, incorrectly, that he was not authorized to spend public money on a search. But the publicity did spur the Army into action. Indian runners were sent to Indian villages north of what was now Fort Yuma offering ransoms for any white prisoners. On February 22, 1856, an Indian named Francisco said he had information that a white woman was being held by the Mohave about a ten-day walk north of Fort Yuma. At the Army's request, he visited the village and arranged for her release. A ransom of a white horse might have been paid but the historical record is unclear.

When Olive learned she would return to white society, the son of Chief

Espaniola, with whose family she lived, took away from her everything she owned while living with the Mohave. These included some strings of beads and pieces of blankets. Olive thought the son was guilty of "littleness and meanness" (McGinty, p. 147) for taking these possessions. When she reached Fort Yuma, news of her return was sent to, among other places, Los Angeles, where the *Star* published an article about her. Someone showed the article to Lorenzo, and he rushed to Fort Yuma. Reunited after five years, brother and sister joined a wagon train headed for the West Coast. Her story would soon make her, along with Mary Jemison and Rachel Plummer, among the most famous white women to live unwillingly with Indians, and would thereby help shape white attitudes towards Indians.

Olive and Lorenzo moved to the Rogue River Valley in Oregon, just north of the California line, about the same time Royal Stratton, a Methodist minister from New York, moved to Yerka, California, just south of the Oregon line.[27] When Stratton learned that someone who lived less than a day's ride away had such an interesting experience, he decided he wanted to write a book about her. The Oatmans, sister and brother, accepted his offer to "help" them write a book, but, as with James Seaver writing about Mary Jemison, the final product, despite being mostly in the first person, is at least as much the work of Stratton as it is of the Oatmans. Even the full title of the book, as it appeared on the title page, indicates how contrived the final product is: *Life Among the Indians: Being an interesting Narrative of the Captivity of the Oatman Girls, Among the Apache and Mohave Indians, containing also An interesting account of the Massacre of the Oatman Family, by the Apache Indians, in 1851; the narrow escape of Lorenzo D. Oatman; the Capture of Olive A. and Mary A. Oatman; the Death by Starvation of the latter; the Five Years Suffering and Captivity of Olive A. Oatman; also, her singular recapture in 1856; as given by Lorenzo D. and Olive A. Oatman, the only surviving members of the family, to the author, R.B. Stratton.* The cover, mercifully, has a shortened version: *Captivity of the Oatman Girls*.

What is missing from the narrative, what is missing from almost all the narratives of white women who lived with Indians and then returned to white society, is any reference to sexual intercourse. Some historians assume that many, probably most, of these women were raped, yet none of the women specifically state that. No doubt that is a reflection of a time when openly discussing rape was considered highly inappropriate. It would be a mistake, however, to assume white women who were raped by Indians were scorned by white society. Quite the opposite, they were typically treated with kindness, although often that kindness degenerated into pity.

The 1956 film *The Searchers*, directed by John Ford, and considered by some critics the finest Western ever produced by Hollywood, offers a view that has little support in the historical record of how white men reacted to a white woman having sex, willingly or unwillingly, with an Indian man. Ethan Edwards (John Wayne) a veteran of the Confederate army, returns to West Texas, where his brother, his brother's wife, and all of their children except a daughter and an adopted son are killed by Comanches. Edwards searches relentlessly for Debbie, the niece who was not killed (she's played by Natalie Wood), telling his brother's adopted son, Martin Pawley (Jeffrey Hunter), "We'll find them, sure as the turnin' of the earth, we'll find them" (Nugent, *The Searchers*). Five years pass before they do, and when Edwards learns Debbie is married to a Comanche man, he aims a rifle at her, and only Pawley's last second intervention saves his half-sister. Edwards's racist comments about both Pawley's half–Cherokee heritage and Debbie's relationship with a Comanche man make his motivation clear. The movie ends with Edwards finally deciding to allow his niece to live. The plot no doubt reflects a modern sense of moral superiority — i.e., today we know you shouldn't kill a white women because she slept with an Indian man — but the movie and the Alan LeMay novel that was the source of the screenplay are based on assumptions about the past, not the historical record.[28]

While there is no mention of sexual relations between Olive and any Mohave man, Stratton did write that "much of that dreadful period is unwritten and will remain forever unwritten" (Stratton, p. 283). Mid–19th century Mohave culture accepted premarital sex as normal. It was, in fact, encouraged, with the assumption that as members of the tribe grew older they would assume responsibilities, from marriage and raising children to hunting and waging war, that would prevent them from ever again enjoying themselves to the same extent. Some historians have suggested that the young man who took beads and pieces of blankets away from Olive before she returned to a white world may have done so because he was her husband and felt she was abandoning him. Even while she lived, many people speculated that Olive may have had children by a Mohave man, children she left behind when the Army ransomed her. This is all speculation, but the speculation reflects an assumption many people make about almost any young woman: she will — willingly or unwillingly — have sexual relations.

Stratton's book went on sale in April 1857, and the first printing of 5,000 copies sold out in three weeks. By the end of the decade, more than 27,000 copies were in print (and presumably most were sold), making its sales less impressive perhaps than Seaver's Mary Jemison book, but still a best-seller for the times. In the summer of 1857, C.E. Bingham, a playwright from San Francisco, wrote a play based on the book — *The Captivity and Massacre of the Oatman Family by the Apache and Mohave Indians* (a word-frugal public called it *The Oatman Family*) — starring Harriet Mace as Olive Oatman and Mace's husband, Junius Brutus Booth, Jr., as a fictional Indian named Langee.[29] (Booth was the older brother of Edwin Booth, perhaps the most famous American actor of his time, and of John Wilkes Booth, who achieved an infamy that far outstripped the fame of anyone else in his family.)

The royalties from the book enabled Olive and Lorenzo to enroll at the University of the Pacific, a Methodist-owned institution in Santa Clara, California. Admission to the university was helped by the fact that the now mildly famous Stratton was appointed to its Visiting Committee. Neither of the Oatmans would complete their degrees. The brother and sister next moved to Chili, just southwest of Rochester, New York, to live with an uncle. Olive used the Rochester area as a base to travel through much of New York and Midwestern states to lecture about her experiences. She became a popular speaker, one of the few women at the time who made her living as a public speaker. At least part of the appeal for audiences was seeing her unusual tattoos. There was no way to remove them. Nor could the ones on her face be easily hidden. Later in life she would apply a great deal of makeup to hide the tattoos on her chin and long sleeves to hide those on her arms, but when she gave a public speech, she knew the tattoos should be visible so her audience would have a clearer picture of what had happened to her.

Her standard speech followed closely what Stratton had written. She always called the tattoos slave marks, but she also always limited her criticism of the Mohave, noting that many of them had shown her considerable kindness. Once, in 1864, she was in New York City to give a lecture and read in a newspaper that a Mohave chief by the name of Irataba was also in town. John Moss, an Arizona prospector, accompanied him. The idea was that the Indian would see white civilization and how many whites there were and conclude that adopting white ways was beneficial and resisting white might was futile. She met with Irataba and spoke to him in the Mohave language. She learned he was the brother of the chief whose family she had lived with, that that chief had died and the brother, Irataba, was now chief. "I learned too," Olive wrote for notes for her standard speech, "that the chiefs daughter was yet living & that she still hoped that I would tire of my pail faced friends & return to her" (McGinty, p. 176). An admission was charged for her lectures and copies of the book were sold before or after she spoke, and Olive made her living on her fame. She was so admired for having suffered and possessing the courage to speak about her suffering that dozens of baby girls were named after her.

During a lecture in Farmington, Michigan, in 1864, Olive met John Brant Fairchild, whose brother Rodney had been killed by Apaches years earlier. That was something he had in common with Olive, who always believed, probably incorrectly, that the murderers of her parents and four siblings were

Apaches. The following year she returned to Michigan to visit Fairchild at his farm, and he proposed to her. She accepted and they were married in Rochester on November 9, 1865. She was 28, he was seven years older. (Five years earlier, Lorenzo, then 24, married 18-year-old Edna Amelia Canfield in Morrison, Illinois.)

Significantly, Royal Byron Stratton was not invited to the wedding. Fairchild, who was well-off, upper-middle class by standards of the time, had enough money to purchase every copy of *Captivity of the Oatman Girls* he could find. Not as souvenirs, but to prevent anyone else from buying and reading them. And he let visitors to their home know he did not want them to mention the book or its subject matter. Although Olive had acquired some money and fame because of the Stratton book, she had come to dislike it intensely. It reminded her of the most painful times in her life. After her marriage, she never again lectured. She had other reminders: The harsh treatment she received from the tribe that kidnapped her and the famine and harsh climate she endured when living with the Mohave damaged her physically. For the rest of her life she suffered from painful eyes, frequent and intense headaches, great nervousness, and what was probably clinical depression.

Stratton, who was now scorned by Olive and John Fairchild, would end up in an institution for the insane in Worcester, Massachusetts, where he died, at age 48, in early 1875. A local newspaper reported the cause of his death as a "disease of the brain" (McGinty, p. 186). (Lorenzo's view of Stratton was kinder. He and his wife, Edna, named a baby boy born in 1883 Royal, after Stratton.)

The Fairchilds moved to Sherman, Texas, in 1872, adopted a baby girl the following year, and lived a life largely out of public view. Olive became an Episcopalian, and she and her husband attended church regularly. Otherwise, she seldom visited town. After her lecturing ceased, she used makeup to cover as best she could the tattoos on her chin. When she did visit town to shop, she always wore long sleeves to cover the tattoos on her arms and usually a veil to cover whatever parts of her facial tattoos the makeup couldn't hide. Olive died while sleeping on March 21, 1903, probably from a heart damaged during the ordeal among the Indians. She was 66 years old. Her husband ordered her coffin enclosed in an iron box because he feared the Mohave might attempt to steal it. Both the Fairchilds would have been dismayed to know that Stratton's *Captivity of the Oatman Girls* was reprinted in 1909, 1935, twice in the 1970s, 1982, 1983, and 1994.

Today we remember the massacres of Indians by whites at Sand Creek in Colorado, at Washita in Oklahoma, and at Wounded Knee in South Dakota (and we should remember the massacre of Shoshoni at Bear River in Idaho), but we give far less historical attention to the Oatman sisters, Rachel Plummer,

Pennsylvania's Wyoming Massacre, Mary Jemison and other stories of atrocities committed by Indians against whites. Remembering them, especially the white fear — based on both tragic experience and arrogant cultural assumptions — that white women might be raped or forced unwillingly into marriage with Indian men, helps us understand part of the motivation for the westward expansion of the American white world. Recognizing the belief that only white occupation of Indian lands, accompanied by the destruction of what was seen as heathen cultures, could assure the purity of white women helps us understand how the West became American.

Fanny Kelly

Most of the approximately 2,700 captivity narratives were short: newspaper or magazine articles or booklets.[30] *Narrative of my Captivity among the Sioux Indians* by Fanny Kelly is one of the few book-length renditions by a white woman or man about time unwillingly spent with Indians. It is also the most consciously *literary* captivity narrative. It is cluttered with enough similes, metaphors, and other literary flourishes to embarrass Zane Grey. There are, in fact, so many attempts in the book to be "literary" that many readers will find it difficult to complete, and for those who do read it in its entirety, the stylistic excesses stretch credibility.

But Fanny Kelly's story contributes significantly to an understanding of the nature of captivity narratives written by white women. It is as melodramatic in its details and style as Rachel Plummer's heart-wrenching tale and, occasionally, as insightful as Mary Jemison's thoughtful observations. It is typical of the better captivity narratives. In many ways, in fact, Fanny Kelly's story is archetypal. It can, that is, serve as a model for the genre.

Kelly was taken captive by Sioux Indians on July 12, 1864, in Wyoming and held for five months until her freedom was arranged by the U.S. Army on December 9. She probably was subjected to sexual abuse during that time, but, as is typical of white women's captivity narratives, the details are suggested and never explicit. In Kelly's case, in fact, she at one point explicitly denies she suffered sexual abuse. She writes in her book, "Surely, the Oglalas (a tribe within the larger Sioux nation) had treated me at times with great harshness and cruelty, yet I had never suffered from any of them the slightest personal or unchaste insult. Let me bear testimony to this redeeming feature in their treatment of me" (Kelly, p. 164).

The book was first published in 1871, although it was mostly written as early as 1865. But in 1868, when she asked the United States Congress for a grant, she wrote, "Your memorialist was ... taken into captivity, and was forced to become the squaw of one of the O-gal-lah-lah chiefs, who treated her in a manner too horrible to mention, and during her captivity was passed from Chief to Chief, and treated in a similar manner" (Kelly, p. 273). It's hard to interpret that as meaning anything other than she was forced into sexual relations with several Sioux men. Was she lying when she said she did not suffer "the slightest personal or unchaste insult" during her five months with the Sioux? Or lying when she told Congress she was "passed from Chief to Chief"?

White women held captive by Indians and who later wrote about it routinely refused to discuss what sexual abuse, if any, they endured. However, phrases like the one Fanny used in her application to Congress—"treated in a manner too horrible to mention"—were common, even standard. Although white women who were raped by Indians were generally treated with sympathy when returned to white society, the social stigma of any sex outside of marriage, whatever the reason, was strong enough that polite society avoided discussing it. What seems most likely, based on the length of time Kelly spent with Indians and the number of male Indians she came in contact with, is that she was forced to have sex with one or more Sioux, lied about it in her book to protect her reputation, but implied the truth with Congress to strengthen her request for money. (Congress gave her $5,000 in 1870 for her claimed role in warning soldiers at Fort Sully in Dakota Territory of an impending attack and another $10,000 in 1872 to compensate her for the loss of personal property when her wagon train was attacked and she was taken captive in 1864).

Fanny Kelly was born either in 1842 (the year on her tombstone) or 1845 (the year she cites in the first sentence of her book) in Orillia, Ontario, Canada, on the shores of either Lake Simcoe or Lake Couchiching. She says only, "Our home was on the lake shore" (Kelly, p. 3); Orillia touches both lakes. These are small points, but they illustrate the difficulties in evaluating Kelly's book. We can't be certain of the year of her birth or which lake she was born along. Her lack of precision makes dozens of points of her book uncertain.

When she was 11 (if we accept 1845 as her birth year), her father, James Wiggins, moved to Geneva, Kansas, but on his way back to Orillia he contracted cholera and died. His wife then took the family to Geneva, where in November 1863 Fanny Wiggins, then aged 18 or 21, married Josiah Shawahan Kelly, who had served the Union army in the still raging Civil War. His year of birth is uncertain, but he was at least 15 years older than Fanny. He was born in Ohio, had worked in the gold mines of California, been a farmer, and ended up in Geneva, with property valued, according to the 1860 U.S. Census, at $300. In 1870, however, one of his brothers insisted Josiah owned property worth up to $10,000. (The Kellys sold the land to buy goods to take on their move westward, and that was the basis of the second payment—for $10,000—from Congress.)

The Kellys adopted a daughter, Mary, who was seven or eight at the time. Mary Hurley was the daughter of Fanny's sister, who may have died or who may have been unable to take proper care of her. Partly because Josiah's health was poor and he thought a different climate might be helpful and partly to seek their fortune, the Kellys decided to move to Idaho Territory. (Today's Idaho was originally part of Oregon Territory, but when Oregon became a state, it became part of Washington Territory, but administering its affairs from Olympia, the territorial capital, proved impractical, so Congress created, in 1863, Idaho Territory, which at the time included all of today's Idaho, Wyoming, and Montana. In 1864, Congress created Montana Territory, leaving an Idaho Territory that consisted of today's Idaho and Wyoming. The details can be confusing, and some historians think the Kellys really had the western part of Montana Territory in mind as their destination, although Fanny Kelly specifically says Idaho in her book. In her letter to Congress, however, she says they were headed for Bannock City, Montana Territory).

On May 17, 1864, the Kellys, with their adopted daughter Mary, two black servants, Andy and Franklin, both former slaves of the Cherokee Indians, and a friend, Gardner Wakefield, started their westward trek. Several days later a Methodist clergyman, a Mr. Sharp, joined them. A few weeks later they met a larger wagon train, but didn't join it. A family from that train, however, the Larimers, joined the Kellys. The Larimer family consisted of a husband, wife, and an eight-year-old son. The wife, Sarah, would play an important role in Fanny's future.

On July 12, about 10 miles south of present-day Douglas, Wyoming, the small wagon train encountered about 250 Sioux headed by a chief Fanny called Ottawa (because no historian has been able to identify him with any known Sioux leader, it's possible Fanny misunderstood his name). At first the Indians seemed friendly. Ottawa called himself "Good Indian, me" (Kelly, p. 14). The Indians at first contented themselves by asking for — demanding really — small gifts, like shoes and sacks of flour, but then they wanted the whites to prepare supper for them. As the whites were doing that, the Indians, without warning, opened fire. Franklin, one of the black servants, was hit by an arrow that pierced both of his legs, pinning them together, and then his head was bashed in by a club. Two other men, Wakefield and a Mr. Taylor, were shot dead. Two Indians violently threw Fanny to the ground, almost breaking her arms and legs. When the shooting stopped, Fanny, little Mary, Sarah Larimer, and Sarah's son were prisoners. Then another wagon appeared. A man, a woman, and a small boy were on it. When the Indians saw it, they raced towards it. The man gave the wagon's reins to the woman, who urged the horses to run as fast as they could. The man threw the wagon's heaviest contents out the back and shot at the Indians with a pistol. After a few minutes, the Indians gave up the chase, and the wagon escaped.

Josiah Kelly also escaped. As had Andy, the other black servant, and Mr. Larimer. After the Indians left with their hostages, Kelly and Andy found each other. They then found a dead body. Fanny is unclear about whose body it was, but it seems to have been that of a man who was with the family in the wagon that successfully fled the Indians. Fanny is very forgiving about her husband's escape. She writes, "The pen is powerless to portray his agony during these frightful moments" (Kelly, pp. 22–23). No doubt he could have done nothing effective to keep his wife and daughter from being taken hostage, but the fact that he fled rather than try hardly earns him our admiration. In fact, while she has some limited praise for Indians, most of what she says about Indians is negative and all of what she says about whites is positive, even when there is clearly room for criticism. The result is to tinge her narrative with racism. The racism extended even to the black servants, whom she generally praises. Josiah and the other whites buried Franklin in a common grave with the two white victims of the attack, and Fanny wrote, "The question of color had occasioned much dissension, and feelings were mixed as to the propriety of allowing black people the privilege of sitting beside their white brethren. Poor Franklin had shared death with our companions, and was not deemed unworthy to share the common grave of his fellow victims" (Kelly, p. 26).

After their husbands escaped, Mrs. Larimer said to Fanny, "The men have all escaped, and left us to the mercy of the savages." Fanny replied, "I do hope they have. What benefit would it be to us to have them here, to suffer this fear and danger with us? They would be killed, and then all hope of rescue for us would be at an end" (Kelly, p. 30). In peril, at least in her memory of that peril, Fanny exhibits an unnatural rationality. Then the Indians began destroying Mrs. Larimer's property. She hoped to run a photography business in her new home, but the Indians spilled chemicals on the ground and smashed "the Daguerrean art" (Kelly, p. 31). Sarah "uttered a wild, despairing cry" (Kelly, p. 31). We're not told what it was, but it annoyed the chief enough that he threatened to kill her. Fanny, as she tells the story, came to Sarah's rescue: "assuming a cheerfulness I was very far from feeling, [I] pleaded successfully for her life" (Kelly, p. 32). The chief then gave Fanny "a wreath of gay feathers from his own head.... I afterward learned, it was a token of his favor and protection" (Kelly, p. 32). Then a young Indian named Wechela indicated the white women should take some clothing with them and that was "the first intimation we had that our immediate massacre was not intended" (Kelly, p. 32).

As so often happens in captivity narratives, Fanny turned to God for help: "The only respite we could claim from despair was the lifting of our trembling hearts upward to the God of mercy" (Kelly, p. 34). Dozens of times in her narrative she either praises God or asks him to save her. Also, as is common in the narratives, she wavers between wanting to live and wanting to die. Twice she expresses a desire to live, five times a desire to die. At one point she writes, "Many persons have since assured me that, to them, death would have been preferable to life with such prospects, saying that rather than have submitted to be carried away by savages to a dark and doubtful doom, they would have taken their own lives. But it is only those who have looked over the dark abyss of death who know how the soul shrinks from meeting the unknown future" (Kelly, p. 36). She does not say who said death would be better, but presumably it was women who feared rape. Sex outside marriage never met with social approval, but it was forgiven, but sex with someone of another race, even unwillingly, was unthinkable. Interestingly, however, each time she hoped for death it was because of a lack of food or water or physical warmth, never because of whatever sexual abuse she suffered.

She was put on a horse with Mary and they rode through the dark. Fanny dropped pieces of paper on the ground so a rescue party would be able to follow them. In the darkness she whispered to Mary, "We are only a few miles from our camp, and the stream we have crossed you can easily wade through. I have dropped letters on the way, you know, to guide our friends in the direction we have taken; they will guide you back again, and it may be your only chance of escape from destruction. Drop gently down and lie on the ground for a little while to avoid being seen; then retrace your steps, and may God in mercy go with you. If I can, I will follow you later" (Kelly, p. 39). In the darkness, certain the Indians could not see her, Fanny dropped Mary to the ground, and the procession moved forward. After a while, Fanny "slipped to the ground under the friendly cover of night, and the horse went on without its rider" (Kelly, p. 40).

After a while, the Indians realized Fanny was gone, so they rode after her and quickly found her. She told them Mary had fallen from the horse and she was only looking for her. "The Indians used great violence toward me" she said (Kelly, p. 41), but doesn't provide details. The Indians then sent a party after Mary. Not until after Fanny was free did she learn what happened next. Mary made her way back to the main road and waited in the hope some whites would pass. In the daylight, she spotted three, perhaps four, soldiers, and they saw her. But they feared she might be a decoy to lure them into a trap. They had been chased the prior day by Indians and had also seen the destroyed wagons and goods from the attack on the Kelly train. So they hesitated, but soon decided to try to rescue the little white girl. Just then they saw the party of Indians sent after Mary. The soldiers, now convinced the girl was indeed part of a trap, fled the scene and went to Deer Creek Station, where there was a small detachment of soldiers.

Either that day or the next, Josiah arrived at Deer Creek Station and heard their story. He asked the officer in charge to send soldiers after his adopted daughter, but the officer, for reasons Fanny doesn't discuss, refused to do so. Probably he too feared a trap and perhaps the station just wasn't large enough to spare any soldiers. Two days later, however, the officer agreed and a "squad" of soldiers was sent to the spot Mary had been seen, eight or ten miles away (Kelly, pp. 211–212). That was July 14. They found Mary. Dead. "Three arrows had pierced her body, and the tomahawk and scalping knife had done their work. When discovered, her body lay with its little hands outstretched as if she had received, while running, the fatal arrows" (Kelly, p. 212). The father buried his daughter on the prairie. Fanny found solace in her religious beliefs: "When she had once gained the great and unspeakable bliss of heaven, it must have blotted out the remembrance of the pain that won it, and made no price too great for such delight" (Kelly, pp. 212–213).

The night she was captured, after she urged Mary to escape, Fanny was instructed "to lie down on the ground near a wounded Indian" (Kelly, p. 45). Other Indians were nearby, and it's unlikely she had sex with the wounded Indian, but certainly thoughts of being sexually violated must have entered her mind. She prayed for deliverance and believed her prayers were answered: "This nerved me to endure and appear submissive" (Kelly, p. 46).

The next night, before going to sleep, she told fellow prisoner Sarah Larimer that she intended to escape. Sarah pleaded that she not be left alone. When Fanny woke in the morning, however, it was Sarah who had fled. As with Mary, she wouldn't know Sarah's fate until months later.

The next day she was ordered to carry the chief's three-foot-long pipe and other "implements" (Kelly, p. 48). The load was so heavy she threw away the pipe, and when the chief found out, he threatened to kill her. "An untamed horse was brought," she wrote, "and they told me I would be placed on it as a target for their deadliest arrows" (Kelly, p. 50). She was saved when she took out some money, $120, and gave it to the Indians. Later, when riding a horse, she was beaten and the chief swore at her in English. Fanny wrote, "Drunkenness, profanity, and dissolute habits are the lessons of civilization to the red men" (Kelly, p. 52).

A few days later, what she saw as an act of kindness resulted in her again being endangered. "The chief's brother-in-law gave me a pair of stockings from his stores, which I gladly accepted," but the chief "immediately after ... shot one of his brother-in-law's horses" (Kelly, p. 59). The two men argued, and when the chief refused to pay for the dead horse, the brother-in-law "aimed his arrow at my heart, determined to have satisfaction for the loss of his horse" (Kelly, p. 60). Just then a young Blackfeet named Jumping Bear grabbed the bow and threw it to the ground. Finally, the chief gave his brother-in-law a horse and the matter was settled.

Fanny, unlike Rachel Plummer or Mary Jemison, kept careful track of dates and knew, for example, that the day they saw a large herd of buffalo was July 21. (At one point she writes, "I missed no count of the rising or setting sun, and knew dates almost as well as if I were in the heart of civilization" [Kelly, p. 116].) Like many observers of 19th century Indian buffalo hunts, and unlike many 21st century commentators who assume an unrealistic relationship between Indians and the environment, Fanny noted the great waste the hunts produced: "The Indians often for the mere sport, make an onslaught, killing great numbers of them.... They use no economy in food. It is always a feast or a famine.... Each man selects the part of the animal he has killed that best suits his own taste, and leaves the rest to decay or be eaten by wolves, thus wasting their own game, and often suffering privation in consequence" (Kelly, p. 69). The Sioux gave Fanny a knife and motioned for her to cut a piece of buffalo to eat, but she wouldn't, "thinking then it would never be possible for me to attempt to eat uncooked meat" (Kelly, p. 69).

The next morning, Jumping Bear rode silently at her side. Clearly he was becoming attached to her.

The day after that she was again offered uncooked meat and again declined, but this time a young Indian cooked some for her, but she ate only a small part of the offering "owing to the filthy manner in which it was prepared" (Kelly, p. 71).

About a third of the way through the book, 60 pages after she reports being taken captive by Ottawa, she tells the reader that "the war chief ... was quite old, over seventy-five, partially blind, and under the medium height" (Kelly, p. 73). Two pages later she notes that he had six wives. All that may explain why she did not have sex with Ottawa. If, indeed, she didn't. Fanny looked forward to arriving at an Indian village because it would afford her some female companionship, but when she finally reached a village, she was frightened by some of the women, who seemed to resent her presence.

In the village she saw several children who she learned had Indian mothers and white fathers. "It was a very sad thought for me," Fanny wrote, "to realize that a parent could part with such a child, committing it forever to live in barbarous ignorance, and rove the woods among savages with the impress of his own superior race, so strongly mingled with his Indian origin" (Kelly, pp. 78–79). If the racism in Fanny's statement is harsh, so too was the racism the half-white-half-Indian children encountered in the village: "On many occasions they are cruelly treated by the full-blooded and larger children because of their unfortunate birth," Fanny wrote (Kelly, p. 70).

Shortly after arriving at the village, despite her fear of the some of the women, Fanny befriended others. "To their great surprise," she wrote, "they discovered my bruised and almost broken limbs that occurred when first taken ... and proceeded at once to dress my wounds" (Kelly, p. 79). The chief later gave Fanny a little girl, one of his own, to raise, to replace the daughter Fanny had lost. The little girl's name was Yellow Bird. Fanny, in fact, became friendly with many Indian children. In addition, she sometimes sang for the adults. She was, despite her desire not to, fitting in among the Sioux. She believed it helped keep her alive. One way she fit in was that, like the Sioux, constantly on the move and unable to provide enough food, she often had little to eat.

Throughout her narrative, Fanny offers observations that vary between insightful and silly. On the reason the Sioux hated whites: "The antipathy of the Indian to the white man's occupation or invasion of its land is very intense and bitter. The felling of timber, killing of buffalo, traveling of a train, or any other indication of permanent possession by the white man excites deadly hostility. It is their last hope; if they yield and give up this, they will have to die or ever after be governed by the white man's laws; consequently they lose no opportunity to kill, steal from, or harass the whites when they can do so" (Kelly, pp. 90–92). But, she saw blankets as a great hindrance to Indian advancement: "The blanket, as worn by the Indian, is an insuperable barrier to his advance in arts or agriculture. When this is forever dispensed with, then his hands will be free to grasp the mechanic's tools or guide the plow. It is both graceful and chaste in their eyes and to adopt the white man's dress is a great obstacle, a requirement too humiliating, for they have personal as well as national pride" (Kelly, p. 180).

Meanwhile, General Alfred Sully was pursing the Sioux across the Dakotas. An Indian was sent to Fanny and told her she would be "burned at the stake.... He said that he had been sent from the council to warm me that it had become necessary to put me to death on account of my white brothers killing so many of their young men recently. He repeated that they were not cruel, for the pleasure of being so; necessity is their first law, and he and the wise chiefs, faithful to their hatred for the white race, were in haste to satisfy their thirst for vengeance; and, further, that the interest of their nation required it" (Kelly, p. 101). Fanny then reports a debate that took place among tribal leaders. "One of the eldest of the chiefs ... who enjoyed a reputation for great wisdom" said, according to Fanny,

> The palefaces, our eternal persecutors, pursue and harass us without intermission, forcing us to abandon to them, one by one, our best hunting grounds, and we are compelled to seek a refuge in the depths of these Bad Lands like timid deer. Many of them even dare to come into the prairies which belong to us, to trap beaver and hunt elk and buffalo, which are our property. These undesirable creatures, the

outcasts of their own people, rob and kill us when they can. Is it just that we should suffer these wrongs without complaining? Shall we allow ourselves to be massacred like timid Assiniboins [a tribe that spoke the same language as the Sioux but whom they considered inferior]...? Does not the law of the Dakotas say, "Justice to our own nation and death to all palefaces?" Let my brothers say if that is just [Kelly, pp. 102–103].

Then he pointed to the stake at which Fanny was to be burned. "Vengeance is always allowable" (Kelly, p. 103), said another chief, Mahpeah (The Sky).

Ottawa then stood and said, "It is the undoubted right of the weak and oppressed; and yet it should be proportioned to the injury that was received. Then why should we put this young, innocent woman to death? Has she not always been kind to us, smiled upon us, and sang for us? Do not all our children love her as a tender sister? Why, then, should we put her to so cruel a death for the crimes of others, even if they are of her nation? Why should we punish an innocent one in place of the guilty?" (Kelly, p. 103).

Fanny silently prayed and her prayers were fulfilled. The council heeded Ottawa and spared her life. She took solace in her belief that no matter what suffering she endured, a benevolent God watched out for her: "While my temporal wants were ... poorly supplied, I was not wholly denied spiritual food. It was a blessed consolation that no earthly foe could interrupt my communion with the heavenly world" (Kelly, p. 105).

Fanny was with a large group of Indians, perhaps several thousand, so it's not surprising that days passed before she realized another white woman was also in the village: "a victim of Indian cruelty, whose fate was even sadder than mine" (Kelly, p. 106). Fanny met the girl while carrying water from a river. She was "a fair-faced, beautiful young girl, sitting there, dejected and worn, like myself, but bearing the marks of loveliness and refinement, despite her neglected covering" (Kelly, p. 106). She had "sad brown eyes" and a "drooping, pallid face" (Kelly, p. 107). Ottawa was nearby and gave Fanny a book, a school primer by Marcus Willson taken from one of the Kellys' wagons. He wanted Fanny to give it to the girl. Fanny did and the girl said, "What book is that?" (Kelly, p. 107). The sound of someone speaking English made Fanny "insensible" (Kelly, p. 107). As so often happens with Kelly's use of words, the reader must pause to figure out exactly what she means. In the next sentence, she writes that "a kindly squaw ... began sprinkling my face with water" (Kelly, p. 107), suggesting that "insensible" meant Fanny fainted.

The girl told Fanny her story: "My name is Mary Boyeau; these people call me Madee. I have been among them since the massacre in Minnesota and am now in my sixteenth year" (Kelly, p. 108).

The Minnesota massacre Mary referred to was probably the great uprising of Santee Sioux in 1862, in which the Indians, upset at white failures to honor treaties, revolted, killing about 500 whites before the state militia destroyed the Sioux ability to wage war. About 2,000 Indians were captured and 308 of them were condemned to death. President Abraham Lincoln personally reviewed each conviction and limited the executions to 38 men who were guilty of murder or rape. The 38 were hung together that year, the day after Christmas. Historians have been unable to trace a Mary Boyeau, and while they don't doubt the essence of the story Fanny relates, the details are sometimes in doubt.[31]

Mary said her parents and some siblings were killed. "We were among the first victims of the massacre, and ... all my family were murdered except myself, and, I fear, one younger sister" (Kelly, p. 108), Mary said. Fanny replied, "You fear! Do you not hope that she escaped?" (Kelly, p. 108), and Mary said — a remark echoed by many white woman captured by Indians — "From a life like mine, death is an escape." She added, it's "a sin to rush unbidden into God's presence, but I cannot live through another frightful winter. No, I must and will die if no relief comes to me. For a year these people regarded me as a child, and then a young man of their tribe gave a horse for me and carried me to his tipi as his wife" (Kelly, p. 109). Fanny asked, "Do you love your husband?" (Kelly, p. 109), and Mary replied, "Love a savage, who bought me to be a drudge and slave! No! I hate him as I hate all that belong to this fearful bondage. He has another wife and a child. Thank God!, that I am not a mother!" (Kelly, p. 109). Fanny asked, "Does he ill treat you?" (Kelly, p. 109), and Mary said, "His wife does. I am forced to do different types of slavish chores, and when my strength fails, I am urged on by blows. Oh! I do so fearfully dread the chilling winters without proper food or clothing; and I long to lie down and die, if God's mercy will only permit me to escape from this hopeless imprisonment" (Kelly, pp. 109–110).

Mary told how an attempt was made by whites to ransom her but her Sioux husband refused the payment as inadequate. The offer evidently included one horse and some other unspecified inducements. Without directly quoting Mary, Fanny says Mary never attempted to escape because of "her dread of soldiers" (Kelly, p. 110). Fanny makes no attempt to explain that dread, but undoubtedly it is a reference to reports, some of them probably true, of white soldiers raping white women they helped free from Indian captivity.

Then Fanny writes, "True, I was like her, a captive torn from home and friends and subject to harsh treatment, but no such personal indignity had fallen to my lot" (Kelly, p. 111). While this statement is consistent with her claim that "I had never suffered from any of them the slightest personal or unchaste insult" (Kelly, p. 164), it is inconsistent with the statement in her petition to Congress that she was "forced to become the squaw of" Ottawa and "passed from Chief to Chief" (Kelly, p. 273).

5. Saving White Women from Indians 141

Mary then told Fanny about some atrocities she saw the Indians commit after her capture. In one, "the Indians entered into a house where they found a woman making bread" and throwing her baby "into the heated oven, its screams torturing the wretched mother, who was then stabbed and cut in many places. Taking the suffering little creature from the oven, they then dashed out its brains against the walls of the house" (Kelly, p. 111). In another, a captive white woman made to carry a heavy burden across a stream fell into the water and was shot and killed while trying to reach the bank. In another, five children of Laura Duley were killed during the 1862 uprising, "one of which was left on the ground in a place where the distracted mother had to pass daily in carrying water from the river; and when they left the camp the body still remained unburied. So terrible were the sufferings of this heartbroken mother that, when she arrived in safety back among the whites, her reason soon became dethroned, and I was told that she was sent to the lunatic asylum, where her distracted husband soon followed" (Kelly, pp. 112–113). Her husband was Captain William J. Duley and he was assigned the "honor" of cutting the rope that resulted in the simultaneous hangings of the 38 Sioux President Lincoln said could be executed.

Fanny gave Mary a book and half a pencil as presents. The Indians were upset that she had given the book away because she had used it to try to teach some of them to read. "I found them apt pupils," Fanny wrote, "willing to learn, and they learned easily and rapidly. Their memory is very retentive — unusually good" (Kelly, p. 113).

While she could praise their ability to learn, much in the culture of the Indians shocked her. One day she saw an Indian carrying, evidently attached to his horse, "a child's scalp of long, fair hair.... I realized that innocent victim's dying agonies. The torture was too great to be endured, and a merciful insensibility quickly interposed between me and madness. I dropped from the saddle as if dead" (Kelly, p. 114). This is the second time Fanny faints, although she never uses that word. When the Indians place her again upon her horse, she asks them to kill her. Throughout her narrative she wavers between wanting to live and wanting to die. She then makes a judgment about the Sioux that today we're tempted to dismiss as racism, but can also be seen as a result of the desperate state she was in: "I had found by experience that the only grief with which this red nation had any sympathy was the sorrow one might feel for a separation from a mother" (Kelly, p. 115). So, to avoid being punished for offering difficulty in being placed back on her horse, she said, "I want to see my dear mother, my poor mother who loves and pines for her unhappy child" (Kelly, p. 115). That seemed to satisfy the Indians.

Shortly after that incident, the band was attacked by a horde of grasshoppers. The Indians, who considered the insects good food, dug holes, heated the holes with fires, removed the flame, and drove the grasshoppers into the holes, where they were baked. Fanny does not indicate if she ate any. She does, however, complain that she did not have enough to eat and tired because of the constant work assigned to her: "I had grown so weak that motion of any kind was exhausting to me and I could scarcely walk. I felt that I must soon die of starvation and sorrow; life had ceased to be dear to me" (Kelly, p. 117). She couldn't do some task — she doesn't say which one — because of her weakness, so the "old squaw" (one of Ottawa's wives) "came flying into the lodge like an enraged fury, flourishing her knife, and vowing she would kill me. I rose immediately and fled, the squaw pursuing me. The chief attempted to interfere, but her rage was too great. He struck her, at which she sprang like an infuriated tiger upon him, stabbing him in several places. Her brother, who at a short distance beheld the fray, and deeming me the cause, fired six shots determining to kill me. One of these shots lodged in the arm of the chief, breaking it near the shoulder" (Kelly, p. 118).

Fanny then fled the village but was caught by several Indians, who gave her to some women, who took her back to the chief's lodge. "He was," she writes, "very weak from loss of blood" (Kelly, p. 119). She adds, "I never saw the wife of the chief afterward" (Kelly, p. 119). Because of his wound, he could no longer hunt or fish and therefore could not provide food for his family, so he "sent his [six] wives to work for themselves while keeping the sisters and myself to attend him" (Kelly, p. 120). That is, the chief's three sisters now lived with him, and, Fanny writes, "with these I continued to live in companionship" (Kelly, p. 119). Was the "old squaw's" rage a result of Fanny being a sexual partner of the chief? Does living "in companionship" with the chief's sister mean, also, living "in companionship" with the chief? And in what way did she "attend" to him? Fanny remains determined throughout her narrative to at points deny having sexual relationships with Ottawa or any other Indians. Only in her letter to Congress does she make an uninhibited acknowledgment of sex with Indians.

She does report an ominous conversation with one of Ottawa's sisters. She repeatedly writes that Indians regularly claimed to be friendly with whites in order to collect food or other supplies promised to them under treaties, but that when away from whites they exhibited nothing but hatred. Fanny asked the sister, "But will they not suspect you? They will surely discover your deceit and punish you some day" (Kelly, p. 119). The sister "laughed derisively" and said, "Our prisoners don't escape to tell tales. Dead people don't talk" (Kelly, p. 119).

Whatever her exact relationship with Ottawa, with his six wives gone, the chief decides he needs another wife, so he "concluded to send an offer of marriage to the daughter of the war chief of another band" (Kelly, p. 120).

He needed a gift to accompany the offer, so, Fanny writes, "he availed himself of my shoes, which happened to be particularly good, and, reducing me to moccasins, sent them as a gift to the expected bride" (Kelly, p. 120). Must have indeed been good shoes, because the woman became a frequent visitor to the chief's lodge, and "as the betrothed continued in favor, the chief evinced it by giving her articles of my clothing" (Kelly, pp. 120–121). Fanny then comments on the relationship between husbands and wives in Sioux culture, generalizing it, as she almost always does, to include all Indians: "An Indian husband's power is absolute even to death. No woman can have more than one husband, but an Indian man can have as many wives as he chooses" (Kelly, p. 121). Actually, many North American Indian nations forbade polygamy.

Fanny later learned that the U.S. Army was looking for her. The Army knew she was a captive of the Sioux and was prepared to offer a ransom. An Indian named Porcupine (it's not certain if he was a Sioux) gave her a letter from Captain Levi Marshall saying Porcupine had been given a horse and provisions for the journey Fanny would need to make to return to white society and that he "had left his three wives, with thirteen others, at the fort as hostages" (Kelly, p. 122). But Ottawa would not agree to let Fanny go. She pleaded with him to take her despite what Ottawa said, but Porcupine replied that "he would report me to be dead or impossible to find" (Kelly, p. 123). Fanny told him that his wives might be killed if he didn't bring her back, but Porcupine said, "The white soldiers are cowards. They never kill women" (Kelly, p. 123).

The young woman Ottawa was about to marry questioned Fanny about her desire to stay with the Sioux, and Fanny was suspicious the questions might be intended to trap her. "There are white people down there" (Kelly, p. 124), the young woman said, indicating some unspecified distant place. Her name was Egosegalonicha.

"How far?" (Kelly, p. 124), Fanny asked.

"About fifty miles. They have great guns and men dressed in many buttons. Their wagons are drawn by horses with long ears" (Kelly, p. 124).

Fanny, "remembering the treacherous nature of the people she was among ... repressed every sign of emotion and tried to look indifferent" (Kelly, p. 124).

"Should you like to see them?" (Kelly, p. 124), asked Egosegalonicha.

"They are strangers to me. I do not know them" (Kelly, p. 124).

"Are you sorry to live with us?" (Kelly, p. 124).

"You do not have such bread as I would like to eat" (Kelly, p. 124).

"And are you dissatisfied with our home?" (Kelly, p. 124).

"You have some meat now; it is better than that at the other camping ground. There we had not food and I suffered" (Kelly, p. 124).

"But your eyes are swollen and red. You do not weep for bread" (Kelly, p. 124).

"Just see how green that wood is" (Kelly, p. 124), Fanny said, trying to evade what she took to be trick questions designed to get her to say something that would bring her punishment.

"But you do not say you are content. Will you stay here always, willingly?" (Kelly, p. 126).

"Come and listen to the birds" (Kelly, p. 126).

A short time later, Fanny "overheard [Egosegalonicha] relating to the chief the amusement she had enjoyed in lying to the white woman" (Kelly, p. 126). Fanny "resolved to take advantage of the affair as a joke, and ... begged to reverse the story. It was the squaw who had implored me to go with her to the white man's fort ... and find her a white warrior for a husband; but, true to my faith with the Indians, I refused" (Kelly, p. 126). Egosegalonicha left the tent, confused. The teasing comment to Ottawa about finding a white husband, of course, might indicate that Fanny saw herself as one of Ottawa's wives.

Meanwhile Porcupine told villagers the whites were offering a large reward for Fanny and at least one, White Tipi, offered to sneak her out of the village and take her to the fort, but when she went to meet him at an appointed spot at night, he saw her and left. She never found out why.

Fanny became friendly with one young woman, in her mid-twenties, who had white parents. An Indian man, Black Bear, discovered her one day, about 25 years earlier, in a wagon with her father, who was dying of cholera. The father asked Black Bear to take care of his daughter, to take her to his home in the East and that he would be given a large reward. Black Bear took the money the father offered and whatever valuables were in the wagon, and he took them and the girl to his home. "She forgot her own language, her name, and everything about her past life," Fanny writes, "but she knew that she was white" (Kelly, p. 131). Fanny adds, "When she was of marriageable age, Black Bear took her for his wife, and they had a child, a boy" (Kelly, p. 131). Fanny, uncharacteristically, does not comment on what in effect is an adoptive father marrying his adopted daughter. She does offer a characteristically racist opinion: "I endeavored to enlighten her, and to do her all the good I could; told her of the white people, and of their kindness and Christianity, trying to impress her with the superiority of the white race, all of which she listened to with great interest" (Kelly, p. 132). But, to Fanny's sadness, if not her surprise, the young woman "was happy and contented with Indian surroundings, for she knew no difference" (Kelly, p. 132).

Fanny also writes of a 14-year-old boy named Charles Sylvester from Quincy, Illinois, who, at age seven, was kidnapped by Indians and thereafter raised as an Indian. Sometime after Fanny met him (and probably after Fanny returned to white society) he accidentally killed a hunting companion and was afraid to return to the village, so he ran away to rejoin white society, but after a while, Fanny writes, "being discontented with his own people, he returned to his adopted friends" (Kelly, p. 133).

At one point, some Indian warriors drew pictures showing Indians defeating white soldiers in combat, and Fanny, annoyed, snatched one of the drawings, tore it in two, threw one half in a fire, clutched the other to her heart, and said she loved white soldiers. "Never did I see a more enraged set of men," Fanny writes. "They assailed me with burning firebrands, burning me severely. They heated the points of their arrows, and burned and threatened me sorely" (Kelly, p. 137). She promised to draw them some new pictures, and that ended the matter. Fanny then makes two comments about the incident, one clearly racist, and one full of obvious truth. First: "They were much like children ... easily offended, but very difficult to please." Second: "I knew not how to get along with them" (Kelly, p. 137).

One day she was summoned to see a dying man, evidently with a wound suffered in combat. Fanny asked him how he got the wound, and he said, "I go to fight white man. He take away land and chase game away; then he take away our squaws. He take away my best squaw" (Kelly, p. 138).

Fanny's stereotyping runs rampant through her narrative. Examples: When someone brought a jar of pickles into the camp, "The result was comical in the extreme, for there is nothing that an Indian abhors more than a strong acid" (Kelly, p. 140). Discussing Indians as warriors: "Ambush ... is their only idea of warfare. Indians are not truly brave, though they are vain of the name of courage. Cunning, stealth, strategy, and deceit are the weapons they use in attack. They endure pain because they are taught from infancy that it is cowardly to flinch, but they will never stand to fight if they can strike secretly and quickly escape" (Kelly, p. 140). And: "Instinct, more than reason, is the guide of the red man. He repudiates improvement and despises manual effort. For ages his heart has been embedded in moral pollution" (Kelly, p. 180). Much harsher: "The Indian ... has none of the kindlier feelings of humanity in him. He is devoid of gratitude as he is hypocritical and treacherous ... the young ... torture birds, turtles, or any other small animal that may fall into their hands. They delight in it, while the pleasure of the adult from torturing his prisoners is unquestionable. They are inveterate beggars, but never give.... His most fiendish murders of the innocent is his sweetest revenge for a wrong that has been done by another" (Kelly, pp. 180–181). The quotes can go on. Fanny Kelly suffered during her five months of captivity by the Sioux, and we can easily understand, even excuse, the bitterness that resulted. Her stereotyping, however, casts doubt on the usefulness, even the accuracy, of her observations.

Not surprisingly, Fanny reports that at some points she outwitted what she saw as intellectually inferior Indians. Most obviously this happened when a detachment of cavalry were known to be nearby and Ottawa ordered Fanny to write a letter for him. The intent of the letter was to tell the soldiers the Indians were friendly and the soldiers should just pass by. Fanny wanted to let the soldiers know she was with the Indians. She writes, "Knowing their malicious designs, I set myself to work to circumvent them; and although the wily chief counted every word he dictated as they were marked on paper, I contrived, by joining them together and condensing the information I gave, to warm the officer of the perfidious intentions of the savages, and tell him briefly of my helpless and unhappy captivity" (Kelly, p. 141). The letter was delivered to the soldiers by an Indian, and after "a reasonable interval the reply arrived, and again my ingenuity was tasked to read the answer corresponding with the number of words that would not condemn me" (Kelly, p. 141). The letter said only that the captain in charge, James Liberty Fisk, did not trust the Indians, and Fanny's hopes of being rescued "were severely crushed" (Kelly, p. 142). The next day, Ottawa had her write another letter, this one assuring the soldiers the Indians were friendly. Fanny "managed to communicate with them, and this time begged them to use their field glasses, and that I would find an excuse for standing on the hills in the afternoon, that they might see for themselves that I was what I represented myself to be—a white woman held in bondage" (Kelly, p. 142).

The message got through, and, according to Fanny, "As soon the soldiers saw that it truly was a woman of their own race, and that I was in the power of their enemies, the excitement of their feelings became so great that they desired immediately to rush to my rescue" (Kelly, p. 142). (Presumably this was something she learned after her release.) She adds, "A gentleman belonging to the train generously offered eight hundred dollars for my ransom.... There was not a man in the train who was not willing to sacrifice all he had for my rescue" (Kelly, p. 142). But Captain Fisk, not trusting the Indians and believing any attempt to rescue Fanny would result in her death, ordered that no rescue attempt be made. Fisk did send a ransom offer of "three wagonloads of stores" (Kelly, p. 145). Fanny writes, "To this the deceitful creatures readily pretended to agree, while I, the tortured captive, who could understand their tongue, heard them making fun of the credulity of white soldiers who did not doubt their promises" (Kelly, p. 143). Fanny wrote again to Fisk "about the futility of ransoming me in that way, and warned him of the treachery intended against his messengers" (Kelly, p. 143). She doesn't explain how this message was delivered. Nor does she make it clear how Fisk reacted, but evidently the wagons were never delivered. Then, she writes, the Indians said "I could not be purchased at any price since they were determined not to part with me"

5. Saving White Women from Indians 147

(Kelly, p. 143). Fisk left the area but spread word among whites about where Fanny was held.

Some civilian members of the group under Captain Fisk's command left some poisoned crackers that the Indians found and ate. The crackers were left by relatives of people killed in the 1862 Minnesota uprising. The poison was strychnine. An estimated 25 Indians died as a result of the poisoning. Captain Fisk denied any role in the poisoning but praised the action.

Fanny suffered her own health problems about the same time. Rheumatism. It was so bad, she writes, "I often prayed fervently to God to give me sweet release in a flight to the land where there are no storms" (Kelly, p. 146).

Despite her low opinion of nearly everything about Indian culture, she reports one incident, in October, that reflects ingenuity, social organization, and courage. A prairie fire suddenly appeared, racing towards the village. "The Indians, old and young, male and female began to pull up the grass by the roots all about the camp, then lassoed the horses and hobbled them in the center, and, in a few moments, a large space was cleared, where the herbs and grass had been pulled up with the feverish rapidity which all display in the fear of death" (Kelly, p. 154). Then on the outer edges of the cleared space they piled the pulled grass and set it on fire. Cleared space and fighting fire with fire worked. "By degrees," Fanny writes, "the flames became less fierce, the air purer; the smoke dispersed, the roaring diminished, and, at length, we were able to recognize each other in the horrible chaos" (Kelly, p. 154). Interestingly, Fanny offers not one word of praise for the ingenuity and effectiveness of the community effort. Unlike her running commentaries on what she saw as negative in Sioux society, this incident is reported journalistically.

Also in early October (Fanny says Oct. 1, although she tells about this incident after she tells us about the prairie fire in the same month) the Oglala Sioux attacked a flatboat on a nearby river. About 20 whites, men, women, and children, were on the boat. The Indians surprised them and killed all the men. "Then followed the torture of the women and children. Horrible thought! From which all will turn with sickened soul and shuddering cry to Heaven, 'How long, O Lord! How long shall such inhuman atrocities go unpunished?' Not a soul was left alive when that black day's work was complete" (Kelly, p. 156).

Fanny later saw "a woman's scalp with heavy chestnut hair, a golden brown, and four feet in length, which had been secured for its beauty. The tempting treasure lost the poor girl her life, which might have been spared; but her glorious locks were needed to hang on the chief's belt" (Kelly, p. 157). Later that day during a victory dance, Fanny saw the "young brave who bore the beautiful locks as his trophy.... He sat alone, looking sad. I approached him and questioned him, and he replied that he regretted his dead victim.

He brought a bloodstained dress from his lodge, and told me it was worn by the girl with the lovely hair, whose eyes haunted him and made him sorry" (Kelly, p. 158).

General Sully, meanwhile, was still pursing the Sioux to punish them for the 1862 uprising, and while Fanny hoped he would rescue her, she worried for her life. "Many of the Indians who had lost relatives in the recent battles with General Sully, were thirsting for my blood" (Kelly, p. 159). There might, however, be a chance to escape. An "Indian, or rather white man or half-breed, as I believe him to have been," Fanny wrote, someone she had not previously seen, "came into a tent where I was and showed me a small pocket Bible that had belonged to my husband, and was presented to him by his now sainted mother many years before" (Kelly, p. 159). The man wanted Fanny to go with him, presumably so he could return her to white society and collect a reward, but she didn't trust him and refused to go. He "threatened to kill me if I would not go with him" (Kelly, p. 160). Still she refused, but pleaded that he give her the Bible, but he wouldn't.

Shortly after that Ottawa and his three sisters went on a journey — Fanny doesn't say where, maybe because she didn't know — and Fanny was sent with Yellow Bird to live in another village, a day's travel away. She "was to live with ... a very old Indian, his squaw, and a young girl" (Kelly, p. 160). The village was small, and Fanny was there for three weeks. She said she was "treated with almost affectionate kindness ... by every member of the little community" (Kelly, p. 160). She described her time in the village as "my brief season of enjoyment" (Kelly, p. 161). But then Ottawa returned and "he seemed to delight in torturing me, often pinching my arms until they were black and blue. Regarding me as the cause of his wounded arm, he was determined that I should suffer with him" (Kelly, p. 161).

Then an Indian named "Man-Afraid-of-His-Horses" (Kelly, p. 161) arrived. He was very well dressed, and Fanny later learned her husband purchased the outfit for him. The idea was that the Indian would help obtain Fanny's release, but he later lied to the whites, telling them the band Fanny lived with had moved.

Also at that time, General Sully threatened some Blackfeet if they did not help obtain Fanny's release. The Blackfeet had approached Sully asking for an end to hostilities, but Sully told them, "I want no peace with you. You hold in captivity a white woman. Deliver her up to us and we will believe in your professions. But unless you do, we will bring soldiers as numerous as the trees on the Missouri River and exterminate the Indians" (Kelly, p. 162). The Blackfeet told Sully they did not have the white woman but that the Oglalas did. Sully, however, offered the Blackfeet a reward for Fanny's return. Perhaps because of the reward, perhaps because of the threat — punishing the wrong Indians was a common practice as the United States expanded westward — the Blackfeet visited the Oglala camp and negotiated for Fanny's return to the whites. For two days the Oglalas debated what to do. They "at last resolved that the Blackfeet should take me as a ruse," Fanny writes, "so as to enable them to enter the fort, and a wholesale slaughter should exterminate the soldiers" (Kelly, p. 163).

Even as Fanny was being put on a horse to be taken to the Blackfeet village, however, the Oglalas argued over whether she should go. Two armed groups of Oglalas argued as Fanny watched. One of them pointed a pistol at her and demanded she get off her horse. Once again, she thought she was about to die, but, she writes, "God willed it otherwise, and to Him I owe my grateful homage" (Kelly, p. 164). Not certain what was going to happen to her, she didn't want to go to the Blackfeet village, because, "my companionship with the sisters of the chief had been such as to protect me from injury or insult" (Kelly, p. 164). The "insult" she refers is clearly sexual assault, because here she makes her point that "I had never suffered from any of them [Oglalas] the slightest personal or unchaste insult" (Kelly, p. 164).

She goes on to explain, "At the time of my capture, I became the exclusive property of Ottawa, the head chief, a man more than seventy-five years old and partially blind, yet whose power over the band was absolute.... I was compelled to become his nurse or medicine woman; and my services as such were so appreciated, that harsh and cruel as he might be, it was dangerous for others to offer me insult or injury; and to this fact, doubtlessly, I owe my escape from a fate worse than death" (Kelly, pp. 164–165). In fact, Ottawa so liked having Fanny around that he "expressed the wish that, if the Great Spirit should summon him away, that I might be killed in order to become his attendant to the spirit land" (Kelly, p. 165). That, of course, might explain why Fanny worked so hard to see that he lived. Despite her reluctance to go with the Blackfeet, she had no choice. She did determine that she would warn the white soldiers of the impending Indian attack before the attack could take place.

At this point, Fanny digresses from her story line and gives us a 15-page chapter on "Indian Customs" (Kelly, Chapter XIX, pp. 166–182) in which she offers dozens of observations about Sioux culture, including the one about blankets hindering their civilization. The chapter is the second longest, out of 28, in the book, and its placement is revealing. It comes just as the climax of the story is about to occur. That is, she lengthens her narrative at the same point a novelist is likely to, when the reader's interest is heightened and he or she is likely to be most tolerant of a digression. Think of a television show in which the hero or heroine is about to be killed and as your attention is so focused you're unlikely to take a bathroom or refrigerator break. What do you get? A commercial, of course. Fanny doesn't give us a commercial, but she uses the timing of the digression to heighten our interest in her story. The point is, Fanny Kelly is a very conscious creator of her story. That is not to accuse her of fabrication, but rather of control of her material. That control, as much as anything that happened to her while she was a captive, helps to explain why her book is among the half dozen most popular captivity narratives ever published.

Among her observations in the "Indian Customs" chapter: "All drudgery ... is performed by the squaws since an Indian brave scorns as degrading all kinds of labor not incident to the chase or the warpath" (Kelly, p. 166). This observation is, of course, consistent with similar ones made by Rachel Plummer (about Comanches), Mary Jemison (about Senecas), and other women held unwillingly by Indians.

In the same chapter she writes about a plant the Sioux used as a purgative, saying it is "*euphorbia corrallata*," and tells us "All the drinks which are given the sick to quench thirst are astringent ... slightly mucilaginous," the most common being red root or "*ceanothus canadensis*" (Kelly, p. 171). The Latinate terms, astringent, mucilaginous? Clearly Fanny did some research, supporting a view that her narrative was not simply written from memory, as Rachel Plummer's clearly was, but was carefully crafted.

Some of her observations are inconsistent, however, with what historians and scientists tell us. She writes, "It is an uncommon occurrence that an Indian woman loses her life in parturition" (Kelly, p. 172), when in fact much evidence suggests death among Native American women during child delivery was very high. (One study of the Anasazi, in the Southwestern United States, a culture that disappeared before whites came to the hemisphere, puts the death rate for females aged 16 to 26 at 80 percent, but for males at half that, 40 percent. Only childbirth could explain the large difference.[32] While the figures for Anasazi are high, the differences in death rates for young male and female Indians is not unusual.) She also writes, "it is said that deformed infants are regarded as unprofitable and a curse from the Great Spirit. They are disposed of by death soon after birth" (Kelly, p. 172). She does not say who says this, Indians or whites, but historians do not believe it was a widespread practice among the Sioux or other prairie tribes. However, the tribes were generally incapable of providing the type of care such people needed and they often died young. Another statement made by Fanny — "Sometimes, at the death of a mother, the infant is also interred" (Kelly, p. 172) — is also unsupported by historical evidence, although that in itself does not prove it never occurred.

Her observations about courting and marriage in mid-19th-century Sioux society, by contrast, are consistent with what most historians believe happened, although few today would agree with Fanny's racist way of telling it:

5. Saving White Women from Indians   151

The wife is sometimes wooed and won, as if there was something of sentiment in the Indian character, but more often is purchased without the wooing. When the desired object is particularly attractive and of a good family, both the courting and purchasing may be required. When a young brave goes courting, he decorates himself in his best attire, instinctively divining that appearances weigh much in the eyes of a forest belle or dusky maiden, who receives him bashfully, for a certain kind of modesty is inherent in Indian girls, which is rather incongruous when considered in relation to their peculiar mode of life. Discretion and propriety are most carefully observed, and the lovers are seated side-by-side in silence. At times he produces presents for her acceptance. These express a variety of sentiment and refer to distinct and separate things; some signifying love; some, strength; some, bravery. Others allude to the life of servitude she is expected to live if she becomes his wife. If they are accepted graciously and the maiden remains seated, it is thought to be equivalent to an assurance of love on her part and is acted upon accordingly. Although no woman's life is made less slavish by the marriage connection, and no one is treated with respect, it is scarcely known in Indian life that a girl has remained unmarried even to middle age. When a chief desires to multiply the number of his wives, he often marries several sisters, if they can be had, not because of any particular fancy he may have for any but the one who first captivated him, but because he thinks there will be more harmony in the household when they are of one family. Not even squaws can live happily together when each has a part interest in the same man as their husband. Polygamy is generally considered inconsistent with the female character, whether in barbarism or civilization" [Kelly, pp. 176–177].

(Mormon men in polygamist marriages in the 19th century sometimes, also, married sisters).

Despite her obvious racism, Fanny does recognize that whites are sometimes unfair to Indians: "The Indians know they are being cheated whenever they barter with the white traders, but they have no remedy as there is no competition, and this causes much of their disaffection" (Kelly, p. 178).

By the time she returns to her impending release from captivity, the reader's appetite for her tale has been whetted.

Now she is in a Blackfeet village. "These savages proved very kind to me ... they showed me nothing but civility and respect" (Kelly, p. 183). Part of understanding Fanny Kelly and other 19th century white commentators on Indians is to recognize the differences in how they and we use the same words. For Fanny and her contemporaries, "savages" was not automatically a derogatory word. It simply meant a people who were not part of a Euro-centric civilization. One morning "a delegation from the Yanktons" (Kelly, p. 185) arrived in the village. "They desired to purchase me," Fanny writes, "offering five of their finest horses for me" (Kelly, p. 185). They evidently were making an attempt to ransom Fanny and return her to whites. The Blackfeet, however, rejected the offer. Fanny thought they were insulted because their horses were as fine as any the Yanktons possessed. Several other offers were made to ransom

Fanny, but the Blackfeet rejected all of them. But then, one day, "a party of [white] traders arrived in the neighborhood with four wagons ... and they wanted to buy me," Fanny writes. "I pretended I did not desire to leave them, but pleaded that I might go with them to see the white men, which was refused, as was also a request that I might write a letter to them. A few days later all but one of the traders were murdered" (Kelly, pp. 186–187). She later learned the attempt to purchase her freedom was arranged by Geminien Beauvais, who ran a trading post not far from Fort Laramie.

Fanny has particular praise for Tall Soldier, the chief in charge of the Blackfeet village, whom she says "displayed at all times the manners and bearing of a natural gentleman" (Kelly, p. 187). She also notes that Tall Soldier held several feasts in her honor and all of the work in preparing for them was done by his wife. "These unceasing toils she performed alone," Fanny writes, "the commands of the chief forbidding me to aid her" (Kelly, p. 188). She says, of Indian women in general, "the squaws are very rebellious, often displaying ungovernable and violent temper. They consider their life a servitude, and being beaten at times like animals, and receiving no sort of sympathy, it acts upon them accordingly" (Kelly, p. 188). She adds that she believes she was treated well because of "my patient submission" (Kelly, p. 189). That is, unlike the Indian women, she did not rebel.

Then there was an attempt by the Yanktons to steal Fanny. She says, "One night I awoke from my slumbers to find an Indian bending over me, cutting through the robes which covered me. Fearing to move, I reached out my hand to the squaw who slept near me [and] she immediately arose and gave the alarm, after which the Indian fled" (Kelly, p. 189).

After she was in captivity for five months, Jumping Bear, a young warrior who months earlier had grabbed a bow and arrow from the hand of Ottawa's brother-in-law, who had been threatening to kill her, told Fanny he loved her. Fanny writes that he said "he had always liked white women, and would be more than a friend to me" (Kelly, p. 191). She told him that "unless he proved his friendship for me, no persuasion could induce me to listen" (Kelly, p. 191). She asked him to take a letter to the fort and give it to the officer in charge. Jumping Bear hesitated, but "the women of the lodge ... used their influence" (Kelly, p. 192), and he agreed to take the letter. Fanny writes that the letter was "a warning to the 'Big Chief' and the soldiers of an intended attack on the fort and the massacre of the garrison, using me as a ruse to enable them to get inside the fort. It was also a desperate plea for them to rescue me, if possible" (Kelly, p. 192). Jumping Bear delivered the letter and was given a letter in return to deliver to Fanny, but she never saw him again. The night before she was to leave for the fort, Fanny overheard Ottawa addressing the village's warriors:

5. Saving White Women from Indians 153

Friends and sons, listen to my words. You are a great and powerful band of our people. The inferior race, who have encroached upon our rights and territories, justly deserve hatred and destruction. These intruders came among us and we took them by the hand. We believed them to be friends and true speakers; they have shown us how false and cruel they can be. They build forts to live and shoot from with their big guns. Our people fall before them. Our game is chased from the hill. Our women are taken from us and made to forsake our lodges. They have been wronged and deceived. It has only four or five moons since they drove us to desperation, killed our brothers, and burned our tipis. The Indian cries for vengeance! There is no truth nor friendship in the white man; deceit and bitterness are in his words. Meet them with equal cunning. Show them no mercy. They are but few, we are many. Whet your knives and string your bows; sharpen the tomahawk and load the rifle. Let the wretches die, who have stolen our lands, and we will be free to roam over the soil that was our fathers'. We will come home bravely from battle. Our songs shall rise among the hills, and every tipi shall be hung with the scalp locks of our foes [Kelly, pp. 193–194].

Ottawa's complaint that whites took Indian women is contrasted by a detail Fanny reports next: "That night, as if in preparation for the work he had planned, the gracious chief beat his poor, tired squaw unmercifully because she murmured at her never-ending labor and heavy tasks" (Kelly, p. 195). She learned a lesson from that: "His deportment to me was as courteous as though he had been educated in civilized life; indeed, had he not betrayed so much ignorance of the extent and power of the American nation in his address to his band, I should have thought him an educated Indian, who had traveled among the whites. Yet in his brutal treatment of his squaw, his savage nature asserted itself and reminded me that, although better served than formerly, I was still among savages" (Kelly, p. 195).

Fanny gave whatever trinkets she had accumulated while with the Sioux to the little girl who had been given to her as a companion. Then she left on her 200-mile journey to Fort Sully. Along the way the party came to a small Indian village, and among its residents was a white man with an Indian wife and children. Fanny spoke to him and learned he was a Southerner who favored the South in the still-raging Civil War, about which Fanny had heard nothing during her captivity. Later, the Sioux sent some young warriors to talk to the white man to see what Fanny had told him. They did not trust her. He told them she "had breathed nothing but kindliness for them" (Kelly, p. 198). As they neared Fort Sully, the Sioux "divided into squads of fifty," Fanny writes, with "several of these squads remaining in ambush among the hills for the purpose of intercepting any who might escape the anticipated massacre at the fort" (Kelly, p. 199). Closer to the fort, "one of the warriors in passing thrust out his hand to salute me," Fanny says. "It was covered by one of my husband's gloves, and the sight of such a memento filled me with inexpressible dread as to his fate" (Kelly, p. 199). She tells us that her husband had been in the Union army and that she still had his discharge papers.

Then she digresses to tell us "I had been obliged to paint daily like the rest of my companions, and narrowly escaped tattooing by pretending to faint away each time I saw the implements for the operation" (Kelly, pp. 199–200). That, of course, contrasts with Olive Oatman, who was tattooed and who spent much of her life after gaining freedom trying to hide the result. Fanny says that whenever she could, she used snow to wash off the "savage adornment" (Kelly, p. 200). That comment is followed by one comparing national adornments: As the party approached within sight of the fort she sees "the glorious flag of our country," and adds, "How insignificant and contemptible by comparison were the flaunting Indian flags that had so long been displayed to me" (Kelly, p. 200). Eight chiefs rode in front, one of them leading Fanny's horse, with hundreds of warriors behind them. The gates of the fort opened, Fanny and the chiefs entered, and Fanny looked at Captain John Logan and murmured, "Am I free, indeed free?" and Logan said, "Yes" (Kelly, p. 201), and then shouted an order for the gates to the fort to be shut. The chiefs were inside, the other warriors were locked out.

Fanny writes that although, at least during her final days with the Sioux, she was well-treated, "their people were not my people"[33] (Kelly, p. 204). She places this remark in quotation marks, but does not credit it to any source. Of course, most readers will recognize it as a paraphrasing of a famous quote from the Book of Ruth in the Old Testament. Ruth is the daughter-in-law of Naomi, whose husband and two sons have died while the family was living in Moab, and she decides to return to live in Bethlehem among her own people, the Jews. She urges her two widowed daughters-in-law to live among their own people, the Moabites. One, Orpah, decides to do that, but Ruth famously tells Naomi, "wither thou goest, I will go; and where thou lodgest, I will lodge; thy people shall be my people; and thy God, my God." Ruth moves to Bethlehem with Naomi and marries a Jewish man, Boaz. In saying the Sioux "were not my people," Fanny is implying that she was not the wife of one of them, that she did not have sexual relations with an Indian. The timing of this passage in Fanny's narrative is significant, because it is closely followed by an incident that occurred two months after she arrived at the fort. She learns an "ambulance" is about to arrive, and a soldier approaches her and says, "Mrs. Kelly, I have news for you. Your husband is in the ambulance" (Kelly, p. 208). The comment about the Sioux not being her people reinforces how she wants her husband to see her.

The comment also is consistent with the religious tone of so many of the captivity narratives. Similarly, immediately after the quote referring to the Book of Ruth, she remarks, "With Alexander Selkirk I could state, 'Better dwell in the midst of alarms, than reign in this horrible place'" (Kelly, p. 204). Selkirk, of course, is famous as Daniel Defoe's probable model for *Robinson Crusoe* (Defoe never said who, if anyone, was his model). Selkirk was stranded on an uninhabited island off the west coast of South America for four years and four months beginning in 1704, before being rescued and returned to Europe. Kelly's quote is actually from a 1782 poem by William Cowper, which is based on Selkirk's experiences and which contains the famous first line that usually serves as the poem's title: "I am the monarch of all I survey." It is an example of the deliberately literary style in Fanny Kelly's *Narrative*.

After she is reunited with her husband, Fanny learned the details of the death of their adopted daughter, Mary. Fanny gives no indication that she blamed her husband for fleeing the scene of her capture.

Josiah, her husband, told Fanny he made several attempts to rescue her, at one point offering the Indians a ransom of 19 horses. The horses were left at Fort Laramie, and two Oglalas, Two Face and Black Foot, unable to locate Fanny, brought in another captive white woman, Lucinda Eubanks (sometimes spelled Ewbanks) and her infant daughter, who had been held by the tribe for 14 months. They offered Mrs. Eubanks to the fort commander, Colonel Thomas O. Moonlight, in exchange for the horses. Moonlight, however, took them prisoner, put them on trial, had Mrs. Eubanks testify against them, and ordered them hung. By chains. Moonlight was drunk at the time. The executions were carried out in the spring of 1865.

Josiah said he and his brothers made other ransom offers, but none of them were accepted. He said he spent $1,075 attempting to rescue his wife and he billed the U.S. government for $50,000 for, according to his 1866 affidavit accompanying the bill, "Damages for my wife's being made prisoner and Slave and suffering Starvation Privation disease frozen limbs and being tormented and suffering all the abuse that those savage devils could invent for five months" (Kelly, p. 216n). The government did not pay.

Fanny then offers a surprising interpretation of how her freedom was obtained: "I believe the destitute condition of the Indians had much to do with my final restoration to freedom. Had there been plenty of food in the Indian villages, none would have gone to Fort Sully to make a treaty" (Kelly, p. 221). This is, of course, inconsistent with her earlier explanation of the Sioux plan to capture Fort Sully, but it is probably more realistic. She did earlier quote several Sioux as complaining that their best hunting grounds had been taken by the whites. The view that the westward expansion of the Euro-centric white society drove many Indian nations into poverty is now widely accepted among historians.[34]

But Fanny's problems were not over. After visiting with her mother (who was grieving both because of her daughter's capture by the Indians and because her 19-year-old son had died, probably a result of disease, while serving in the Union army), she and her husband moved to Ellsworth, Kansas, where they opened a hotel and, Fanny writes, "were prospering when fears of the Indians again harassed us" (Kelly, p. 226). The Army was conducting a punitive expedition against Indians and the Kellys feared the town might be attacked in retaliation. "We lived in a continual state of alarm" (Kelly, p. 227), she writes, and in fact the Indians did attack the town at least once, although they were driven away. Soldiers were sent to protect the town, but they brought cholera with them. Josiah died from the disease on July 28, 1867. Fanny then moved to St. George, Kansas, where, she writes, "my little one was ushered into this world of sorrow" (Kelly, p. 228). That is, she was pregnant when her husband died. After an unspecified amount of time, she visited Fort Hays, also in Kansas, where "I came upon two Indians who recognized me, and I also knew them" (Kelly, p. 230). Later she was told a group of Indians approached a train as it was leaving town. Fanny writes, "They told the people that I belonged to them, and they would take my papoose and me way off to their own country; we were their property and must go with them. It was supposed that if I had been in the cars the Indians would have attempted to take the train" (Kelly, pp. 230–231). There is, of course, the clear suggestion that the Indians were saying that Fanny's baby had an Indian father, although the timing would be wrong for that to be true, since she had been freed from captivity more than two years earlier.

The story of Fanny's captivity by the Sioux pretty much ends there, except she has three more chapters in her book. One of those tells about the "Fates of Other Captives" (Kelly, Chapter 26, pp. 232–243), and among these is the story of Elizabeth Blackwell, whose parents were Mormons in Salt Lake City. When Elizabeth's father took a second wife, the first wife protested, a fight broke out, and Elizabeth, trying to protect her mother, "was struck by her brute of a father with a knife," Fanny writes, "and one of her eyes was destroyed" (Kelly, p. 232). The mother and her three daughters then fled the home and went into the mountains where the mother and two daughters died from exposure. An Indian — Fanny doesn't say from which tribe, but if it was in the Wasatch Mountains of Utah it would probably be a Shoshoni, and if it were the Unita Mountains, it would probably be a Ute — found Elizabeth and took her to a village, where she was cared for. She then went to some unspecified place in the East, where both legs were amputated above the knee. She then returned to the mountains to live among the Indians who had helped her.

Fanny evidently met Elizabeth after she married and moved to Cincinnati. Elizabeth told her a story of another captured white woman. She had been taken from a "train" (probably a wagon train) and taken to the village where Elizabeth stayed. As an Indian was trying to help this woman from a horse, the woman shot the Indian in the hand. As Fanny tells the story, "This so enraged the savages that they cut her body in gashes, filled them with powder and then set fire to it. The sight of the woman's terrible suffering was too much for Elizabeth to endure and she begged the savages to put a merciful end to the victim at once, which accordingly was done" (Kelly, pp. 233–234).

In another story Fanny tells, a 10-year-old girl whose last name was Boxx "was compelled to stand on a bed of live coals in order to torture the mother" (Kelly, p. 235) and two older sisters. In still another story, Cheyennes attacked a wagon train in eastern Colorado. After a brief battle in which several men on the wagon train were killed, the other men fled, leaving women, children, and wounded men behind. The wounded men were killed and the women and children taken captive. Among these were Clara Blynn, whose husband had been killed in the attack, and her two-year-old son, Willie. The leader of the Cheyenne, a chief named Santana, was annoyed by Willie's crying, grabbed him by the heels, and was about to bash his head into the ground, but the mother grabbed her son and fought with Santana. The chief for a few moments tried to wrestle the boy away from his mother, but then laughed and allowed the boy to live. Mrs. Blynn was later tortured by Cheyenne women, who burned her with hot sticks, and Willie was similarly tortured as she was forced to watch.

Fanny reports that Mrs. Blynn was in a Cheyenne village along the Washita River, in the Oklahoma panhandle, when the U.S. Seventh Cavalry under Lieutenant Colonel George Armstrong Custer attacked the village on Nov. 27, 1868, killing 103 men, women, and children (some reports put the numbers of Indian dead as low as 27) in one of the most famous massacres of Indians in history.[35] Clara Blynn (this is Fanny's spelling; more commonly her name is spelled Blinn) and Willie were killed by the Cheyenne in retaliation at the time of the attack. Fanny believes they were killed in the village that was the main point of Custer's attack, although many historians believe Mrs. Blynn and Willie were at another Cheyenne village, perhaps five miles away. There is agreement she was killed by Cheyenne on the day of the attack. They were buried by white soldiers and went, in Fanny's words, to "the land where captivity is unknown" (Kelly, p. 243).

Fanny's woes, it seems, just never stopped. She said her husband's body was robbed "of the sum of five hundred dollars on the day of his death" (Kelly, p. 244), although she gives no details. She then moved to Wyoming to live with Sarah and William Larimer, who were traveling with the Kellys when Fanny was taken captive. William escaped at the time of the attack and Sarah escaped the next day. They had moved to Sherman Station, Wyoming, and were running a photography business. Once there, however, according to

Fanny, Sarah stole the manuscript Fanny was writing about her captivity. The manuscript was then published, Fanny says, "as the experience of my false friend, who, by the aid of an Indian, escaped after the duration of but a single day and night" (Kelly, pp. 244–245). After a year in Wyoming, she moved to Washington where she was "resolved to present a claim to the Government for losses sustained at the hands of the Indians" (Kelly, p. 245). She was invited to meet with President Ulysses S. Grant, and several members of Congress — "realizing that some compensation was due me" (Kelly, p. 245) — introduced a bill that would give her $5,000. Although she claims "this was handled without my having any knowledge of it until the bill had passed both houses of Congress and become law" (Kelly, p. 246), she had, in fact, written a petition to Congress asking for the money.

It is in that petition that she writes, referring to herself in the third person, that she was "taken into captivity, and was forced to become the squaw of one of the O-gal-lah-lah chiefs, who treated her in a manner too horrible to mention, and during her captivity was passed from Chief to Chief, and treated in a similar manner" (Kelly, p. 273). She adds the immodest claim that her narrative is "evidence of her valuable services to the United States troops" (Kelly, p. 273) that she "contributed largely to saving that garrison [Fort Sully] from total massacre" (Kelly, p. 274). She concludes by saying she is "now in destitute circumstances ... alone in the world ... and [deserving of] some compensation in such sum as may seem mete" (Kelly, p. 274).

The petition was accompanied by a letter signed by the X's of four Brule Sioux chiefs, although it was not the Brule who had held her captive: Spotted Tail, Swift Bear, Fast Bear, and Yellow Hair. Their letter says they desire that Fanny "be paid ... out of any moneys now due our nation, or that may become due us by annuity" (Kelly, p. 271, Google Books version). Several officers and enlisted men at Fort Sully also signed letters supporting Fanny's request for compensation.

While Fanny was in Washington, Red Cloud, a famous Sioux chief, was also there with other Dakotas. Fanny says she arranged for the Indians to be invited to attend a church service where there would be a "great organ" and "fine music," and some of the Indian women did go, but "Red Cloud replied with dignity that he did not have to go to the big house to talk to the Great Spirit, he could sit in his tipi or room and the Great Sprit would listen. The Great Spirit was not where the big music was. No, he would not go" (Kelly, p. 246).

Red Cloud, however, did support her request for money. In a meeting with Secretary of Interior Jacob Cox and Commissioner of Indian Affairs Ely Parker (a Seneca and the first Indian to hold that position), Red Cloud said, "Look at the woman; she was captured by Silver Horn's party. I wish you to pay her what her captors owe her. I am a man true to what I say, and want to keep my promise. I speak for all my nation. The Indians robbed that lady there, and through your influence I want her to be paid out of the first money due to us. Pay her out of our money; do not give the money into any but her own hands; then the right one will get it" (Kelly, p. 247).

Her final chapter, briefly outlining some military actions taken by the Army against Indians, is most notable for its attitude. Consider this, in defending General William Harney, who, Fanny admits, "slaughtered indiscriminately" (Kelly, p. 249) Sioux at the battle of Ash Hollow in 1857: "The punishment inflicted made the name of General Harney a terror to the Indians, and at the same time, brought upon his head the execration of thin-skinned philanthropists, who thought savages — the 'noble red men' as they imagined — should be conquered only by a sugarplum and rosewater policy" (Kelly, pp. 249–250). And consider her use of the word "graced" in this defense of an action taken by General Alfred Sully: "General Sully afterward had their heads cut off; and when the command left camp next morning, they graced two pointed stakes on the bank of the river, placed there as a warning to all straggling Indians, bent on murder or mayhem" (Kelly, p. 251).

Fanny Kelly offered throughout her narrative harsh judgments of the Oglala Sioux who held her captive, and that's to be expected, but her harshest judgments come at the end of her book. And just a few hundred words from the end of her narrative of nearly 70,000 words, she offers a contrasting judgment of the soldiers who fought the Indians. Of Captain James L. Fisk learning that a wagon train was under attack by Indians, she writes that he "thrilled with an earnest desire to save the women and children of that apparently doomed train" (Kelly, p. 258). And of the men under Fisk's command, when they learn that a white woman is held captive by the Indians, she writes, "Every man would have been willing to risk his life for her rescue" (Kelly, p. 258).

Fanny's narrative ends there. Later, on July 28, 1867, her husband died from cholera, and a few days later her son was born.[36] She named him Josiah, after his father. She then went to live with Sarah Larimer, who had been captured with her but escaped the first day, and her husband, William, in Sherman Station, Wyoming, between Cheyenne and Laramie. According to Fanny, she and Sarah agreed to jointly write a memoir of their experiences and that it would be published with both of them listed as authors, but Sarah, with the help of her husband, stole the manuscript and took it to Philadelphia, where it was published with only Sarah's name on it. Fanny filed suit against both of them in a court in Allen County, Kansas. That book, *The Capture and Escape; Or, Life among the Sioux,* was published by Claxton, Remsen and Haffelfinger in 1870. It included a note saying, "For want of room in this volume, which has already exceeded the limits originally contemplated, I am compelled to omit the highly interesting experience of Mrs. Kelly, but issue it in a book entitled, 'Mrs. Kelly's Experience Among the Indians'" (Kelly, p. 265). Claxton did print that second book, but never bound it, and the publisher, at Fanny's insistence, eventually destroyed all copies of it.

At the Kansas trial, the Larimers argued that Fanny, as a married woman who did not have an occupation, could not enter into a legal contract and therefore could not contractually agree to have a book published. The court rejected that argument. The heart of the Larimers' argument was a claim that Fanny's manuscript had been destroyed in a fire and that Fanny had stolen copies of Sarah's manuscript. Fanny's argument was that Sarah stole her manuscript. The jury's verdict favored Fanny and the judge awarded her $5,000. The Larimers appealed and the case was sent back to court because, the higher court said, Fanny had not established the value of her manuscript. There was a change of venue to Woodson District, and Fanny won again, although this time the verdict was only $285.50. The Larimers again appealed, this time saying a juror was drunk when the verdict was rendered. The Kansas Supreme Court rejected that appeal, and in mid-1876 the parties reached an out-of-court settlement. The details of that settlement are uncertain, but evidently included an agreement that the Larimers would pay Fanny's legal expenses of about $2,000. There's no evidence that the Larimers made the payments.

In 1871, Fanny's book was published by Witstach, Baldwin and Company in Cincinnati, and later that year was republished by the much larger Mutual Publishing Company of Hartford, Connecticut. Fanny wrote a second book, *Afterwards of Life and Trials Subsequent to My Captivity Among the Sioux, with an Account of the Litigation Concerning My History, in Which Truth is Stranger than Fiction*. That book never reached publication. In 1880, Fanny married William Gordon, a writer from Kansas. She died in 1904 at either age 59 or 62 and is buried in Washington, D.C.

Fanny Kelly, in the final chapters of her captivity narrative, captures the underlying role these stories played in America's westward expansion. In its simplest terms, these stories almost always involve a three-part plot that reflected white attitudes: (1) a white woman is captured by Indians; (2) while the white woman almost always directly or indirectly denies she was sexually abused, she strongly hints that she was; (3) white men come to her rescue, often killing the Indians in the process. That is, the captivity narratives presented a justification for killing Indians. Settling the West, going beyond exploration and religious proselytizing, required that families move into the West. And that required that white women be protected from Indians. The captivity narratives contributed significantly to the belief that women, and thus families, could be protected only by killing Indians.

6

Sexual Exodus

No religion in American history has suffered as much persecution as the Church of Jesus Christ of Latter-day Saints, the Mormons. Formed in Upstate New York, near Palmyra, in 1830, by Joseph Smith,[1] the son of a dirt-poor farmer, the founder and the church were products of the Jacksonian Era.[2] The first six presidents of the United States were all patricians, members of the privileged class who led the American Revolution, men who assumed they would always produce the country's leaders. When Andrew Jackson, a coarse, poorly schooled, often ill-tempered man from a poverty-ridden family was elected president, he both represented and spurred a new national attitude. With Jackson originated the national belief anyone can grow up to be president. And if anyone could grow up to be president, why couldn't anyone grow up to start his own church? Joseph Smith did.

Smith and his church were also products of the Second Great Awakening. The First Great Awakening was in the early 1740s. Fire and brimstone preachers attracted large crowds of the religiously oriented who were in some way dissatisfied with existing religions or, at least, religious leaders in their home towns. New churches were started, old churches split in two. Dartmouth College and Princeton University were outgrowths of the First Great Awakening because some people were not satisfied with how existing institutions educated future preachers. The Second Great Awakening (actually maybe it was the third, if you count the Salem witch trials of 1692, and maybe there have been a third and a fourth — historians agree about as often as economists do) began in the very late 18th century and extended until just before the Civil War, but it reached its zenith in the late 1820s and early 1830s, and no where was it more fervent than in the Erie Canal towns of upstate New York. Towns like Palmyra. So many preachers passed through warning local residents of the danger of spending eternity in the fires of Hell that the area east and west of Rochester, including Palmyra, came to be known as the Burned Over District. It was a time and a movement not noted for restraint. Just like the sex life of Joseph Smith.

Smith and his followers numbered a few hundred within a year. Partly because of that success, partly because Smith repeatedly denounced surrounding churches, including Methodists and Presbyterians, as "abominations in the sight of God" (Remini, p. 175), partly because much of the developing theology of the new church seemed downright silly to non–Mormons (including a claim the Book of Mormon, which said American Indians were descendants of one of the lost tribes of Israel, was a third holy book, equal to the Old and New Testaments), Mormons were repeatedly denounced, ridiculed, and otherwise made to feel unwelcome in and around Palmyra. Smith claimed church members were in danger of physical violence, although mostly they were assaulted with ridicule. So Smith led an exodus to Kirtland, Ohio, just east of Cleveland.

There they encountered the same criticisms, faced the same ridicule. But this time there were also complaints of financial shenanigans. The church started its own bank and the bank issued its own currency, which for a while a bank could legally do in the United States. But some non–Mormon residents of the area found the bank's dealings suspect and the currency worthless. Smith was tarred and feathered and he and his followers fled to Columbia, Missouri.

Once there they prospered. A little too much for their non–Mormon neighbors. Especially onerous to the neighbors was the tendency of Smith and his followers to engage in block-voting.[3] The, by now, thousands of Mormons in the area voted for whoever Smith told them to vote for. They bought up a lot of the best farmland in the area and were often unneighborly. The result this time went far beyond ridicule and tar and feathers. Governor Lilburn Boggs on October 27, 1838, issued a written order that said all Mormons must be out of Missouri within 48 hours. If they weren't, the order said, they were to be exterminated. A militia of 200 men attacked a Mormon settlement at Haun's Mills and slaughtered 18 men and boys. Other militia units concentrated on rounding up church leaders, including Smith. In an incredible achievement, a high-ranking church official little known to Missouri authorities quickly and efficiently organized a mass exodus eastward, rescuing thousands of Mormons. They crossed the Mississippi River and were welcomed by residents of Illinois who were outraged by Boggs's murderous order. The organizer's name was Brigham Young.

The Missouri militia meanwhile arrested Smith and nine other top church officials. General Samuel Lucas, head of the state militia, ordered General Alexander Doniphan to execute Smith and the others. Doniphan, far more honorable than Lucas or Boggs, refused to carry out the order. Further, he informed Lucas he would hold him personally responsible for murder if anyone carried out the order. Doniphan's courage saved the lives of Smith and the other Mormon leaders. After six months in jail, with a nation, including many powerful members of Congress, outraged at the extermination order, Smith and others found someone had left their cell door unlocked. At first they feared a trick but soon realized this was a real invitation to escape. It was the best, if awkward, way Missouri officials could rid themselves of a self-created embarrassment. Smith joined his followers in Illinois and while there said he had the revelation that would cause more hostility towards Mormons than anything they encountered previously. It would also satisfy his lust, lead to his murder, and result in the first major American settlements in the West.

Plural Marriage

Joseph Smith married Emma Hale on January 18, 1827. It was an elopement because Emma's father did not approve of Joseph. Eight months later he told his son-in-law, "You have stolen my daughter and married her. I had much rather have followed her to her grave" (Brodie, *No Man Knows My History*, p. 32, and Remini, p. 51). Young Joseph, 21 at the time, a year younger than Emma, was a handsome man who many women found appealing. Except for a large nose — the largeness visible only in profile — he was striking, with thick, dark hair, large eyes, long eyelashes, and prominent cheekbones. He possessed an ability to speak quickly and smoothly on nearly any subject. Whether he knew what he was talking about didn't matter; he sounded like he did. Emma was pretty but very shy and seemed to fear the possibility of never marrying. Yet, she clearly was as attracted to Joseph, as were other woman. Joseph had an innate ability to attract women.

The marriage was neither less nor more happy than most. Emma clearly didn't like the life of poverty they lived, or living with his parents in Palmyra. And when he told her about golden plates he found and read by looking through stones but wouldn't let her see either the plates or the stones, she wasn't pleased. He found the golden plates, he said, buried in the Hill Cumorah, just south of Palmyra, the location having been shown to him by an angel named Moroni, who was the son of another angel, named Mormon, who had written things on the plates, written them in something like Egyptian hieroglyphics, and to translate them into English (into the Book of Mormon) Joseph was given two stones, which he called the Urim and Thummim, and he looked through them at the plates and.... Well, devout Mormons believe this story and Emma would eventually become one, but at the time she wasn't and it's not hard to understand not only that she was skeptical but that she wasn't happy with her new husband for not letting her share his secrets. If he truly loved her, as he claimed, he would let her see the plates, let her hold the special stones. But, Joseph insisted, God didn't want her to.

Despite the poverty, despite the lack of trust, the marriage lasted, as did almost all marriages in the United States in the early 19th century. But Smith — to use a term we would use today — cheated on his wife. To use a term that would become common among Mormons once they moved to Nauvoo, he engaged in plural marriage. The practice started in Kirtland, Ohio.

While the hostility that led to the tar and feathering in Ohio was no doubt caused by the shady financial dealings of the church, the immediate cause seems to have been a belief by a man named Eli Johnson that Smith had sex with his sister, Nancy Marinda Johnson. In fact, Johnson even persuaded a doctor to castrate Smith to make certain the dalliance wouldn't be repeated, but the doctor, at the final moment, decided not to perform the operation. Smith, instead, was badly beaten. The evidence Smith and Nancy Marinda Johnson slept together consists entirely of her brother's claim. But Nancy Marinda Johnson later became one of Smith's many wives, even though by then she was married to a man named Orson Hyde, who may have approved of her plural marriage to Smith. Whether he did while she was alive is unclear, but more than a decade after Smith was murdered he arranged to have her married to Smith for all eternity in a Mormon Temple ceremony.

There's no evidence Emma knew about Nancy in Kirtland, but she did know about Fanny Alger. Fanny was a pretty, charming girl, an orphan whom Emma took into her household. Fanny may have become pregnant with a child by Joseph, or she and Joseph may have been seen together in an uncompromising position, but, whatever the reason, a rumor the two had an adulterous relationship soon spread throughout Kirtland. That was spurred by the fact Emma demanded Fanny get out of her house. What she did or said to Joseph is unknown. It is known Oliver Cowdery, one of the earliest converts to the church, was confronted by Smith about spreading the rumor of the affair and refused to back down. Cowdery was soon excommunicated for, among other reasons, accusing Smith of adultery.

Some people who lived in Kirtland at the time later claimed the formal beginnings of plural marriage, the Mormon term for polygamy, began with Fanny Alger, that she and Smith were actually married in a church-sanctioned ceremony. If so, there is no known record of the marriage. Which is not surprising. Polygamy then, as now, was illegal, so, being already married to Emma, Smith could not get a marriage license from the state of Ohio, or from anywhere else in the United States, to marry another woman. There were thousands of plural marriages in the fifty-plus years the practice was sanctioned by the church, and except for the first wife of each husband, not one of them was legal from the view of a state or federal or other government. Even today there are hundreds of women living as plural wives, largely in southern Utah and northern Arizona, but also elsewhere throughout the West, and in Canada and Mexico, members of churches that claim to have originated in the teachings of Smith (but not affiliated with the one that has its headquarters in Salt Lake City), and not one of them, other than the first wife, has a government-issued marriage certificate. And whatever marriages were sanctioned by the church in Ohio and later Missouri are usually without church records, also, since there was a reluctance to create a document that could be used in a court of law to prosecute someone. Later church records were kept but they are usually kept secret by church officials.

Long before the Mormons were driven from Kirtland, Smith preached that God told him they should move to Missouri, where Christ would return to Earth. Smith, in fact, visited Missouri, returned to Ohio, and then moved to Missouri. While there he stayed in the home of Lucinda Harris, who, other than Smith himself, may at the time have been the most famous member of the church. Her fame derived from the fact her first husband, William Morgan, was the victim in the most publicized murder in the United States before the assassination of Abraham Lincoln in 1865.

Revealing Secrets

When 52-year-old William Morgan of Batavia, New York, halfway between Rochester and Buffalo, borrowed a shirt and a piece of neckwear from an innkeeper in Canandaigua, a pretty little town on the northern tip of one of the Finger Lakes, he sealed his fate, changed presidential politics, and took the first step in the first American murder case to capture national attention. Morgan was in most ways an unremarkable man, 5 feet 6 inches tall, with brown hair and a high forehead. A veteran of the War of 1812, he claimed, inaccurately, that he had received a battlefield commission from Andrew Jackson himself. He called himself Captain Morgan. He was, in two ways, a mason. He made his living, when he worked, which was not often, as a stonemason. The closest he came to fame in that occupation was as the principal mason on the last home owned by Colonel Nathaniel Rochester, founder of the area's largest city, which he immodesty named after himself.

Morgan was also a member of the Freemasons, a secretive organization that grew out of Europe's stonemason guilds during the Middle Ages.[4] The first Freemasonry lodge was organized in 1717 in London. America's first Masonic lodge was formed in Philadelphia in 1730. George Washington and a dozen other presidents were Freemasons, as were Benjamin Franklin and Rudyard Kipling. In many ways a fraternal organization, Freemasonry mainly introduced members to one another. In Morgan's day they did a lot of drinking and Morgan did as much as anyone. More than most. The Freemasons often enabled members to make useful business contacts, and Morgan obtained jobs as a stonemason in Batavia and nearby Le Roy. The Freemasons had a secret handshake, a secret organizational structure, and, their most ardent critics claimed, a secret plan to take over the world. They were a politically cohesive group, and in some towns it was difficult to be elected to local office if the Masons didn't like the candidate. New York Governor DeWitt Clinton was among the nation's most prominent Freemasons.

Morgan belonged to the Le Roy Masonic Lodge, but he wanted to also join a newly formed lodge in Batavia. The decision on who could join was made by Masonic leaders in Rochester, and they rejected Morgan's application because of his heavy drinking. It was an odd charge because many Freemasons were heavy drinkers. Morgan was irate. The insult, particularly after a few drinks in a Batavia tavern, was too much to endure. He took his complaint to David Miller, editor of Batavia's *The Republican Advocate*. Miller, once a Mason, had grown to distrust the organization. Miller was about to reprint *Jachin and Boaz*,[5] an out-of-print book that had exposed some Masonic secrets. Over the centuries there had been a dozen or more such books, and none of them were much noticed. Morgan offered to write a new one, and Miller arranged for two Batavia residents, Russell Dyer and John Davids, to finance the project. So in the spring of 1826, partly as an act of revenge for having been snubbed and partly as a shot at becoming a rich and famous author, Morgan began writing *Illustrations of Masonry by One of the Fraternity Who Has Devoted Thirty Years to the Subject*.[6]

Two years earlier, Morgan's wife, Lucinda, 27 years his junior, had given birth to a boy, and Morgan, at the time staying at a Canandaigua tavern, had accepted an offer from the tavern owner, David Kingsley, to borrow a clean shirt and cravat so he would be presentable visiting his newborn son. Morgan eventually returned home to Batavia with his wife and son without returning Kingsley's clothing. Kingsley didn't mind, at least not for two years, but when word of Morgan's book-in-progress spread, he, like hundreds of other Masons in New York, became irate. Rochester Masons, the regional leaders, were so angry they sent Daniel John, a Canadian, to spy on Morgan and Miller. Advertisements in local newspapers openly denounced Morgan, his life was threatened, and he was harassed by government officials who were Masons. At one point he was jailed for failure to pay a debt. The arrest was timed for when the sheriff was out of town, and since no one else could accept bail, Morgan had to spend the weekend in jail. Miller's print shop was set on fire one night, but saved by a group of teamsters working nearby who rushed to extinguish the flames.

6. Sexual Exodus

The Masons' spy, Daniel John, stole parts of Morgan's manuscript in August. It was rushed to New York City and presented to the General Grand Chapter with a request for help: What should be done about Morgan? DeWitt Clinton, the Grand Chapter's presiding officer and the country's best known Mason, was aghast. The manuscript was stolen property, and he ordered it returned immediately to its rightful owners, Morgan and Miller. The manuscript disappeared, but Clinton at least was free of it. Clinton, however, did make a mid–August trip to Batavia to visit with Judge Henry Brown, the commander of the Batavia Lodge. The meeting was private, but local Masons interpreted Clinton's visit as a certificate of approval for their continued harassment of Morgan and Miller. Kingsley, the Canandaigua innkeeper, joined in the harassment. He charged Morgan with stealing his shirt and cravat, and Morgan was seized on the streets of Batavia, rushed into a carriage, and driven at high speed over 50 miles of dusty, bumpy, dirt roads to Canandaigua. The charge, of course, was silly, and the Canandaigua magistrate accepted Morgan's version that he had merely forgotten to return the clothing. The instant he was freed of that charge, a Batavia Mason stepped forward and charged Morgan with not paying a $2.68 bill. Morgan was immediately rearrested. He didn't have money to pay the debt, a fine, or bail, so he was jailed for the night.

Fearing he would be freed in the morning, two Masons, Nicholas Cheesboro and Loton Lawson, paid Morgan's fine. As soon as he stepped onto the cobblestone street, they grabbed him, forced him into a yellow carriage driven by another Mason, Colonel Samuel Sawyer, and drove off with him. When news of the kidnapping reached Governor Clinton, he was stunned and ordered a $2,000 reward for the arrest of the kidnappers. He also ordered a state grand jury impaneled to investigate the kidnapping.

Over the next five years more than 20 grand juries in five counties looked into the kidnapping. The testimony given was inconsistent, but there was widespread agreement on some facts. Morgan was taken, probably bound and gagged, to Rochester, where he spent the night; the next day he was taken to Fort Niagara, where the Niagara River flows into Lake Ontario, and hidden in a block house. The kidnappers were under the impression Canadian Masons had agreed to take Morgan as a prisoner and allow him to live a comfortable life on the twin conditions he never return to the United States and that he make no attempt to publish his book. However, late the next night, when Morgan was taken across the river, either the Canadians changed their minds or, more likely, were hearing about the plan for the first time. They refused to be partners in the kidnapping, and Morgan was taken back across the Niagara River and returned to the Fort Niagara blockhouse.

Not knowing what to do with him, the kidnappers may have panicked.

Possibly they had an alternative plan all along, or they may have asked for guidance from higher ranking Masons. In any case, Morgan was never seen alive again. It's not even clear Morgan was ever seen dead again. About 13 months later, a badly decomposed body turned up at the point where Oak Orchard Creek, just east of the Niagara River, flows into Lake Ontario. Lucinda Morgan identified it as her husband's body; so did Batavia editor Miller and Thurlow Weed, editor of an anti–Masonic newspaper, *The Rochester Telegraph*, and a leader of the state's anti–Masonic movement. The body was interred in a Batavia cemetery. There was no insurance money or other financial reason for any of these three to lie, but Masons insisted they did. They even insisted there was no proof Morgan was dead. A Canadian woman, whose husband had disappeared while fishing at about the same time Morgan did, asked that the body be exhumed and identified it as that of her missing spouse. A tombstone with Morgan's name was removed from the grave and replaced with one with the name Timothy Munroe.

Whether the body was that of Morgan or not did not stop the nation from being outraged. Freemasonry as a political force in America was as dead as whoever rested in the grave. Anti-Masons rallied to form a third political party, calling themselves the Anti-Masonic Party, and in 1832 fielded a presidential candidate, William Wirt, who won few votes, less than eight percent nationally, but who seemed to have taken votes away from Henry Clark, thus helping Andrew Jackson win reelection.[7] The Anti-Masonic Party was the first third party in American presidential campaigns. The three men who snared Morgan from the Canandaigua jail were convicted of kidnapping, then only a misdemeanor. Each was sentenced to a few months in jail. No one was ever charged with murder. Morgan's book was published in December following his disappearance and for a while sold briskly.

Lucinda Morgan later married George Washington Harris, a widower, and moved with him to Terre Haute, Indiana. At some point they became Mormons and moved to Far West, Missouri, and Joseph Smith, founder of the Mormon church, stayed with the family for a while. Lucinda Morgan Harris was short, with light hair and blue eyes, and — said everyone who saw her — beautiful. One day, probably in 1842, Sarah Pratt, a married woman and a friend of Lucinda's, told her that Smith had made an improper proposal to her, and Lucinda laughed and said, "How foolish you are. Why, I am his mistress since four years" (Brodie, *No Man Knows My History*, p. 460). Lucinda and Joseph were married in a secret ceremony, probably with her husband's knowledge, in 1838. In January 1846, a year and a half after Smith was murdered, Joseph Smith and Lucinda Morgan Harris were married in the Nauvoo Temple. George Harris stood in as proxy for Smith.

Celibacy and Sharing Wives

If husbands sanctioning their wives having sex with a religious leader seems odd, consider other religious experiences that grew out of the Second Great Awakening. Near Putney, Vermont, John Humphrey Noyes[8] created a farming community of several dozen men, women, and children that stressed community sharing to the point that husbands shared wives with each other. When disapproving neighbors hounded them out of the area in 1848, they moved to north-central New York and established the Oneida Community[9] (today about an hour's drive from Smith's Palmyra). One of the features of this community, which lasted until 1880, was "mutual criticism" (Thomas, pp. 164, 165) meetings in which members told an individual what his or her faults were so the individual could improve. The most common criticism was that someone became jealous of any affection shown by someone else to his or her spouse. Sex lives, like everything else in the communal society, were for the community to share. The community called the arrangement complex marriage. Noyes, not surprisingly, felt it was his duty to be the first to have sex with young females. The community fell apart only when Noyes, at age 68, feared he might be arrested for statutory rape and fled to Canada.

Not all new religions developed leaders who seemed excessively lustful to outsiders. Sometimes, the religious fervor produced an attitude towards sex that was exactly the opposite and just as odd from the non-believer's view. The United Society of Believers in Christ's Second Coming, better known as the Shakers,[10] because of a habit of trembling adopted by many members during ceremonies, practiced celibacy. The religion originated in Great Britain but came to the United States in the late 18th century. Its earliest communities, not surprisingly, were in upstate New York, at Watervliet and New Lebanon. Although Shaker communities spread throughout the Northeast and the religion eventually numbered about 6,000 members, its ability to expand was limited to conversions. Men slept in one large room, women in another. The major source of new believers came from adoption of orphans. Not surprisingly, the religion could not obtain new converts as fast as old ones died off, and by the end of the 19th century the Shaker religion was all but extinct.

A similar group, at least when viewed by non-members, was the Harmony Society,[11] which originated in Germany, moved to the United States to establish the town of Harmony in western Pennsylvania, and then the town of New Harmony in Indiana. They too practiced celibacy and their religion, also, lasted only a few decades.

There were, in fact, dozens of religious-communal societies started in the United States during the Second Great Awakening. Almost all of them adopted attitudes towards sex that the rest of America, then and now, considered odd. The primary difference with the Mormons is that Mormonism survived. In fact, an often quoted prediction by Rodney Stark, a non–Mormon sociologist who teaches at Baylor University in Waco, Texas, a Baptist institution, states the Mormon church will have reached more than 250,000,000 members by 2080, making it the first major new world religion since Islam was founded 1,400 years ago. Stark argues there is no such entity as "the Protestant church," or "Protestantism" (see Stark, p. 140), and says none of the individual denominations will be as large as the Mormon church in 2080.[12]

What God Wants

Smith next married Prescindia Huntington Buell, whose husband, Norman, was so upset that he left the church and even forbade his wife to mention the church in his presence, although he later rejoined. Prescindia is the only woman, other than Emma, Smith's only legal wife, we can be certain had a child by Smith, a son, although there certainly must have been others. He also married Clarissa Reed Hancock, wife of Levi Hancock, Zina Diantha Huntington Jacobs, wife of Henry Jacobs, Mary Elizabeth Rollins Lightner, wife of Adam Lightner, and the list goes on and on and on. Smith married at least 22 women. Probably 30. Maybe 48. One study puts the number at either 66 or 67 while he was alive and 149 who married him after he died.[13]

Mormon marriages then, and today, are of two kinds. A couple married in a Mormon meeting house, the church Mormons attend on Sundays, are married for "time" (Ostling, p. 165). That is, they are married as long as both of them are alive. Meeting houses are open to everyone, including non–Mormons. Weddings held in a Temple, however, are for "eternity" (Ostling, p. 166) and will last beyond death. Only Mormons are allowed in Temples (there are more than 100 of them around the globe), and not even all Mormons. You must have a "Temple recommend" (Ostling, pp. 187–188), a card that says your bishop (roughly the equivalent of a parish priest in the Roman Catholic church) believes you are a good and faithful Mormon, that, for example, you do not smoke or drink alcohol (these prohibitions came into existence decades after Smith died; Smith considered himself a connoisseur of fine wines and Brigham Young owned a brewery). More and more the paper card used for the Temple recommend is being replaced by an encoded credit card–size card.

All of Smith's marriages seem to have been Temple marriages, so he should have 215 or 216 wives for eternity. Many of the marriages of his wives to other men, all of which predated his marriages to him, were "for time." In most cases the husbands did not know of their wives' marriages to Smith, and without exception, where a record exists revealing their reactions, they were irate. Some left the church. Some confronted Smith. Some later rejoined the church and some later agreed to the marriage of their wives to Smith.

How did Smith get away with this sexual shenanigans? A letter written by Lucy Walker, perhaps wife number 26, is revealing.[14] It says,

> President Joseph Smith sought an interview with me and said, "I have a message for you. I have been commanded of God to take another wife, and you are the woman." My astonishment knew no bounds. This announcement was indeed a thunderbolt to me. He asked me if I believed him to be the Prophet of God, "Most assuredly I do," I replied.... "What have you to say?" he asked. "Nothing." ... He said, "If you pray sincerely for light and understanding ... you will receive a testimony of the correctness of this principle." ... I was tempted and tortured beyond endurance until life was not desirable.... He also said..., "I will give you until tomorrow to decide this matter. If you reject this message the gate will be closed forever against you" ... I stood fearless before him, and looked him in the eye. I felt at this moment that I was called to place myself upon the altar a living sacrifice.... [I] said: Although you are a Prophet of God you could not induce me to take a step of so great importance, unless I know that God approved my course. I would rather die [Brodie, *No Man Knows My History*, p. 478].

The next morning while lying in bed, she went on, she was overcome with "a calm, sweet peace" (Brodie, *No Man Knows My History*, p. 478). She interpreted that to mean God approved of her marriage to Smith. She was unmarried and 17 at the time.

Lucy Walker's experience was not unusual. Several of Smith's plural wives wrote or told others Smith put great pressure on them. They believed him to be a prophet, which in Mormon belief is a person to whom God speaks directly. For the devout, especially the young and inexperienced devout, the pressure was beyond endurance. Smith's good looks and his charm helped, no doubt, in his seductions, but nothing was as effective as his telling a woman God commanded her to have sex with him. And sex is precisely what most of these marriages amounted to. Some of his plural wives lived for short periods, weeks at the most, in his household, and one or two or three were given, with their husbands, homes close to his in Nauvoo, but only Emma lived with him openly as his wife and only Emma lived with him an extended period. Men for centuries have seduced women with promises of marriage. Joseph Smith one-upped them. He married them as part of the seduction.

Many Mormon apologists have attempted to explain Smith's actions in a manner designed to make him seem less lustful. Some Mormon historians have denied he had more than one wife (a claim never made about Brigham Young, who lived openly with his many wives). More recently, the defense against the charge of lustfulness has taken a new tack. Richard Lyman Bushman, retired as a history professor at Columbia University, wrote in his highly admiring biography of Smith, "There is no certain evidence that Joseph had sexual relations with any of the wives who were married to other men" (Bushman, p. 439).[15] What, an objective skeptic might ask, does Bushman want as proof, video tapes? He adds, "The marriages were numerous enough to indicate an impersonal bond. Joseph did not marry women to form a warm, human companionship, but to create a network of related wives, children, and kinsmen that would endure into the eternities" (Bushman, p. 440). Sounds like a husband telling his wife, "But honey, she's just someone I work with, a business associate."

Not all women acceded to his sexual suggestions, and not all who had sex with him felt happy about it, and not all husbands were forgiving, and that led to Smith's death and the first large American settlements in the West.

Lying About Lying

With so many women seduced by Smith and so many husbands irate, Smith had to devise an explanation. Being a religious leader, he came up with a religious explanation. There were many men in the Old Testament who had many wives, including Abraham, Solomon, and Jacob, and the book does not condemn polygamy. Smith often quoted a passage in Exodus: "And if a man entice a maid that is not betrothed, and lie with her, he shall surely endow her to be his wife" (Exodus, Chapter 22, Verse 16). There's no limitation on the number of wives in the passage, only a requirement that if a man and a woman have sex, they must be married. But Smith's defense of polygamy went far beyond whatever justification he found in the Bible. A good Mormon, one who obeys the word of God, in the theology Smith developed, can become a god with his own universe. As Smith preached at the funeral of a friend, King Follett, "God himself was once as we are now, and is an exalted Man ... you have got to learn how to be Gods yourselves ... the same as all Gods have done before you" (Brodie, *No Man Knows My History*, p. 300; Bushman, p. 534; Ostling, p. 295–296).

On other occasions he said part of what needs to be done is to have many wives and many children. In fact, once you die, you should still continue to have children in heaven. Thus, having many wives and many children was a path to becoming a god. To help explain that this was a commandment from God and not just the rationalizations of his own lust, he told Lorenzo Snow, one of his most ardent followers, that once "an angel of God stood by him with a drawn sword and told him that, unless he moved forward and established plural marriage, his Priesthood would be taken from him and he should be destroyed" (Brodie, *No Man Knows My History*, p. 303n). The official justification thus became not lust but God's will. Or as those Mormons today who still practice polygamy in isolated sects scattered around the West are fond of saying, sex is for procreation, not recreation.

But the rationalization was for the ears only of the most prominent Mormon leaders, those who would also marry multiple wives, and, of course, the women Smith and the others wed. For others there were lies. Repeatedly, Smith and other church leaders denied polygamy existed in or was sanctioned by the church. A formal statement of denial was issued in Kirtland. In Nauvoo, Smith had some of the church's most prominent members sign a statement of denial. All the signatories but one knew the statement to be a lie. The exception was Emma, Joseph's only legal wife. She knew, of course, that her husband was guilty of sexual indiscretions, but at the time she signed the document she seems to have not suspected he actually married other women. For others the denials sometimes seemed odd. At least two men, Harrison Sagers and Hiram Brown, were driven from the church because they publicly advocated polygamy. Practicing polygamy was acceptable; advocating it was not.

In his book *History of the Church*,[16] Smith wrote, "What a thing for a man to be accused of committing adultery, and having seven wives, when I can find only one" (Brodie, *No Man Knows My History*, p. 374). His most important denial, however, came in June 1844 in Nauvoo when he ordered a newspaper, not the editors or writers, but a newspaper, put on trial for accusing him of polygamy. That denial was part of a series of incendiary events that led to his murder and to Mormons inadvertently making the West part of the United States.

Putting a Newspaper on Trial for Murder

As rumors spread in Kirtland and later the Mormon communities in northwestern Missouri and then in Nauvoo that Smith had more than one wife, even his denials to the faithful were not always convincing. So Smith let them in on the secret and, to make certain they accepted the idea, told them they too should have plural lives. Not everyone he told accepted what he said. Among others, his younger brother, Don Carlos, objected strongly, saying, "Any man who will preach and practice spiritual wifery will go to hell, no matter if it is my brother Joseph" (Brodie, *No Man Knows My History*, p. 303). Others accepted the concept reluctantly, or so they later claimed. Brigham Young said that when Smith first told him about plural marriage, "It was the first time in my life that I desired the grave, and I could hardly get over it for a long time. And when I saw a funeral, I felt to envy the corpse its situation" (Ostling, p. 57). But Young did get over it. He married 56 women.

In the spring of 1844 in Nauvoo, however, opposition to plural marriage took what should have been an expected turn. Robert Foster, a physician, arrived home to find his wife having dinner with Smith. When Smith left, Foster threatened to shoot his wife if she didn't tell him what was going on. She told him Smith had revealed the doctrine of plural marriage to her and tried to seduce her. Foster met at a small grocery store with other Mormons who were upset with Smith for similar reasons. Two men at the meeting told Smith what happened and Smith, in what he must have thought was a stroke of genius, ordered an account of the accusations against him, including the attempt to seduce Dr. Foster's wife, be published in the *Nauvoo Neighbor*, a newspaper he controlled. Three days later there was to be a trial of Foster, presumably for slandering Smith, but when Smith learned Foster had gathered 41 men and women to testify in his behalf and against Smith, the trial was canceled and instead a church council was convened and Foster was excommunicated. So were Jane Law, who earlier that year Smith had unsuccessfully attempted to seduce, her husband William, and William's brother Wilson.

The Laws and Foster struck back by starting their own newspaper, the *Nauvoo Expositor*. The first and only issue of the paper, on June 7, 1844, reported that polygamy existed in Nauvoo. The majority of the people in the city had no doubt heard rumors, but this was the first published account within the city. Smith felt threatened. He even seriously considered not just denying polygamy existed within the church but denouncing it and excommunicating everyone who continued to practice it. But, for a man who was in effect the dictator of the city, it's not surprising he employed a far more forceful method to solve his problem. He summoned a meeting of the city council and demanded the *Expositor* be put on trial.

It was, and he and a bunch of other church leaders accused the newspaper's editors of crimes ranging from counterfeiting and theft to pandering and murder, although it's not clear who they were supposed to have killed.[17] City council, which always did Smith's bidding, found the paper guilty, and with that legal technicality, Smith declared the paper a public nuisance. He called out the Nauvoo Legion, his personal militia, which destroyed the newspaper office, including the press, and burned all copies of the paper they could find. Destroying newspapers in that era was actually rather common. In particular, pro-slavery forces often burned down anti-slavery newspapers. Most people involved in these crimes escaped unpunished. That's what Smith expected to happen to him. He was, after all, the law in Nauvoo. In all his life he was never so wrong.

The Laws and Foster fled for their lives to the nearby cities of Warsaw and Carthage. In an article in a Warsaw newspaper, Foster wrote about the Nauvoo Legion destroying his press. And about Smith ordering one of his henchmen, Porter Rockwell, to murder Governor Boggs of Missouri in retaliation for the extermination order. And about Smith's seduction of the female faithful. A few days later the editor of the same paper, the *Warsaw Signal*, published an editorial calling for the extermination of Mormon leaders ("War and Extermination Is Inevitable!" [Brodie, *No Man Knows My History*, p. 378]). Smith, near panic, wrote a letter to Illinois Governor Thomas Ford defending the Legion's destruction of the *Nauvoo Expositor*, and he instructed the Legion to prepare to defend his city.

William Law and Foster swore out complaints against Smith. He was in danger of being arrested if he left the confines of Nauvoo. Reports came in that crowds of angry citizens denouncing his highhanded tactics were meeting in Warsaw and Carthage, and that people were coming across the Mississippi River from Missouri and Iowa to join them. Block voting, rumors of polygamy, deliberate isolation from neighboring communities, and, most of all, a sense that Mormons were different mixed together in a pot waiting to boil over. Smith's destruction of the newspaper office was like lighting a fire beneath the pot.

Governor Thomas Ford, trying to avoid a civil war between Mormons and anti–Mormons, wrote a letter to Smith urging him to surrender for trial: "If you, by refusing to submit, shall make it necessary to call out the militia, I have great fears that your city will be destroyed, and your people many of them exterminated" (Brodie, *No Man Knows My History*, pp. 382–383). Smith and his brother Hyrum fled across the Mississippi to Iowa, but fearing Nauvoo would be sacked in a search for him, he decided to return. Ford ordered that the Nauvoo Legion surrender its arms, and Smith agreed, although he ordered a few weapons retained in secret. Members of the state militia escorted Joseph and Hyrum to Carthage, where they were given a perfunctory preliminary hearing and then placed in the town jail.

The governor visited Smith in jail and told him he was wrong for ordering the newspaper office destroyed, but Smith insisted anyone in a position of authority would have done the same thing. A friend of Smith's, Dan Jones, was told by a guard Smith would be killed once the governor left town. Jones found the governor and told him what he had heard, but Ford didn't believe him. He made plans to go to Nauvoo to speak to the Mormons and ordered a company of militia to guard the jail. When Smith learned Ford had left Carthage, he panicked and quickly wrote a letter to a leader of the Nauvoo Legion ordering him to have the Mormon militia march on the jail and free him, but the man he sent it to, Jonathan Dunham, either believed he had more time or for some other reason failed to call out the Legion. Joseph and several friends visiting him in jail drank some wine to relax.

Not long after that, the state militia broke into the jail. Friends had smuggled pistols into the Smith brothers, but they were of little use. Hyrum was shot dead in the first volley. Joseph emptied his six-shooter, probably hitting three of the attackers, and then ran for the window of his second floor cell, where he was hit in the back by a bullet. He jumped or fell to the ground, where a member of the militia took hold of him and placed him against a curb. The leader of the militia ordered his men to fire and they did. Joseph Smith, founder of what would grow into the largest church originating on American soil, was dead, the victim of a legal militia transformed into a murderous mob.

A Country for Mormons

Smith was murdered June 27, 1844. Within days struggle for control of the church commenced.[18] Hyrum, Joseph's older brother and principal advisor and confidant, probably would have assumed leadership, but he was murdered the same day. Emma, Joseph's only legal wife, argued their oldest child, Joseph III, age 11, had been designated by his father to assume leadership of the church, but there were powerful forces, led by Brigham Young, who had other ideas. Joseph III did eventually come to head a separate church, known for a century and a half as the Reorganized Church of Latter Day Saints (in 2000 the church changed its name to Community of Christ). For the rest of his life Joseph III denied, as did his mother, that his father ever had more than one wife.

While the Community of Christ shares much in common with the Church of Jesus Christ of Latter-day Saints (including tracing its origins to Joseph Smith and accepting the Book of Mormon, along with the Bible, as holy scripture), it has long differed in many important respects, including having never accepted polygamy. The church, based in Independence, Missouri, unlike the church based in Salt Lake City, allows everyone, not just church members, to enter its temple and permits women to become priests. About 140,000 Americans belong to the church, compared to more than 5,000,000 Americans, and another 6,000,000 around the world, who belong to the Salt Lake City–based Mormon church, as of the end of the first decade of the 21st century.

Brigham Young decided the church must move to an area where the non–Mormon population was not hostile. He considered Texas and Oregon, but eventually settled on what is now Utah. Its very isolation was its primary appeal. At the time, the area was claimed by Mexico, although that country had no outposts as far north as the area Young would select, the Great Salt Lake valley. Young, in fact, intended to start his own country. Mexico, he knew, was too weak to exercise control over any sizable population that far north, hundreds of miles beyond Santa Fe, the closest significant Mexican military outpost.

Unfortunately for Young and his plans, James Polk was elected president in 1844 and assumed office the next year. Polk was the most expansionist-minded man ever to hold the office. Texas had declared its independence from Mexico in 1836, but Mexico never officially recognized that claim. The American transplants, largely slave owners from Southern states, who led the Texas war for independence, wanted to become part of the United States, but anti-slavery forces blocked any annexation for nearly a decade. Meanwhile, Polk convinced Great Britain to give up its claims to what would become the states of Oregon and Washington. With what would become, sometime in the future, anti-slavery states, Polk, a slave owner from Tennessee, was able to convince Congress to admit Texas as a slave state.[19]

Immediately Mexican authorities protested and both countries sent armies to the area. When a minor clash in southern Texas resulted in some American soldiers being wounded, Polk asked Congress for a declaration of war. American blood had been shed on American soil, Polk said, and among those opposed to war with a weak neighbor was a young Congressman from Illinois who sarcastically asked the president to show him the blood. But the Congressman, Abraham Lincoln, was in the minority and war was declared. It wasn't an even match. The larger, better armed, better disciplined American army, fighting its first war beyond U.S. borders, invaded Mexico and in less than two years had wrested control of what would become California, Nevada, Arizona, New Mexico, and Utah, and parts of Colorado, Kansas, Oklahoma, and Wyoming, roughly half of Mexico, increasing the size of United States territory by about 50 percent.

While the war was being fought, Brigham Young was moving Mormons to Utah by the thousands, hoping and expecting to establish Deseret, as he called the area, as an independent country. It was an American exodus led by an American Moses.[20] From the beginning of the war, however, he realized there wasn't much hope of that happening. Creating his own country in the northernmost reaches of Mexico, far beyond the effective control of a government in Mexico City, was one thing. Doing the same thing in the United States was another. Recognizing the futility of his plans, he even agreed to the establishment of the Mormon Battalion, several hundred young Mormon men who joined the U.S. Army, marched across the deserts of the southwest, the longest land march in American military history, to help secure San Diego, arriving after the job was completed, and nearly all of them agreeing to send their pay to the church. Well, if Young couldn't establish his own country, he would do the next best thing. He ran it as if it was his own country. Polygamy was illegal everywhere in the United States, including its territories, but that didn't bother Young. This was Deseret. This was, for all practical purposes, the same as an independent Mormon nation.

Young had none of the charisma of Smith. He was powerfully built with a permanent look of harshness on his face. Today he could pass for a professional football player (just like his great-great-great grandson, Steve Young, the Hall of Fame quarterback for the San Francisco Forty-Niners in the 1990s). He could not captivate an audience with a speech. The most famous speech he made is when he stood in front of a crowd of Mormons in Nauvoo six weeks after Smith's murder and explained why he should he become leader of the church. According to Mormon mythology he took on the mantle of Joseph Smith, sounded and looked like Joseph Smith. While devout Mormons cite this speech as proof Smith wanted Young, not Joseph Smith III, to head the church, it is also unwittingly an acknowledgment that Brigham Young was not charismatically equal to Joseph Smith. Where Smith was imaginative, Young was doctrinaire. Where Smith developed a creative theology supported by what one historian called "one of the earliest examples of frontier fiction"—the Book of Mormon—(Brodie, *No Man Knows My History*, p. 67), Young was an organizational genius. Today Smith might be a movie director. Or maybe a movie star, since he constantly performed. Young would be a producer. Smith would be an inventor, Young a CEO. But Young knew how to wield power and, as Henry Kissinger said more than a century later, power is an aphrodisiac.

Once Young established the beginnings of his Mormon kingdom in the Great Salt Lake Valley, he felt emboldened enough to announce publicly what most of the world knew, the male leaders of his religion were marrying more than one woman. The first public, formal admission came in 1852. In addition to what Young and other church leaders considered a sanctioning of the practice by their interpretation of the Old Testament and Smith's claim that God revealed to him that it was required, other, sometimes silly defenses were offered. Heber C. Kimball, one of Young's top assistants, said in 1857, "I have noticed that a man who has but one wife, and is inclined to that doctrine, soon begins to wither and dry up, while a man who goes into plurality looks fresh, young, and sprightly. Why is this? Because God loves that man, and because he honors His work and word" (Kimball, p. 22).[21]

Mormon revisionist historians have sometimes put the percentage of 19th century Utah marriages that included multiple wives at two or three percent and also claimed there were far more women living in the territory than men because it was a hard time and men often died young. Both claims are lies. The actual percentage of polygamous marriages in Utah in the 19th century was probably 30 percent, although, because of the illegality of the practice and the secretiveness of the church, exact figures are impossible to determine. Two out of three polygamist marriages involved one husband and two wives. More were just too expensive. Kimball had 45 wives, which means that by his own logic he must have been sprightly indeed. Brigham Young married 56 times but did not live with more than 27 wives at any one time. Must have kept him sprightly, too.

Similarly, census figures show the male/female ratio in Utah was, as it generally is worldwide, 50/50. Because Smith's practice of marrying (often for short-term sexual dalliances) women who already had husbands was abandoned in Utah, the excesses of Young, Kimball, and others, in fact, doomed hundreds, maybe thousands, of young men to unwilling bachelorhood.

Young, like Smith, send missionaries to the East and to Europe to convert men and women to the religion. They were particularly successful among the poorest people in the cities of the East and in Northern England and Scandinavia. Most of the converts to new religions traditionally come from the least satisfied members of society. If the God of the prevailing religions has destined them to a life of hard work and poverty and little social status, looking for a new God makes sense. By the thousands they crossed the Atlantic, joined thousands of others from the American Eastern seaboard, and crossed the continent. When the church couldn't afford enough wagons, Young ordered handcarts built. These brave men, women, and children pulled the carts, laden with hundreds of pounds of food and supplies. Five handcart companies crossed the plains and mountains in 1856. The first three made it safely. The next two did not. The thousand people in the two companies encountered an early winter in central Wyoming. The handcart decision was among Young's biggest mistakes. His hubris, that he had planned so carefully nothing could go wrong, killed more than 400 converts seeking to join him in their Zion.

As converts set out from Boston, New York, Philadelphia, and other Eastern cities, including those who arrived from Europe, church officials met and guided them. Some of these mid-ranking church officials selected the most attractive young women as brides. That happened so often higher ranking officials in Utah complained none of the good looking women were left for them.

Mark Twain made a similar but broader observation. When the Civil War ended his career as a riverboat pilot on the Mississippi, he accepted an invitation from his older brother, Orion, to travel with him on his way to Nevada. Along the way, in 1861, they spent two days in Salt Lake City, where they chatted with Brigham Young, who ignored young Sam Clemens but listened intently to the older brother. Sam, who relates the anecdote in *Roughing It* (1872), says he was trying to ask Young about politics. At the end of the meeting, Young stood up, placed his hand on Sam's head, looked at Orion, and said, "Ah — your child, I presume? Boy, or girl?" (Twain, *Roughing It*, p. 94). Perhaps it was because of the comment, but more likely because Twain never met a person or culture he wasn't willing to make fun of, that *Roughing It* devotes three chapters and two appendices to what he saw as the foibles of Mormons. He wrote that before visiting Salt Lake City he was prepared to denounce polygamy, but that once he saw what Mormon women looked like, he concluded, "The man that marries one of them has done an act of Christian charity ... and the man that marries sixty of them has done a deed of open-handed generosity so sublime that the nations should stand uncovered in his presence and worship in silence" (Twain, *Roughing It*, p. 97).

James Polk, having made the United States a continental country stretching from ocean to ocean, was an extraordinarily popular president. Nearly everyone in the country, it seemed, wanted him to be reelected. Except Polk. He hated the job. It exhausted him. He wrote in his diary on December 29, 1848, near the end of his term, "The public have no idea of the constant accumulation of business requiring the President's attention. No President who performs his duty faithfully and conscientiously can have any leisure. If he entrusts the details and smaller matters to subordinates, constant errors will occur. I prefer to supervise the whole operations of the Government myself rather than entrust the public business to subordinates, and this makes my duties very great" (Borneman, p. 319). Before being elected, he had promised to serve only one term, and his exhaustion made it easy and prudent that he chose not to run for reelection. Less than three and a half months after leaving office, he died. He had the shortest ex-presidency in American history. Zachary Taylor, a hero of the war that stole nearly half of Mexico, was elected to replace him, but he died of what was called "acute indigestion" after less than a year and a half in office (Hicks, *The Federal Union*, p. 570, says the cause of death was "probably ... cholera morbus"), and his vice president, Millard Fillmore, became president. Fillmore, preoccupied with trying to avoid a civil war between the North and South, was anxious to have the newly acquired territories in the West stabilized. For Utah, that meant appointing someone to run the territory who knew the people. So Brigham Young was named governor.

Meanwhile, gold had been discovered in California in 1848, encouraging thousands of Americans to cross the continent to seek their fortunes. Thousands more moved to the verdant farmlands and forests of the Northwest. The three major wagon train routes across the western part of the continent largely followed the same route, from Omaha, across southern Nebraska hugging the flat land along the Platte River, into Wyoming, northwest to the South Pass, the only place the Rockies flattened enough to make crossing the

6. Sexual Exodus 181

mountains practical, and did not split until western Wyoming and southern Idaho. Thousands then turned southwest to seek gold in California (the California Trail); thousands went northwest for free or cheap land in Oregon Territory (the Oregon Trail), and thousands headed into Utah hoping to find religious freedom (the Mormon Trail). Before the Civil War more than 40,000 people, almost all of them Mormons, had moved to Utah.

About half of Fillmore's presidential appointees in Utah, which Young insisted on calling Deseret (a word from the Book of Mormon with an unclear translation, although it is often said to mean Land of Milk and Honey) were Mormons. Congress did not want the territory to have a Mormon name and instead named it after the Ute tribe that lived there and in Colorado. The Mormon appointees did what Young told them to, including not prosecuting anyone for polygamy. Young ignored the others. Utah was run, for all practical purposes, as an independent country. Young referred to Mormons as the Saints and to everyone else in any area controlled by the United States as Americans. Fillmore's successor, Franklin Pierce, probably America's least effective president, offered the Utah governorship to Edward Steptoe, a career Army officer then stationed in the territory, but he turned it down, believing any non–Mormon would be incapable of administering anything from Salt Lake City. So, Pierce — whose primary goals were consoling his grieving wife (they saw their young son killed in a train wreck after Pierce was elected but before he took office) and placating his best friend from his Senate days, South Carolina Senator Jefferson Davis — re-appointed Young. After that, Pierce paid virtually no attention to Young's Mormon kingdom 2,000 miles to the west.

Pierce's successor, however, was different. James Buchanan opposed slavery but was determined to keep Southern states from seceding. Demonstrating there was only one United States might help achieve that. So he went to war against Utah. That is, Buchanan sent the U.S. Army to make certain his appointees were allowed to take office and that they were listened to once they did. He named Alfred Cumming, a former mayor of Augusta, Georgia, as Utah's governor in 1857. Cumming and three non–Mormon federal judges were accompanied to Utah by 2,500 soldiers, but they got started late and had to spend the winter at Fort Bridger, Wyoming. The Rockies were impassable by large groups in the winter. Brigham Young panicked. He put the entire territory under martial law and ordered that no one was to trade with gentiles, the term Mormons used to describe anyone who did not belong to their religion.

A wagon train of more than 120 men, women, and children from Arkansas on the way to California passed through Salt Lake City and camped in southwestern Utah, at Mountain Meadows, near Cedar City, to graze livestock, replenish water, and rest. They were attacked by Mormons, some disguised as Paiute Indians, reacting in the aura of hysteria created by Young's panic-inspired order. After a three-day siege, the attackers offered to allow the people in the wagon train to have safe passage. They were told if they put down their weapons and if all the male adults left the encircled wagons single file they would be escorted to a safe place. The people in the wagon train encampment knew that sounded suspicious, but they had been cut off from water for three days and had no choice. As the men filed down the road, each alongside a Mormon man, one of the Mormon leaders called out, "Halt!, do your duty" (Brooks, p. 74), and most turned and with a gun or knife killed the Arkansas man next to him. Then other men rushed to the encircled wagons and killed all the women and older children. Only the younger children were allowed to live, those too young to be reliable witnesses in a court of law. They were kidnapped by Mormon families who raised them. Then the murderers took a holy vow never to tell anyone what happened. The exact number of dead is uncertain (at least 110, maybe up to 130), but killed with them was any hope Mormons may have had to keep polygamy alive.

The date of the mass murder was September 11, 1857. The first 9–11 act of terrorism in American history. It was the second largest massacre in the 19th century in the United States. More people died that day than did in the famous massacres of Indians at Wounded Knee, Sandy Creek, and Washita. Only the Bear River Massacre, in January 1863, in southeastern Idaho resulted in more deaths. That massacre, by the U.S. Army responding to complaints from Mormon farmers and ranchers that Shoshoni Indians were sometimes stealing their crops and cattle, resulted in at least 200 dead men, women, and children. The figure may be as high as 400. Mormons had moved into Cache Valley in northern Utah and southern Idaho and appropriated Shoshoni hunting and food gathering lands, driving the once prosperous tribe into poverty. So the Shoshoni stole cattle to eat, and the local Mormons asked the army for help. The result was the massacre at Bear River, near present-day Preston, Idaho.)

The vow of silence taken by the murderers and witnesses at Mountain Meadows was very effective, but not complete. Federal investigations quickly established what happened, but getting convictions in Young's Utah, with Mormon juries, was impossible without Young's approval. The U.S. Army that had camped the winter in Wyoming entered Utah the following spring to find Salt Lake City deserted. Young, his panic continuing, ordered the city's tens of thousands of residents to go into hiding in the mountains and deserts. And hide they did, for Young was a dictator not to be defied. The Mormon War, other than the murders at Mountain Meadows, consisted of Mormons driving off Army cattle and trying, unsuccessfully, to hinder the advancement of the soldiers.

Once the soldiers occupied Utah, however, Young realized he didn't have a choice. He acquiesced to Cumming assuming the office of governor and changed his political plans. Rather than run Utah as a Mormon kingdom, he would seek statehood. But Congress would have nothing of it for decades. First, Congress and the nation demanded someone must be punished for what happened at Mountain Meadows, and, second, polygamy must be abolished. Without Mountain Meadows, chances are good some type of accommodation might have been possible on polygamy, perhaps a don't-ask-don't-tell approach. But Young would not acknowledge any complicity in Mountain Meadows. He was not a man to admit to faults or mistakes. So for 20 years, no one was punished and Young saw his political influence fade slowly but irrevocably into oblivion. Then he offered up his adopted son. John D. Lee, whom Young had adopted as an adult, a practice then common among Mormon church leaders, had been at Mountain Meadows, the third in command. Young sent out word Lee could be charged and that a Mormon jury should find him guilty. The trial was held and Lee was condemned. He was — 20 years after the murders in which he played a role, but not the leading part — taken back to Mountain Meadows and executed by firing squad at the scene of his crime. No one else was ever punished. Not until 1990 would the state of Utah, where politics and the Mormon church are inseparable, even agree to place a historical marker at Mountain Meadows telling people what had happened. And when the marker went up, it listed the names of all the known victims, but it did not say — still does not say — that Mormons did the killing.

Only after Brigham Young died in 1877 and one of his successors as church President, Seer, Prophet, and Revelator (all four titles go with the position) Wilford Woodruff, declared in 1890 that God had informed him polygamy should no longer be practiced on Earth (later in heaven it would be all right) was Utah found acceptable for statehood. Admission to the union as a state came in 1896, five decades after church leaders first tried to create an independent nation where they could have as many wives as they wanted. Statehood was the only way they could have some political self-control.

Joseph Smith's lust led to the adoption of polygamy as a formal church doctrine, and that led to Smith's murder and driving the Mormons beyond the then-borders of the United States, only to quickly find themselves, because of President Polk's expansionist policies, back in the country they had fled. They built the first American cities in the mountains and deserts of the West. Acting as an independent country led to a near-war in which the only people killed were 120 innocent men, women, and children, victims of Brigham Young's panic. The other victim was Mormon polygamy. When that died, Utah became part of the United States.

7.

End of the Sex Drive

No doubt it is just a coincidence, but it is easy to see significance in the fact that the same year the U.S. Census Bureau declared that there was no longer an American frontier is the same year the Mormon church declared that no member of that church should practice polygamy. Thus, in a real sense, the expansion of the American empire westward ended at the same time one of the principal institutions in the country ended one of the key policies that contributed to that expansion.

More generally, just as historian Frederick Jackson Turner theorized that the closing of the frontier foretold a changing in the American character, so too did the end of Westward expansion foretell an inevitable change in American attitudes about sex.

In what may be the single most influential scholarly paper ever written by an American historian, "The Significance of the Frontier in American History," which he first read to a meeting of the American Historical Association at an 1893 meeting held during the Chicago World's Fair, Turner outlined what came to be known as the Frontier Thesis. (In 1921 it was published as the first chapter in his book, *The Frontier in American History*.)[1] Essentially the thesis argued that the American character was shaped by the existence for centuries of a frontier. As Americans moved farther west, the thesis argues, they moved further away from European influences. What became the core of American character, the thesis held, was what Westerners contributed to it: a stress on individuality rather than community, violence as a solution to problems rather than comity, rejection of rigid class structures, self-initiative, and informality.

Much of American historiography was dominated by Turner's thesis for decades. Even historians who disagreed with it felt a need to spend time refuting it. His views are clearly reflected in many American art forms. The movies of John Ford, the novels of Zane Grey, the paintings of Frederick Remington, all, knowingly or unknowingly, are consistent with Turner's views, and as a result much of what the general public thinks about the American frontier

7. End of the Sex Drive

experience has been shaped by Turner. Even among those who never heard of him.[2]

Beginning in the mid–20th century many historians criticized Turner for seemingly ignoring the roles played by gender, race, ethnicity, and other factors in both American westward expansion and in defining the American character.[3] Turner's view of the American character, ironically, while explaining how Americans became less European, was essentially Euro-centric. His critics argued that Turner failed to see similarities between American westward expansion and European colonialism and that he overemphasized what has come to be known as American exceptionalism, the view that the United States is in important ways different from any other country that has ever existed.

Historian George Wilson Pierson in 1942 published an article titled "The Frontier and American Institutions: A Criticism of the Turner Thesis," in which he sought to revise Turner's views, arguing they were not so much wrong as they were too narrow. In 1959 historian Richard C. Wade argued in his book *The Urban Frontier* that Turner's views needed to be revised to put more emphasis on what were once frontier cities like Pittsburgh, Cincinnati, and Louisville. In 1987 historian Patricia Nelson Limerick, in her book *The Legacy of Conquest: The Unbroken Past of the American West*, sought to revise Turner's views by arguing that, in effect, the frontier still exists and still shapes the American character. Cumulatively, these historians are doing what historians have always done, revising their colleagues. Turner has not so much been rejected as he has been reevaluated, and in the reevaluation some of what he argued has been accepted, some of it found too limited, some of it placed in new contexts. That is, the author of perhaps the single most influential scholarly paper on American history has been and continues to be revised.

This book has been a continuation of that process. It argues that Turner ignored, or perhaps more kindly, did not examine, the role played by the human sex drive in pushing white Americans farther and farther West. There is nothing in Turner's famous essay that is inconsistent with the role sex played, nothing in any of his writings that would suggest he would be in disagreement with an analysis of westward American expansion that considered sex an important contributing factor. There is, of course, also nothing in his writings that would enable a contemporary historian to determine how much weight Turner would give to the sex drive if he had considered it. Perhaps he would have considered it insignificant, perhaps a dominating influence, perhaps argue that it was by implication already incorporated in his thesis by a form of literary osmosis.

But the cumulative evidence is there, in the historical record. It appears in Jefferson's instructions to Lewis to study the marital habits of Indian tribes, in Lewis's warm invitation to his friend Clark to join the expedition, in the numerous references in the journals of Lewis and Clark to sexual practices and sexual diseases among the Indians; in the sexual relations between white mountain men and Indian women; in the condemnation by Catholic and Protestant missionaries of premarital sex, polygamy, and easy divorce among some Indian tribes; in the fear of rape and forced marriage to Indian men by white women on the frontier, and in the harassment of Mormons because, among other reasons, of their belief in plural marriage.

Sex helped drive white Americans west. And sex helped push the frontier farther west. There would not have been a frontier if everyone thought of the edges of their communities as fences that could not be crossed. Many, of course, did think that way, but they were not the ones who made America a continental country. The complacent do not shape history. That role is filled by the dissatisfied, by those who cross the fences, who travel beyond the edges of community. And to the extent that many of those found the sexual mores of their communities too restrictive, too fencing-in, they too helped shape a United States of America that stretched from the Atlantic Ocean to the Pacific. The sex drive helped make the West American.

Appendices

Containing A. "Annexation" by John O'Sullivan: The First Mention of "Manifest Destiny"; B. Thomas Jefferson's Letter of Instructions to Meriwether Lewis; C. Meriwether Lewis's Invitation to William Clark; D. Excerpts from Letters Written by Marcus Whitman; E. Fanny Kelly's Petition to Congress; F. Joseph Smith's Revelation on Plural Marriage; G. Mormon Church Ban on Polygamy. (Most of the original spelling and punctuation in these appendices has been retained. A very few changes have been made to improve their readability.)

A. "Annexation" by John O'Sullivan: The First Mention of "Manifest Destiny"

John O'Sullivan, "Annexation," *United States Magazine and Democratic Review 17,* No. 1 (July–August 1845), pp. 5–10. This is the article in which O'Sullivan first used the phrase "manifest destiny." The phrase appears in the third paragraph. The article primarily calls for the annexation of Texas, but it also predicts that California will become part of the United States, that a transcontinental railroad will be built, and that the U.S. will achieve a population of 300,000,000 by 1945, a century after the article is written.

"Annexation"

It is now time for the opposition to the Annexation of Texas to cease, all further agitation of the waters of bitterness and strife, at least in connexion with this question,—even though it may perhaps be required of us as a necessary condition of the freedom of our institutions, that we must live on for ever in a state of unpausing struggle and excitement upon some subject of party division or other. But, in regard to Texas, enough has now been given to party. It is time for the common duty of Patriotism to the Country to succeed;— or if this claim will not be recognized, it is at least time for common sense to acquiesce with decent grace in the inevitable and the irrevocable.

Texas is now ours. Already, before these words are written, her Convention has undoubtedly ratified the acceptance, by her Congress, of our proffered invitation into the Union; and made the requisite changes in her already republican form of constitution to adapt it to its future federal relations. Her star and her stripe may already be said to have taken their place in the glorious blazon of our common nationality; and the sweep of our eagle's wing already includes within its circuit the wide extent of her fair and fertile land. She is no longer to us a mere geographical space — a certain combination of coast, plain, mountain, valley, forest and stream. She is no longer to us a mere country on the map. She comes within the dear and sacred designation of Our Country; no longer a "*pays,*" she is a part of "*la patrie*"; and that which is at once a sentiment and a virtue, Patriotism, already begins to thrill for her too within the national heart. It is time then that all should cease to treat her as alien, and even adverse — cease to denounce and vilify all and everything connected with her accession — cease to thwart and oppose the remaining steps for its consummation; or where such efforts are felt to be unavailing, at least to embitter the hour of reception by all the most ungracious frowns of aversion and words of unwelcome. There has been enough of all this. It has had its fitting day during the period when, in common with every other possible question of practical policy that can arise, it unfortunately became one of the leading topics of party division, of presidential electioneering. But that period has passed, and with it let its prejudices and its passions, its discords and its denunciations, pass away too. The next session of Congress will see the representatives of the new young State in their places in both our halls of national legislation, side by side with those of the old Thirteen. Let their reception into "the family" be frank, kindly, and cheerful, as befits such an occasion, as comports not less with our own self-respect than patriotic duty towards them. Ill betide those foul birds that delight to file their own nest, and disgust the ear with perpetual discord of ill-omened croak.

Why, were other reasoning wanting, in favor of now elevating this question of the reception of Texas into the Union, out of the lower region of our past party dissensions, up to its proper level of a high and broad nationality, it surely is to be found, found abundantly, in the manner in which other nations have undertaken to intrude themselves into it, between us and the proper parties to the case, in a spirit of hostile interference against us, for the avowed object of thwarting our policy and hampering our power, limiting our greatness and checking the fulfillment of our manifest destiny to overspread the continent allotted by Providence for the free development of our yearly multiplying millions. This we have seen done by England, our old rival and enemy; and by France, strangely coupled with her against us, under the influence of the Anglicism strongly tinging the policy of her present prime minister, Guizot. The zealous activity with which this effort to defeat us was pushed by the representatives of those governments, together with the character of intrigue accompanying it, fully constituted that case of foreign interference, which Mr. Clay himself declared should, and would unite us all in maintaining the common cause of our country against foreigner and the foe. We are only astonished that this effect has not been more fully and strongly produced, and that the burst of indignation against this unauthorized, insolent and hostile interference against us, has not been more general even among the party before opposed to Annexation, and has not rallied the national spirit and national pride unanimously upon that policy. We are very sure that if Mr. Clay himself were now to add another letter to his former Texas correspondence, he would express this sentiment, and carry out the idea already strongly stated in one of them, in a manner which would tax all the powers of blushing belonging to some of his party adherents.

It is wholly untrue, and unjust to ourselves, the pretence that the Annexation has been a measure of spoliation, unrightful and unrighteous — of military conquest under forms of peace and law — of territorial aggrandizement at the expense of justice, and justice due by a double sanctity to the weak. This view of the question is wholly unfounded, and has been before so amply refuted in these pages, as well as in a thousand other modes, that we shall not again dwell upon it. The independence of Texas was complete and absolute. It was an independence, not only in fact, but of right. No obligation of duty towards Mexico tended in the least degree to restrain our right to effect the desired recovery of the fair province once our own — whatever motives of policy might have prompted a more deferential consideration of her feelings and her pride, as involved in the question. If Texas became peopled with an American population; it was by no contrivance of our government, but on the express invitation of that of Mexico herself; accompanied with such guaranties of State independence, and the maintenance of a federal system analogous to our own, as constituted a compact fully justifying the strongest measures of redress on the part of those afterwards deceived in this guaranty, and sought to be enslaved under the yoke imposed by its violation. She was released, rightfully and absolutely released, from all Mexican allegiance, or duty of cohesion to the Mexican political body, by the acts and fault of Mexico herself, and Mexico alone. There never was a clearer case. It was not revolution; it was resistance to revolution: and resistance under such circumstances as left independence the necessary resulting state, caused by the abandonment of those with whom her former federal association had existed. What then can be more preposterous than all this clamor by Mexico and the Mexican interest, against Annexation, as a violation of any rights of hers, any duties of ours?

We would not be understood as approving in all its features the expediency or propriety of the mode in which the measure, rightful and wise as it is in itself, has been carried into effect. Its history has been a sad tissue of diplomatic blundering. How much better it might have been managed — how much more smoothly, satisfactorily, and successfully! Instead of our present relations with Mexico — instead of the serious risks which have been run, and those plausibilities of opprobrium which we have had to combat, not without great difficulty, nor with entire success — instead of the difficulties which now throng the path to a satisfactory settlement of all our unsettled questions with Mexico — Texas might, by a more judicious and conciliatory diplomacy, have been as securely in the Union as she is now — her boundaries defined — California probably ours — and Mexico and ourselves united by closer ties than ever; of mutual friendship and mutual support in resistance to the intrusion of European interference in the affairs of the American republics. All this might have been, we little doubt, already secured, had counsels less violent, less rude, less one-sided, less eager in precipitation from motives widely foreign to the national question, presided over the earlier stages of its history. We cannot too deeply regret the mismanagement which has disfigured the history of this question; and especially the neglect of the means which would have been so easy of satisfying even the unreasonable pretensions and the excited pride and passion of Mexico. The singular result has been produced, that while our neighbor has, in truth, no real right to blame or complain — when all the wrong is on her side, and there has been on ours a degree of delay and forbearance, in deference to her pretensions, which is to be paralleled by few precedents in the history of other nations — we have yet laid ourselves open to a great deal of denunciation hard to repel, and impossible to silence; and all history will carry it down as a certain fact, that Mexico would have declared war against us, and would have waged it seriously, if she had not been prevented by that very weakness which should have constituted her best defence.

We plead guilty to a degree of sensitive annoyance — for the sake of the honor of our country, and its estimation in the public opinion of the world — which does not find even in satisfied conscience full consolation for the very necessity of seeking consolation there. And it is for this state of things that we hold responsible that gratuitous mismanagement — wholly apart from the main substantial rights and merits of the question, to which alone it is to be ascribed; and which had its origin in its earlier stages, before the accession of Mr. Calhoun to the department of State.

California probably, next fall away from the loose adhesion which, in such a country as Mexico, holds a remote province in a slight equivocal kind of dependence on the metropolis. Imbecile and distracted, Mexico never can exert any real governmental authority over such a country. The impotence of the one and the distance of the other, must make the relation one of virtual independence; unless, by stunting the province of all natural growth, and forbidding that immigration which can alone develop its capabilities and fulfil the purposes of its creation, tyranny may retain a military dominion, which is no government in the, legitimate sense of the term. In the case of California this is now impossible. The Anglo-Saxon foot is already on its borders. Already the advance guard of the irresistible army of Anglo-Saxon emigration has begun to pour down upon it, armed with the plough and the rifle, and marking its trail with schools and colleges, courts and representative halls, mills and meeting-houses. A population will soon be in actual occupation of California, over which it will be idle for Mexico to dream of dominion. They will necessarily become independent. All this without agency of our government, without responsibility of our people — in the natural flow of events, the spontaneous working of principles, and the adaptation of the tendencies and wants of the human race to the elemental circumstances in the midst of which they find themselves placed. And they will have a right to independence — to self-government — to the possession of the homes conquered from the wilderness by their own labors and dangers, sufferings and sacrifices — a better and a truer right than the artificial tide of sovereignty in Mexico, a thousand miles distant, inheriting from Spain a title good only against those who have none better. Their right to independence will be the natural right of self-government belonging to any community strong enough to maintain it — distinct in position, origin and character, and free from any mutual obligations of membership of a common political body, binding it to others by the duty of loyalty and compact of public faith. This will be their title to independence; and by this title, there can be no doubt that the population now fast streaming down upon California will both assert and maintain that independence. Whether they will then attach themselves to our Union or not, is not to be predicted with any certainty. Unless the projected railroad across the continent to the Pacific be carried into effect, perhaps they may not; though even in that case, the day is not distant when the Empires of the Atlantic and Pacific would again flow together into one, as soon as their inland border should approach each other. But that great work, colossal as appears the plan on its first suggestion, cannot remain long unbuilt. Its necessity for this very purpose of binding and holding together in its iron clasp our fast-settling Pacific region with that of the Mississippi valley — the natural facility of the route — the ease with which any amount of labor for the construction can be drawn in from the overcrowded populations of Europe, to be paid in die lands made valuable by the progress of the work itself — and its immense utility to the commerce of the world with the whole eastern Asia, alone almost sufficient for the support of such a road — these coast of considerations give assurance that the day cannot be distant which shall witness the conveyance of the representatives from Oregon and California to Washington within less time than a few years ago was devoted to a similar journey by those from Ohio; while the magnetic telegraph will enable the editors of the "San Francisco Union," the "Astoria Evening Post," or the "Nootka Morning News," to set up in type the first half of the President's Inaugural before the echoes of the latter half shall have died away beneath the lofty porch of the Capitol, as spoken from his lips.

Away, then, with all idle French talk of *balances of power* on the American Continent. There is no growth in Spanish America! Whatever progress of population there may be in the British Canadas, is only for their own early severance of their present colonial relation to the little island three thousand miles across the Atlantic; soon to be followed by Annexation, and destined to swell the still accumulating momentum of our progress. And whosoever may hold the balance, though they should cast into the opposite scale all the bayonets and cannon, not only of France and England, but of Europe entire, how would it kick the beam against the simple, solid weight of the two hundred and fifty, or three hundred millions — and American millions — destined to gather beneath the flutter of the stripes and stars, in the fast hastening year of the Lord 1945!

B. Thomas Jefferson's Letter of Instructions to Meriwether Lewis

Excerpted from *Letters of the Lewis and Clark Expedition With Related Documents, 1783–1854*, edited by Donald Jackson, University of Illinois Press, Urbana, 1962, pp. 61–66. These excerpts concentrate on Jefferson's interest in Indian ethnology, which by implication include his interest in their sex lives. The letter is dated, in its final sentence, June 20, 1803.

Excerpts

To Meriwether Lewis, esquire, captain of the first regiment of infantry of the United States of America:

Your situation as secratary of the president of the United States, has made you aquainted with the objects of my confidential message of January 18, 1803, to the legislature; you have seen the act they passed, which, though expressed in general terms, was meant to sanction those objects, and you are appointed to carry them to execution....

The object of your mission is to explore the Missouri River, and such principal streams of it, as, by its course and communication with the waters of the Pacific Ocean, whether the Columbia, Oregan, Colrado, or any other river, may offer the most direct and practible water-communication across the continent, for the purposes of commerce....

Your observations are to be taken with great pains and accuracy;...

The commerce which may be carried on with the people inhabiting the line you will pursue, renders a knowledge of those people important. You will therefore endeavour to make yourself acquainted, as far as a diligent pursuit of your journey shall admit, with the names of the nations and their numbers;

The extent and limits of their possessions;
Their relations with other tribes or nations;
Their language, traditions, monuments;
Their ordinary occupations in agriculture, fishing, hunting, war, arts, and the implements for these;
Their food, clothing, and domestic accommodations;
The diseases prevalent among them, and the remedies they use;
Moral and physical circumstances which distinguish them from the tribes we know;
Peculiarities in their laws, customs, and dispositions;
And articles of commerce they may need or furnish, and to what extent.

And, considering the interest which every nation has in extending and strengthening the authority of reason and justice among the people around them, it will be useful to acquire what knowledge you can of the state of morality, religion, and information amoung them; as it may better enable those who may endeavour to civilize and instruct them, to adapt their measures to the existing notions and practices of those on whom they are to operate....

In all your intercourse with the natives, treat them in the most friendly and conciliatory manner which their own conduct will admit; allay all jealousies as to the object of your journey; satisfy them of its innocence; make them acquainted with the position, extent, character, peaceable and commercial dispositions of the United States; of our wish to be neighbourly; friendly, and useful to them, and of our dispositions to a commercial intercourse with them; confer with them on the points most convenient as mutual emporiums, and the articles of most desirable interchange for them and us. If a few of their influential chiefs, within practicable distance, wish to visit us, arrange such a visit with them, and furnish them with authority to call on our officers on their entering the United States, to have them conveyed to this place at the public expense. If any of them should wish to have some of their young people brought up with us, and taught such arts as may be useful to them, we will receive, instruct, and take care of them. Such a mission, whether of influential chiefs, or of young people, would give some security to your own party. Carry with you some matter of the kine-pox; inform those of them with whom you may be of its efficacy as a preservative from the small-pox, and instruct and encourage them in the use of it. This may be especially done wherever you winter.

As it is impossible for us to foresee in what manner you will be received by those people, whether with hospitality or hostility, so is it impossible to prescribe the exact degree of perseverance with which you are to pursue your journey. We value too much the lives of citizens to offer them to probable destruction. Your numbers will be sufficient to secure you against the unauthorized opposition of individuals, or of small parties; but if a superior force, authorized, or not authorized, by a nation, should be arrayed against your further passage, and inflexibly determined to arrest it, you must decline its further pursuit and return. In the loss of yourselves we should lose also the information you will have acquired. By returning safely with that, you may enable us to renew the essay with better calculated means. To your own discretion, therefore, must be left the degree of danger you may risk, and the point at which you should decline, only saying, we wish you to err on the side of your safety, and to bring back your party safe, even if it be with less information....

Should you find it safe to return by the way you go, after sending two of our party round by sea, or with your whole party, if no conveyance by sea can be found, do so; making such observations on your return as may serve to supply, correct, or confirm those made on your outward journey....

To provide, on the accident of your death, against anarchy, dispersion, and the consequent danger to your party, and total failure of the enterprise, you are hereby authorized, by any instrument signed and written in your own hand, to name the person among them who shall succeed to the command on your decease, and by like instruments to change the nomination, from time to time, as further experience of the characters accompanying you shall point out superior fitness; and all the powers and authorities given to yourself are, in the event of your death, transferred to, and vested in the successor so named, with further power to him and his successors, in like manner to name each his successor, who, on the death of his predecessor, shall be invested with all the powers and authorities given to yourself. Given under my hand at the city of Washington, this twentieth day of June, 1803.

Thomas Jefferson
President of the United States of America

C. Meriwether Lewis's Invitation to William Clark

Excerpts from Lewis's letter inviting William Clark to join him in exploring the West. *From Letters of the Lewis and Clark Expedition with Related Documents, 1783–1854,* edited by Donald Jackson, University of Illinois Press, Urbana, 1962, pp. 57–60.

Excerpts

Washington, June 19th, 1803
Dear Clark,...

From the long and uninterrupted friendship and confidence which has subsisted between us I feel no hesitation in making to you the following communication under the fulest impression that it will be held by you inviolably secret until I see you, or you shall hear again from me.

During the last session of Congress a law was passed in conformity to a private message of the President of the United States, intitled "An Act making an appropriation for extending the external commerce of the United Sates." The object of this Act as understood by its framers was to give the sanction of the government to exploring the interior of the continent of North America, or that part of it bordering on the Missourie & Columbie Rivers. This enterprise has been confided to me by the President, and in consequence since the beginning of March I have been engaged in making the necessary preparations for the tour, these arrangements being now nearly completed, I shall set out for Pittsburgh (the intended point of embarkation) about the last of this month, and as soon after as from the state of the water you can reasonably expect me I shall be with you, say about the 10th of August....

Thus my friend you have so far as leasure will at this time permit me to give it you, a summary view of the plan, the means and the objects of this expedition. If therefore there is anything under those circumstances, in this enterprise, which would induce you to participate with me in its fatigues, its dangers and its honors, believe me there is no man on earth with whom I should feel equal pleasure in sharing them as with yourself; I make this communication to you with the privity of the President, who expresses an anxious wish that you would consent to join me in this enterprise; he has authorized me to say that in the event of our accepting this proposition he will grant you a Captain's commission which of course will intitle you to the pay and emoluments attached to that office and will equally with myself intitle you to such portion of land as was granted to officers of similar rank for their Revolutionary services; the commission with which he proposes to furnish you is not to be considered temporary but permanent if you wish it; your situation if joined with me in this mission will in all respects be precisely such as my own. Pray write to me on this subject as early as possible and direct to me at Pittsburgh. Should you feel disposed not to attatch yourself to this party in an official character, and at the same time feel a disposition to accompany me as a friend any part of the way up the Missouri I should be extremely happy in your company, and will furnish you with every aid for your return from any point you might wish it. With sincere and affectionate regard Your friend & humbl Sevt.

Meriwether Lewis

D. Excerpts from Letters Written by Marcus Whitman

(Excerpts from letters written by Narcissa Whitman appear in Chapter 3, "The Missionary, Saving the Indian from Sex.")

The following excerpt from an undated letter, probably written in 1843, presents Marcus Whitman's clearest statement justifying the occupation of Indian lands by whites.

Mr. Edward Prentiss
Quincy, Illinois
My Dear Father and Mother: ...

As I hold the settlement of this country by Americans rather than by an English colony most important, I am happy to have been the means of landing so large an emigration on to the shores of the Columbia, with their wagons, families and stock, all in safety....

It does not concern me so much what is to become of any particular set of Indians, as to give them the offer of salvation through the gospel and the opportunity of civilization, and then I am content to do good to all men as "I have opportunity." I have no doubt our greatest work is to be to aid the white settlement of this country and help to found its religious institutions. Providence has its full share in all these events. Although the Indians have made, and are making, rapid advance in religious knowledge and civilization, yet it cannot be hoped that time will be allowed to mature either the work of Christianization or civilization before the white settlers will demand the soil and seek the removal of both the Indians and the Mission. What Americans desire of this kind they always effect, and it is equally useless to oppose or desire it otherwise. To guide, as far as can be done, and direct these tendencies for the best, is evidently the part of wisdom. Indeed, I am fully convinced that when a people refuse or neglect to fill the designs of Providence, they ought not to complain at the results; and so it is equally useless for Christians to be anxious on their account. The Indians have in no case obeyed the command to multiply and replenish the earth, and they cannot stand in the way of others in doing so. A place will be left them to do this as fully as their ability to obey will permit, and the more we can do for them the more fully will this be realized. No exclusiveness can be asked for any portion of the human family. The exercise of his rights are all that can be desired. In order for this to its proper extent in regard to the Indians, it is necessary that they seek to preserve their rights by peaceable means only. Any violations of this rule will be visited with only evil results to themselves.

The Indians are anxious about the consequence of settlers among them, but I hope there will be no acts of violence on either hand....

Your affectionate son,
Marcus Whitman

(In this letter to his wife's sister and brother-in-law, Marcus Whitman makes clear the importance he attaches to marriage.)

Miss Jane A. Prentiss
Quincy, Adams Co., Illinois, U.S.A.
Waiilatpu
May 15th, 1846
Edward and Jane Prentiss, My Dear Brother and Sister: ...

Narcissa wants Jane to come and I want Edward, but it is not for us that you should come but for yourselves and the Lord. Edward would do well to have a wife and then come, and Jane will be agreeable with or without a husband, as suits her best; but if she comes without one, I shall try to convince her of her duty to marry. This country needs those who are able and willing to found and support society, religion, and schools....

I am your affectionate brother,
Marcus Whitman

E. Fanny Kelly's Petition to Congress

To the Senators and Members of the
House of Representatives of Congress (1868)

Your memorialist, Mrs. Fanny Kelly, a citizen of the United States, and residing in the State of Kansas, respectfully petitioning your Honorable bodies, represents:

That during the summer months of the year 1864, your memorialist, in company with her husband, Josiah Kelly, (now deceased), and a party consisting of Wm. J. Larimer, wife and child, Mr. Sharp, Mr. Taylor, Mr. Wakefield, and the adopted daughter of your memorialist, Mary J. Hurley, left different portions of the State of Kansas to go to Montana Territory. The party united at a point west of the Northwestern border of Kansas, and journeyed together. Your memorialist and her husband had in their possession, and owned at the time, certain valuable goods and chattels (a full exhibit of which, with the market value thereof, is hereto attached and made part hereof, marked exhibit "A"). Your memorialist's husband was removing to Bannock City, Montana, with these goods, with a view to enter into trade.

On the 12th day of July, 1864, our party had reached a point some 80 miles west of Fort Laramie. While encamped a mixed party of Indians came into our camp, and deporting themselves in a friendly manner (by shaking hands and other demonstrations of friendship) asked us for supper. During its preparation, the number of Indians increased to nearly one hundred. They were composed of O-gal-lal-lah, and Yank-ton Sioux, Black-feet, and Rees and Gro-rout Indians (the later called "farmer Indians"), also some Hunc-pa-pas.

It had been represented to our party by the Military Commanders along the route of travel, that there was no danger to be apprehended from Indians, that we were entirely secure from attack, and we continued our journey without any fear.

While these preparations for supper were being made, the Indians, who had asked our hospitality, fired upon the men of our party. Mr. Sharp, Mr. Taylor, and the Negro boy fell dead at the first fire. Mr. Wakefield and Mr. Larimer were dangerously wounded, and hobbled off to the bushes. Your memorialist's husband was gathering wood at the time, and succeeded in escaping without injury. The Indians then surrounded the wagons for the purpose of plunder. They sacked the wagons, burned and destroyed what they could not carry away, and took the survivors of the party prisoners. Your memorialist was dragged rudely from one of the wagons and severely injured, from which she suffered for many months. Your memorialist was then taken into captivity, and was forced to become the squaw of one of the O-gal-lal-lah Chiefs, who treated her in a manner too horrible to mention, and during her captivity was passed from Chief to Chief, and treated in a similar manner. Your memorialist kept as full a memoranda of her captivity, and the incidents thereof, as was possible, and has, since her return to her home, reduced the same to a narrative form, embracing the entire period from date of capture to date of release. Your memorialist begs to refer your Honorable bodies to this narrative, as showing in detail something of her sufferings, privations and perils, and especially as presenting the evidence of her valuable services to the United States troops, which after her capture, entered the warpath against the Indians.

During her captivity, which lasted from July 12, 1864, until December 9, 1864, your memorialist acquired somewhat of the language of the Indians, which numbered two or three thousand, banded for plunder and murder, and was enabled to understand their plans and designs. These your memorialist contrived to communicate, from time to time, to emigrant and freight trains, and to troops and your memorialist would especially call attention to her valuable service rendered the garrison at Fort Sully, which, it will be seen, contributed largely to saving that garrison from total massacre. Your memorialist refers to her narrative as exhibit "B," and to letters and other evidences herewith submitted to show your Honorable bodies the truth of her statement.

Your memorialist says that some of her captors claimed to be *annuity* Indians, and boasted that they were drawing money and clothing from the white man, while at the same time they had certain of the white prisoners. The circumstances showing that some of my captors were *annuity* Indians, appear in my narrative.

Your memorialist respectfully urges upon your Honorable bodies, that she is now in destitute circumstances; that all her earthly effects were taken and destroyed by the Indians; that her husband has since died, leaving her helpless and poor; that her adopted daughter was cruelly murdered by her captors, and your memorialist is now alone in the world. She urges that her services to emigrants, traders and United States troops, while she was a captive, often sacrificing her own comfort, and endangering her life, and certainly prolonging her captivity, to render these services, will surely commend her cause to your Honorable bodies. Your memorialist asks some compensation in such sum as may seem mete, and she will, as in duty bound, ever pray.

Fanny Kelly

F. Joseph Smith's Revelation on Plural Marriage

Joseph Smith, founder of the Mormon Church, recorded the following "Revelation" in *Doctrine and Covenants* on July 12, 1843. It is the official church document authorizing polygamy, usually called plural marriage by Mormons.

"Revelation"

[Section] 132

[Paragraph] 59. Verily, if a man be called of my Father, as was Aaron, by mine own voice, and by the voice of him that sent me, and I have endowed him with the keys of the power of this priesthood, if he do anything in my name, and according to my law and by my word, he will not commit sin, and I will justify him.

60. Let no one, therefore, set on my servant Joseph; for I will justify him; for he shall do the sacrifice which I require at his hands for his transgressions, saith the Lord your God.

61. And again, as pertaining to the law of the priesthood if any man espouse a virgin, and desire to espouse another, and the first give her consent, and if he espouse the second, and they are virgins, and have vowed to no other man, then is he justified; he cannot commit adultery for they are given unto him; for he cannot commit adultery with that that belongeth unto him and to no one else.

62. And if he have ten virgins given unto him by this law, he cannot commit adultery, for they belong to him, and they are given unto him; therefore is he justified.

63. But if one or either of the ten virgins, after she is espoused, shall be with another man, she has committed adultery, and shall be destroyed; for they are given unto him to multiply and replenish the earth, according to my commandment, and to fulfil the promise which was given by my Father before the foundation of the world, and for their exaltation in the eternal worlds, that they may bear the souls of men; for herein is the work of my Father continued, that he may be glorified.

64. And again, verily, verily, I say unto you, if any man have a wife, who holds the keys of this power, and he teaches unto her the law of my priesthood, as pertaining to these things, then shall she believe and administer unto him, or she shall be destroyed, saith the Lord your God; for I will destroy her; for I will magnify my name upon all those who receive and abide in my law.

65. Therefore, it shall be lawful in me, if she receive not this law, for him to receive all things whatsoever I, the Lord his God, will give unto him, because she did not believe and administer unto him according to my word; and she then becomes the transgressor; and he is exempt from the law of Sarah, who administered unto Abraham according to the law when I commanded Abraham to take Hagar to wife.

66. And now, as pertaining to this law, verily, verily, I say unto you, I will reveal more unto you, hereafter; therefore, let this suffice for the present. Behold, I am Alpha and Omega. Amen.

G. Mormon Church Ban on Polygamy

Wilford Woodruff, president of the Church of Jesus Christ of Latter-day Saints, issued a manifesto in September 1890 that says church members must obey laws that ban polygamy. It did not dissolve existing "plural" marriages that had been sanctioned by the church, of which there were several thousand. It had the practical effect of making statehood for Utah acceptable to members of the U.S. Congress, and, in fact, statehood was granted effective January 4, 1896. Woodruff's statement is widely known within the church as the 1890 Manifesto or, more often, The Manifesto. The Utah Commission referred to in The Manifesto was a body appointed by Congress to determine whether or not polygamy was, in fact, being practiced in Utah Territory.

Manifesto

To Whom It May Concern:

Press dispatches having been sent from Salt Lake City, which have been widely published for political purposes, to the effect that the Utah Commission, in their recent report to the Secretary of the Interior, alleges that plural marriages are still being solemnized, and that forty or more such marriages have been contracted in Utah since last June or during the last year, also that in public discourses the leaders of the Church have taught, encouraged and urged the continuance of the practice of polygamy—

I, therefore, as President of the Church of Latter-day Saints, do hereby in the most solemn manner, declare that the charges are false. We are not teaching polygamy or plural marriage, nor permitting any person to enter into its practice and I deny that either forty or any other number of plural marriages have, during that period, been solemnized in our temples or any other place in the Territory. One case has been reported in which the parties alleged that the marriage was performed in the Endowment House in Salt Lake City, in the spring of 1889. But whatever was done in the matter was done without my knowledge. In consequence of this alleged occurrence Endowment House was by my instructions taken down without delay.

Inasmuch as laws have been enacted by Congress forbidding plural marriages, which laws have already been pronounced constitutional by the court of last resort, I do hereby declare my intention to submit to those laws and to use all my influence with the members of the Church over which I preside to have them do likewise. There is nothing in my teachings to the Church or in those of my associates, during the time specified, which can reasonably be construed to inculcate or encourage polygamy, and when any Elder of the Church has used language which appeared to convey such teachings he has been promptly reproved; and I now publicly declare that my advice to the Latter-day Saints is to refrain from contracting any marriage forbidden by the law of the land.

       Wilford Woodruff
       President of the Church of Jesus Christ of Latter-day Saints.

Chapter Notes

Introduction

1. For a detailed biography of O'Sullivan, see Sampson, *John L. O'Sullivan*; Sampson discusses and dismisses in an endnote a claim by historian Linda S. Hudson that the annexation editorial was written not by O'Sullivan but by Jane McManus Storms Cazneau.

2. For a detailed discussion of *High Noon* and, to a lesser extent, *Rio Bravo*, see Byman, *Showdown at High Noon*. See also Weidhorn, "*High Noon*: Liberal Classic? Conservative Screed?"

3. Many books detail the rapid growth of California following the discovery of gold in 1848. See, for example, Hicks, Mowry and Burke, *The Federal Union*, pp. 563–565.

4. Many books discuss the low numbers of actual cowboys in the American West and comment on the high numbers in movies, novels, and other cultural outlets. See, for example, Starrs, *Let the Cowboy Ride*.

5. Diner's essay appears in *Jewish Life in the American West*, edited by Ava F. Kahn.

Chapter 1

1. Jefferson discusses some of his plans for exploring the West in "Jefferson to Paul Allen, Aug. 18, 1813, Letter Number 362," in *Letters of the Lewis and Clark Expedition*, edited by Donald Jackson, pp. 586–593. Many, but not all, biographies of Jefferson and books about the Louisiana Purchase also discuss those plans. For example, see Ambrose, *Undaunted Courage*; Cerami, *Jefferson's Great Gamble*; Channing, *The Jeffersonian System*; Jackson, *Thomas Jefferson and the Stony Mountains*; Kukla, *A Wilderness So Immense*; and Sprague, *So Vast, So Beautiful a Land*.

2. Jefferson discusses Andrea Michaux in "Jefferson to Paul Allen, Aug. 18, 1813, Letter Number 362," in *Letters of the Lewis and Clark Expedition*, edited by Donald Jackson, p. 586–593; the discussion of Michaux appears on p. 589.

3. Jefferson's plan to have George Rogers Clark explore the West is examined by Ambrose, *Undaunted Courage*, pp. 68–69.

4. Jefferson discusses Ledyard in "Jefferson to Paul Allen, Aug. 18, 1813, Letter Number 362," in *Letters of the Lewis and Clark Expedition*, edited by Donald Jackson, pp. 586–593; the discussion of Ledyard appears on pp. 588–589. See also Ambrose, *Undaunted Courage*, p. 69.

5. For details about the Freeman and Custis Expedition, see Flores, editor, *Southern Counterpart to Lewis and Clark*.

6. Most biographies of Thomas Jefferson devote some space to his interests in science. See, for example, Brodie, *Thomas Jefferson: An Intimate History*; Burstein, *Jefferson's Secrets: Death and Desire*; and Jackson, *Thomas Jefferson and the Stony Mountains*.

7. The story of the Louisiana Purchase has been told in hundreds of books and thousands of articles. See, for example, Cerami, *Jefferson's Great Gamble*; Kukla, *A Wilderness So Immense*; and Sprague, *So Vast, So Beautiful a Land*.

8. For discussions of Jefferson's plans for Lewis to explore the West see the three

sources listed in the previous note and Ambrose, *Undaunted Courage*, pp. 68–92.

9. "Jefferson's Instructions to Lewis" (June 20, 1803), is letter number 47, in *Letters of the Lewis and Clark Expedition*, edited by Donald Jackson, pp. 61–66. Excerpts from this letter appear in Appendix B.

10. "Lewis to Clark, June 19th 1803" is letter number 46, in *Letters of the Lewis and Clark Expedition*, edited by Donald Jackson, pp. 57–60. Excerpts from this letter appear in Appendix C.

11. For information about smallpox and the Lewis and Clark Expedition see, Paton, *Lewis and Clark: Doctors in the Wilderness*, pp. 36, 42, 43–45, 140–141, 211; Ambrose, *Undaunted Courage*, pp. 20, 160, 178, 183, 286, 326, 337; Jackson, editor, *Letters of the Lewis and Clark Expedition*, pp. 35 (April 17, 1803 letter from Attorney General Levi Lincoln to Jefferson), 64 (Jefferson's June 20, 1803, instructions to Lewis), 130 (October 3, 1803 letter from Lewis to Jefferson), 246 (May 27, 1805, letter from William Henry Harrison [governor of Indiana Territory, later President] to Jefferson).

12. All quotes from the Lewis and Clark journals are from Moulton, *The Lewis and Clark Journals*. However, because even most large public libraries do not have the full edition, interested readers might want to consult the full text on the Gutenberg Project. For ease in locating the quotes cited, dates of entry rather than page numbers are used.

13. See Gass's journal of the Lewis and Clark Expedition.

14. For details about medical treatment received by members of the Lewis and Clark expedition, see Paton, *Lewis and Clark: Doctors in the Wilderness*.

15. Details about gonorrhea and syphilis come from Paton, *Lewis and Clark: Doctors in the Wilderness*, pp. 50, 51, and 169, and from Ambrose, *Undaunted Courage*, pp. 180, 196–197, 202, 223, 241n, 243, 286, 297, 325–326.

16. For the use of mercury pills to treat venereal disease on the Lewis and Clark Expedition see Paton, *Lewis and Clark: Doctors in the Wilderness*, p. 51, and Ambrose, *Undaunted Courage*, pp. 197, 325n, and Lewis's entry in the Journals for March 8, 1806.

17. See note 26, below, this chapter.

18. See Moulton, *Journals of Lewis and Clark*.

19. Little is known with certainty about Sacagawea expect what appears in the *Journals of Lewis and Clark*. Nearly everything else is speculation. She and everyone who knew her who was not a member of the expedition were illiterate and therefore incapable of recording their knowledge about her. Oral tradition regarding her is highly inconsistent, with no agreement on when or where she died, how many children she had, or anything else about her.

20. Doctoring skills of Lewis and Clark are discussed in Chuinard, *Only One Man Died*, and Paton, *Lewis and Clark: Doctors in the Wilderness*.

21. One possibility is that Sacagawea was raped by Hidatsa men, but there is nothing in the *Journals of Lewis and Clark*, the only reliable source of information about her, to suggest she was raped. Of course, their knowledge of the young Shoshoni woman was limited.

22. Although historians widely accept the fact that Clark referred to Sacajawea as Janey, only once in the *Journals* does he use that nickname in reference to her, on Nov. 24, 1805.

23. The script was written by Winston Miller and based on *Sacajawea of the Shoshones*, a novel by Della Gould Emmons. The movie was directed by Rudolph Mate. Oddly, although there have been many television documentaries on the Lewis and Clark expedition, *The Far Horizons* remains the only feature length film ever made about what is undoubtedly the most famous trip ever made by Americans prior to the 1969 moon landings.

24. For a history of the Shoshoni (sometimes spelled Shoshone) see Madsen, *The Lemhi: Sacajawea's People*, and Mann, *Sacajawea's People: The Lemhi Shoshones and the Salmon River Country*.

25. Discussions of the origins of venereal diseases appear in Paton, *Lewis and Clark: Doctors in the Wilderness*, pp. 50–51; Ambrose, *Undaunted Courage*, p. 286. Anyone interested in an in-depth exploration of the issue might consider consulting Powell and Cook, *The Myth of Syphilis*.

26. Ambrose, in *Undaunted Courage*, pp. 196–197, notes that the phrase "mad as a hatter" refers to the fact that hat makers who used mercury in their trade often became "a bit crazy" from breathing mercury fumes. Morris in *The Fate of the Corps* notes that the causes of death of both Goodrich and Gibson are unknown (pp. 193–194). Paton, in *Lewis and Clark: Doctors in the Wilderness*, notes the use of mercury to treat venereal disease but does not discuss its possible negative effects (p. 51).

27. http://www.calpoison.org/hcp/2011/callusvol9no1.htm.

28. Morris, *The Fate of the Corps*, pp. 187–202.

29. Kathleen A. Dahl, an anthropologist at Eastern Oregon University, notes it is highly unlikely that a Nez Percé woman could give birth to a child with red hair and blue eyes. According to Dahl, "Unless the woman was a mixed blood who carried the necessary recessive genes for red hair and blue eyes — unlikely, given the lack of contact between the Nez Percé and white Europeans or Americans up to this point — Clark's Native American son would have been dark-haired and dark-eyed like his mother." (She spells the alleged son's name Tzi-Kal-Tza.) See http://lewisandclarktrailwatch.blogspot.com/2005/11/did-william-clark-have-native-american.html.

30. With few exceptions, Clark's descriptions of the physical appearance of Native Americans are highly negative. He does not comment on Sacajawea's appearance, but skeptics who doubt he was in love with her can point to his overall view of the appearance of Indians in general.

31. Harry Charger's angry denial that his great-great-grandfather was the illegitimate son of William Clark is quoted on the website of the NATHPO, the National Association of Tribal Historic Preservation Officers, http://www.nathpo.org/Many_Nations/mn_news12.html.

32. The Joseph Lewis DeSmet story is discussed on the NATHPO website (see previous note); the website includes a photograph of the headstone.

33. For a history of how homosexuals have been punished throughout the ages, see Fone, *Homophobia*.

34. "Lewis to Clark, June 19th 1803," letter number 46, in *Letters of the Lewis and Clark Expedition*, edited by Donald Jackson, pp. 57–60; the cited quote appears on p. 60.

35. Hall, *I Should Be Extremely Happy in Your Company*.

36. Guice, editor, *By His Own Hand?* This book contains four essays. Clay Jenkinson, a Lewis biographer, and historian James Holmberg believe Lewis committed suicide; Guice, an academic historian, believes he was murdered; while Jay Buckley, also an academic, doesn't take a definite stand. Stephen Ambrose in *Undaunted Courage* argues that Lewis committed suicide, pp. 461–474. Morris, in *The Fate of the Corps*, discusses but does not reach a firm conclusion on Lewis's death (see Morris, pp. 54–74).

37. Jefferson's brief biography of Lewis is based on his personal knowledge. They were neighbors in central Virginia.

38. The term *berdaches* was later applied by anthropologists to indicate men who assumed the role of women in various societies, but since that word, of French origin, suggests the person is a prostitute, it has generally replaced by the less prejudicial "two-spirited."

39. Ambrose, among other historians, cites Jackson's sentence with approval. See Ambrose, p. 97.

40. For Clark naming his first child after Lewis see Ambrose, *Undaunted Courage*, p. 460.

41. For a summary of Lewis's attempts to find a wife see Ambrose, *Undaunted Courage*, pp. 437–441. Ambrose is not among the biographers who suspected Lewis was homosexual. Although he does not directly discuss the possibility, he does write (p. 441) that "Lewis wanted a wife to fill a void in his heart. He never got one."

42. There is nothing in either the *Journals* or in Jackson, *Letters*, to reveal what views, if any, Clark had about homosexuality.

43. Jefferson's comments on Lewis's depression are contained in "Jefferson to Paul Allen, Aug. 18, 1813," in Jackson, *Letters of the Lewis and Clark Expedition*, pp. 591–592.

Chapter 2

1. For an overview history of the roles played by mountain men in westward American expansion, see Utley, *A Life Wild and Perilous: Mountain Men and the Paths to the Pacific.* For an overview of famous Western explorers, see Moring, *Men With Sand: Great Explorers of the North American West.* For an overview that focuses on Hispanic explorers in the Southwest, see Sanchez, *Explorers, Traders, and Slavers: Forging the Old Spanish Trail, 1678–1850.*

2. Because much of Frémont's importance in Western exploration is connected to his relationship with Kit Carson, a particularly good book on his life is the biography of both by David Roberts, *A Newer World: Kit Carson, John C. Fremont, and the Claiming of the American West.* Among the best biographies focusing primarily on Frémont is Rolle, *John Charles Fremont: Character as Destiny.*

3. For Poinsett's relation to Frémont, see Roberts, *A Newer World,* pp. 115–120. For a full-length biography of Poinsett, see Rippy, *Joel R. Poinsett.*

4. Thomas Hart Benton's sometimes stormy relationship with his son-in-law Frémont is covered extensively throughout Roberts, *A Newer World.* For a full-length biography of Benton, see Chambers, *Old Bullion Benton, Senator From the New West: Thomas Hart Benton.*

5. Jessie (Benton) Frémont's relationship to her husband, John C. Frémont, is covered throughout Roberts, *A Newer World.* For a full-length dual biography of John and Jessie Frémont, see Denton, *Passion and Principle.*

6. For Jessie Frémont's admiration of Sir Walter Scott's writing, see Roberts, *A Newer World,* p. 186. For Mark Twain's negative views on Sir Walter Scott's influence on Americans, see *Life on the Mississippi,* Chapters 40 and 46 (pp. 184–185 and 207–210 in the Dover edition).

7. The friendship between Frémont and Kit Carson is the subject of Roberts, *A Newer World.*

8. Frémont's book about his explorations of the West has been reprinted several times under different titles. In 1843 it was published as *A Report on an Exploration of the Country Lying Between the Missouri River and the Rocky Mountains.* In 1845 Congress arranged to have it published as *Report on the Exploring Expeditions to the Rocky Mountains in the Year 1842, and to Oregon and North California in the Years 1843–'44, By Bevit Capt. J.C. Fremont.* In 1856 it was published by a commercial printer, Miller, Orton and Mulligan, which had offices in New York City and Auburn, N.Y., as *The Life of Col. John Charles Fremont, and His Narrative of Explorations and Adventures, in Kansas, Nebraska, Oregon and California.* It has also been published several times in abbreviated editions.

9. Longfellow, not surprisingly, was a great admirer of the novels and poems of Sir Walter Scott, the same writer who so influenced Jessie Benton, who in turn rewrote much of her husband's prose.

10. Much of what is known about Kit Carson comes directly or indirectly from his "autobiography," but the story of that "autobiography" is complicated. Carson was illiterate, and in 1856 he dictated his life story to Jesse B. Turly. Somehow the manuscript came into the possession of De Witt C. Peters, an army doctor, whom Carson authorized to write a biography of him. In 1858 Peters published *The Life and Adventures of Kit Carson, the Nestor of the Rocky Mountains from Facts Narrated by Himself,* which incorporated the Turly manuscript but which was five times longer. The extra material seems to be a combination of information Peters obtained from conversation with Peters and Peters' assumptions or creations. In 1926 Blanche Chloe Grant edited and published the original Turly manuscript, and in 1935 Lakeside Press published the Quaife version, which is widely considered the standard version. It was republished in 1966 by the University of Nebraska Press.

11. For the often strained relations between the United States and, first, Spain and, then, Mexico, in the early 19th century see Sanchez, *Explorers, Traders, and Slavers,* pp. 119–133; Roberts, *A Newer World,* p. 57, and Moring, *Men With Sand,* pp. 130–146.

12. Details on Carson at the 1835 and subsequent mountain men rendezvous are

found in Roberts, *A Newer World*, pp. 66–74.

13. See Simmons, *Kit Carson and His Three Wives: A Family History*.

14. See Beckwourth, *The Life and Adventures of James P. Beckwourth*.

15. For details on Carson at Bent's Fort see Roberts, *A Newer World*, pp. 19, 32, 72, 99–102, 123, 139, 141, 142, 144 183, 184, 188–189, 196, 257.

16. Carson's marriage to Making Out Road is covered in Simmons, *Kit Carson and His Three Wives: A Family History*, pp. 31–52.

17. Willa Cather's view of Kit Carson in *Death Comes for the Archbishop* is more complicated than her view of his wife. She portrays Carson, first, as someone who understands and helps Indians and later as a soldier who takes part in repressing them.

18. For an overview of mountain men see note 1 in this chapter.

19. Charles Rath is discussed in Simmons, *Kit Carson and His Three Wives*, pp. 37, 40 (photo of his children with Making Out Road), 45, 126.

20. John Colter is the subject of Chapters 1 and 2 (pp. 1–22) in Utley, *A Life Wild and Perilous*. He is also the subject of a footnote in Bradbury, *Travels in the Interior of America*, which was the basis for the character of Colter in *Astoria*, a novel by Washington Irving, first published in 1836.

21. Jedediah Smith is the subject of Chapters 4, 5, and 7 (pp. 39–67 and 83–102) in Utley, *A Life Wild and Perilous*. See also "James Clyman, Witness to History" in Froncek, *Voices From the Wilderness*, pp. 179–198, which is an excerpt from Clyman's diaries.

22. Hugh Glass is discussed in Utley, *A Life Wild and Perilous*, pp. 48, 50, 57–58, 73, 84, 63, 132, 142, 328. *The Revenant*, a novel by Michael Punke, is based on the life of Hugh Glass. See also "Hugh Glass: The Will to Endure" in Froncek, pp. 199–210, which is an excerpt from "The Chronicles of George C. Yount," edited by Charles L. Camp, published in the *California Historical Society Quarterly* in 1923.

23. Jim Bridger is the subject of Chapter 13 (pp. 173–183) in Utley, *A Life Wild and Perilous*. Stansbury, *An Expedition to the Valley of the Great Salt Lake*, pp. 239–240, 252–254, contains a firsthand account by an admirer of Bridger.

24. A credible biography of Beckwourth is Wilson, *Jim Beckwourth: Black Mountain Man and War Chief of the Crows*. See next note.

25. While Beckwourth's autobiography, written by T.D. Bonner from Beckwourth's dictation, is entertaining but far from credible, it does reflect the attitudes many mountain men held toward Indian women.

26. Biographical information on Russell is from Haines, "Editor's Preface" in Russell, *Journal of a Trapper*, pp. i–ii.

27. The letter is in the Beinecki Rae Book and Manuscript Library of Yale University Library (thanks to Kathryn James of the Yale University Library for providing a copy of the letter).

Chapter 3

1. For an overview history of missionaries in the 19th century American West see Furtwangler, *Bringing Indians to the Book*.

2. Biographical information on Marcus and Narcissa Whitman is from Jeffrey, *Converting the West*, and Jones, *The Great Command*.

3. Henry Spalding is discussed in both of the biographies listed in the previous endnote and also in Drury, *Henry Harmon Spalding*.

4. Borneman, *Polk: The Man Who Transformed the Presidency and America*.

5. Deloria, *Custer Died for Your Sins*. Deloria's negative view of missionaries extends throughout much of his writings. For example, in an article titled "The Missionary in a Cultural Trap," he wrote, "Missionaries have been chosen — and wisely so — as targets in the War on Ignorance conducted by the Indian people of this country. The good of the country as a whole demands such action, since these people can be the breeding ground for doctrines of intolerance, arrogance and unwise policies regarding the American Indian." The article appears as an appendix in Deloria, *For This Land* (pp. 284–294; the cited quote is on p. 284).

6. Biographical information for Father de Smet comes from Carriker, *Father Peter John de Smet: Jesuit in the West*; Carriker, "Pierre-Jean De Smet," *Encyclopedia of the Great Plains*, and John J. Killoren, "*Come Blackrobe," De Smet and the Indian Tragedy*.

7. See de Smet, *Oregon Missions*.

8. Information on Hurons and Jesuits comes from Anderson, "As Gentle As Little Lambs"; Sagard, *The Long Journey to the Country of the Hurons*; Talbot, *Saint Among the Hurons*; Tooker, *An Ethnography of the Huron Indians: 1615–1649*; Trigger, *Huron: Farmers of the North*; and Trigger, *The Children of Aataentsic: A History of the Huron People to 1660*. See also Calloway, *One Vast Winter Count*, p. 223; Calloway writes, "The Jesuits criticized Huron sexual practices (premarital intercourse was regarded as normal), gender relations (women enjoyed considerable freedom and sexual freedom).... The Jesuits won few converts."

9. Lewis Henry Morgan's study of the Iroquois was first published in 1851 in Rochester, New York, under the title *League of the Ho-De-No-Sau-Nee, Iroquois*. More modern editions tend to use the title *League of the Iroquois*. It was and remains a book that is highly influential; it set a standard for future American ethnologists in its extensive detail and its willingness to adopt a point of view and avoid pure objectivity. In his preface he wrote that he wanted "to encourage a kinder feeling towards the Indian," and that sentiment can be detected throughout. Some of his conclusions, however, are no longer widely accepted, most notably his belief that the Iroquois Confederacy was in some way a centralized governing body with control over its five (and later six) member nations. Today the more common view is that the Confederacy was an agreement not to war upon each other (an agreement that was not always honored) and was otherwise largely ceremonial. (See, for example, William N. Fenton's Introduction to the 1993 Citadel Press edition, which is the one used for my research; Fenton notes that notable historians such as Francis Parkman and George Hunt disagreed with Morgan's assessment on this point.) Morgan's assessments on Iroquois sexual mores, more pertinent to this book, have either largely gone unaddressed by other historians or are mostly accepted as accurate.

10. Morgan, *League of the Iroquois*. The book is in fact "inscribed" (i.e., dedicated) to Ha-sa-no-an-da, Parker's Seneca name.

11. For biographical information on Ely Parker see Armstrong, *Warrior in Two Camps*.

12. Morgan, *Ancient Society*.

13. For the history of the Metis see Harrison, *Metis: People Between Two Worlds*, and Purich, *The Metis*.

14. For the history of the Hudson Bay Company see Binnema, "Hudson's Bay Company," and Newman, *Empire of the Bay*.

15. For a history of the North West Fur Company see Campbell, *The North West Company*. For biographical information on Alexander Mackenzie see Hayes, *First Crossing*.

16. Le Page Du Pratz's story of Moncache-ape's was first printed in *History of Louisiana* in 1758; in that book Du Pratz was seeking to prove the theory that American Indians originated in Asia, a view that is now, of course, widely accepted because of both linguistic and DNA evidence. The part about Moncache-ape is reprinted in *Great Documents in American Indian History*, pp. 16–19.

17. See Hamalainen, "Seven Oaks Massacre." The Battle of Seven Oaks is also covered in Campbell, *The North West Company*, and Newman, *Empire of the Bay*.

18. See Huel, "Louis Riel," and Howard, *Strange Empire*.

19. See Furtwangler, *Bringing Indians to the Book*.

20. For a brief history of the 1675 Pueblo rebellion (and other smaller revolts) see Shoumatoff, *Legends of the American Desert*, pp. 40, 218, 237–41, 404, 407; for a longer, more detailed history see Roberts, *The Pueblo Revolt*.

21. For biographies of Junipero Serra see Omer Englebert, *The Last of the Conquistadors*, and Fogel, *Junipero Serra, The Vatican, and Enslavement Theology*.

22. For Dona Eulalia Callis's divorce from Governor Pedro Fages see Hackel, *Children of Coyote*, pp. 72, 224–225, 240,

290–291, and Beebe, *Lands of Promise and Despair*, pp. 236–238.

23. For the Whitmans see Jeffrey, *Converting the West: A Biography of Narcissa Whitman*, and Jones, *The Great Command: The Story of Marcus and Narcissa Whitman and the Oregon Country Pioneers*.

Chapter 4

1. Carlyle's quote is from his 1841 book *On Heroes, Hero Worship and the Heroic in History*, which is a collection of six lectures he delivered the previous year. The quote appears, in various forms, at least a dozen times throughout the book.
2. For biographical information on Houston, see Haley, *Sam Houston*, and Terrell, "Recollections."
3. For Sam Houston's wound in Indian fighting see Brands, *Andrew Jackson*, pp. 212–213, 218.
4. For Sam Houston's relationship with Eliza Allen see Haley, *Sam Houston*, pp. 49, 51–63, 73–74, 89, 98, 164–179, 307, 314, 331–332, 401, 431n, 452n. Also, Brands, *Andrew Jackson*, pp. 426–428.
5. For Sam Houston's Cherokee wife see Anderson, *The Conquest of Texas*, pp. 401n, 442n.
6. For biographical information on Andrew Jackson see, Brands, *Andrew Jackson*.
7. For a dual biography of Andrew and Rachel Jackson see, Brady, *A Being So Gentle*.

Chapter 5

1. See Plummer, *Rachel Plummer's Narrative of Twenty-one Months' Servitude as a Prisoner Among the Comanche Indians*. See also Anderson, *The Conquest of Texas*, pp. 129, 136–137. Anderson believes Plummer was badly treated but suggests she was probably not raped ("no evidence suggests rape even after the party reached Indian villages").
2. For biographical information on Cynthia Parker see Exley, *Frontier Blood*, and Robston, *Ride the Wind*. For biographical information on Quanah Parker see Gwynne, *Empire of the Summer Moon*. Cynthia, the mother, and Quanah, the son, are of course both discussed extensively in all three books. See also, Anderson, *The Conquest of Texas*, pp. 23, 119, 128–130, 162, 174, 332, 348, 358, 457n.
3. For details about Indian brutality against male captives see Osborn, *The Wild Frontier*. Osborn's book, subtitled *Atrocities During the American-Indian War From Jamestown Colony to Wounded Knee*, seeks to provide a balanced view of atrocities committed by both whites and Indians in the 400 years it took Europeans to subdue native American cultures. He accuses Dee Brown, in his classic *Bury My Heart at Wounded Knee*, of revisionism (see Osborn, p. 272). He does not deny that whites committed atrocities but says Indians had for most of the history of white settlements in America a well-deserved reputation for brutality. He notes for example that one of the complaints Thomas Jefferson listed against King George III in the Declaration of Independence is that the king "had endeavored to bring on the inhabitants of our frontiers, the merciless Indian Savages whose known rule of warfare is an undistinguished destruction of all ages, sexes and conditions" (Osborn, p. 6).
4. For a literary overview of captivity narratives see the "Introduction," pp. vi–xxxi, in VanDerBeets, editor, *Held Captive by Indians*.
5. For details on William Donoho purchasing Rachel Plummer's freedom see Plummer, pp. 361–363, in VanDerBeets, *Held Captive by Indians*. See also Dary, *The Santa Fe Trail*, pp. 136–137.
6. For the story of the Hall sisters see Edwards, "Narrative of the Capture and Providential Escape of Misses Frances and Alira Hall."
7. For the story of Phillip Brigdon, see Edwards, "Narrative." The Brigdon story immediately follows the story of the Hall sisters.
8. Edwards' report on torture by Indians constitutes the third part of his "Narrative."
9. For biographical information on George Catlin see Hausdoerffer, *Catlin's Lament*, and Dippie, "Catlin, George."
10. For the high death rate for children

among Indians see Gregg and Gregg, *Dry Bones*. As one example, the Greggs report that about 41 percent of the skeletons found at one archeological site in South Dakota (the Larson site) were of children who died before the age of one (see Chapter 8).

11. For Catlin's views on the workload of 19th century American Indians see Hausdoerffer, *Catlin's Lament*, pp. 40, 158.

12. For how the arrival of whites increased the workload of Indian women see Wishart, "Native American Gender Roles." See also Calloway, *One Vast Winter Count*. Calloway writes that when Plains Indians obtained horses from whites, "Women's status seems to have declined in the individualistic, male-dominated herding and equestrian hunting culture that developed, especially as it became linked to the European hide trade. In prehorse days, communal hunts involved collective effort and collective ownership. Now men's arrows, shot from horseback, marked the kill as property; women butchered it.... At a time when male losses were increasing in the escalating horseback warfare, successful hunters sometimes took several wives" (pp. 274–275).

13. For the story of John Minto see McLynn, *Wagons West*, pp. 25, 36, 42, 45, 150, 187–192, 196–198, 209–210, 212–214, 216–217, 231. Minto went on to serve four terms as a Republican member of the Oregon legislature.

14. See Seaver, *Mary Jemison*.

15. The French and Indian War in North America was part of a larger global war known as the Seven Years' War and which involved most of the major military powers in Europe. Much of the war was fought in the colonies of those powers in North and Central America, Africa, and Asia. See Anderson, *Crucible of War*.

16. The role of the Seneca during the American Revolution is discussed in Morgan, *League of the Iroquois*, Sever, *Mary Jemison*, and Anderson, *Crucible of War*.

17. For the Wyoming Massacre see Jenkins, "Historical Address." This is a speech given on July 3, 1878, the 100th anniversary of, and at the site of, the massacre. See also Seaver, *Mary Jemison*, Appendix.

18. For Sullivan's March and General Sullivan see *Journals of the Military Expedition of Major General John Sullivan*. See also Seaver, *Mary Jemison*, Chapter 7.

19. For John O'Bail and Cornplanter see Seaver, *Mary Jemison*, Chapter 7. (Seaver spells Cornplanter as Corn Planter).

20. For Ebenezer Allen see Seaver, *Mary Jemison*, Chapters 8, 14, and 16.

21. For land speculators in Western New York see Sisby, *The Holland Land Company*. The Holland Land Company was the major land speculator in Western New York. An earlier and important speculator in the same area was Nathaniel Rochester, who named the city of Rochester after himself. A great deal of information about the role of land speculators in settling Western New York can be found at the Holland Land Office Museum in Batavia, New York. The museum focuses on the role that speculators, interested, of course, in financial profit, played in moving America's Euro-centric population westward.

22. The practice of inviting Indian leaders to Washington, D.C., as a way of impressing them with the number and power of whites was a common practice for more than a century. Ambrose, in Undaunted Courage, discusses the topic no less than 19 times (pp. 126, 130, 133, 136, 137, 200–201, 342–43, 345–346, 350, 351–52, 363, 366, 377–378, 399, 400, 402, 417, 420). Marks, in *In a Barren Land*, discusses it 12 times (pp. 79, 189, 193, 228, 240, 250, 252, 268, 285–286, 303, 334, 338). Hundreds of Indian leaders made the trip to Washington in the 18th and 19th centuries, and the trips continued even into the 20th century, although by then they were less often by invitation and more by Indian initiative in attempts to influence federal policies toward Indian nations.

23. A majority of Indians in the United States were, in fact, citizens of the United States prior to 1924 by virtue of having served in the U.S. military, assimilation into white society, or by other means. The 1924 Indian Citizenship Act, widely called the Snyder Act (for Homer P. Snyder, the Republican congressman from New York who was its principal sponsor) granted citizenship to any Indians born in the U.S. after 1924.

Not until 1940, under the Nationality Act, were all Indians born in the U.S., regardless of date, made U.S. citizens.

24. For the story of Charlotte Brown see Igle, "Charlotte L. Brown" and "Affidavit of Oral Testimony." See also Welke, "Rights of Passage."

25. For the splits in the Mormon church when Smith was murdered, see McGinity, *The Oatman Massacre*, pp. 30–36. See also Alexander, *The Right Place*, pp. 87–91; Russell, "King James Strang"; Speek, "God Has Made Us a Kingdom"; Ostling, *Mormon America*, pp. 334–350.

26. For the Oatman family see McGinty, *The Oatman Massacre*.

27. For biographical information on Royal Stratton see McGinty, *The Oatman Massacre*. For Stratton's book about the Oatman sisters see Stratton, *Captivity of the Oatman Girls*.

28. "The Searchers" was released in 1956, directed by John Ford, with screenplay by Frank Nugent, and starred John Wayne, Jeffrey Hunter, Natalie Wood, Ward Bond, and Vera Miles. It was based on the novel of the same name by Alan LeMay.

29. For C.E. Bingham play's about the Oatman sisters see McGinty, *The Oatman Massacre*.

30. For captivity narratives see "Introduction," pp. vi–xxxi, in VanDerBeets, editor, *Held Captive by Indians*. See also, Spence, "Prologue" in Kelly, *Narrative of My Captivity*, pp. ix–xliv, and Hans, "Captivity Narratives."

31. For the Sioux uprising in Minnesota see Yenne, *Indian Wars*, pp. 95–100, 186; Brown, *Bury My Heart at Wounded Knee*, pp. 37–65, and Osborn, *Wild Frontier*, pp. 12, 35n, 84, 87–88, 202–207, 209, 210, 241, 244, 266, 272, 279.

32. See Alexander, *Utah: The Right Place*. He notes that studies of the Anasazi burial site near the Delores River in Western Colorado "show that 80 percent of the females died between ages 16 and 26, many probably in childbirth" (p. 34).

33. The quote is from Book of Ruth, Chapter 1, Verse 16, in the King James Version of the Bible.

34. Madsen in *The Shoshoni Frontier* and the Bear River Massacre argues that when Mormons moved into what is now Northern Utah and Southern Idaho, they took over the most important food gathering and hunting areas and forced the Shoshoni into poverty. In particular, he notes, grazing by cattle and other white-owned animals destroyed so much seed that the Shoshoni had used for food that starvation became widespread in the native population.

35. For a history of the massacre at Washita, see Greene, *Washita*.

36. Biographical information about Fanny Kelly not contained in her narrative comes from Spence, "Prologue" and "Epilogue," in the Barnes and Noble edition of her narrative. Several websites contain all or part of Kelly's narrative. Careful researchers may note that sometimes the wording in the varying editions differs. For example, on p. 164, the Spences, editors of the Barnes and Noble edition have "After so many prior escapes from death," while the Google Books website (p. 170) has "After so many escapes from death." Similarly, the Barnes and Noble edition on p. 178 has "The Indians know they are being cheated whenever...." while the Google Books version (p. 185) has "The Indians know they are cheated whenever...." There are dozens of differences, but all are minor and none affect Kelly's meaning. Wording in this book follows that used in the Barnes and Noble edition unless otherwise indicated.

Chapter 6

1. For biographical information on Joseph Smith, see Brodie, *No Man Knows My History* (the most widely read biography of Smith, it resulted in Brodie being excommunicated from the Mormon church); Bushman, *Joseph Smith: Rough Stone Rolling* (a highly detailed biography by a prominent historian who is a devout Mormon); Remini, *Joseph Smith* (a brief biography that argues Smith was a product of Jacksonian America); Vogel, *Joseph Smith: The Making of a Prophet*, and Swinton, *American Prophet*.

2. For details about the early history of the Mormon church, see any of the biographies in note 1 above; also, Ostling, *Mormon America*, pp. 1–76.

3. For Mormons in Missouri seen by their neighbors as voting in a bloc see Remini, p. 132, Brodie, pp. 225–227, and Bushman, p. 357.

4. For the Masons and William Morgan see Naparsteck, "The Morgan Affair," and Hicks, *The Federal Union*, pp. 452–454. For similarities between Masonic and Mormon rituals see Remini, p. 157.

5. Jachin and Boaz are the names of two 27-foot-high brass pillars in Solomon's Temple, the first Jewish temple in Jerusalem. There are two references to them in the Old Testament, in the First Book of Kings, Chapter 7, Verses 13–22 and Verses 41–42, and in Jeremiah, Chapter 52, Verses 21–23.

6. For Morgan's book see William Morgan, *Illustrations of Masonry*, "Printed for the Proprietor" (according to the copyright page), Rochester, New York, 1827. Available online at the Project Gutenberg Web site under the title *The Mysteries of Freemasonry*, http://www.gutenberg.org/files/18136/18136-h/18136-h.htm.

7. For the presidential election of 1832 see Brands, *Andrew Jackson*, pp. 473–475. See also sources in note 4 above, this chapter.

8. For biographical information on John Humphrey Noyes see Thomas, *The Man Who Would be Perfect*.

9. For the Oneida Community see Klaw, *Without Sin*.

10. For the Shakers see Stein, *The Shaker Experience in America*, and Stein, "The Shakers."

11. For the Harmony Society see Arndt, *George Rapp's Harmony Society*.

12. See Stark, *The Rise of Mormonism*, pp. 139–146. Stark writes (p. 142), "Projections require assumptions.... If, for example, we assume they will grow by a conservative 30 percent per decade, then in 2080 there will be nearly 64 million Later-day Saints. But, since World War II, the LDS growth rate has been far higher than 30 percent per decade. If we set the rate at 50 percent, then in 2080 there will be 267 million Mormons."

13. Historians have generally found it difficult to determine the exact number of wives Joseph Smith had or the order in which he married them because, since polygamy was illegal, official government records were not kept. The same is true of Brigham Young and other high-ranking Mormons who had numerous wives. Typically, the first marriage was recorded in a government office, but subsequent marriages were either not recorded or recorded only in church records which, generally, have not been made available to non–Mormon historians. Brodie, who did have some access to church records (until she was excommunicated for writing *No Man Knows My History*, provides a list of 49 wives (pp. 335–336). She places Lucy Walker at number 26.

14. For Lucy Walker's letter see Brodie, pp. 477–479.

15. See Bushman, *Joseph Smith: Rough Stone Rolling*. Bushman's defense of Smith's plural marriages appears on pp. 323–327, 437–446, 490–496, 498–499.

16. Although by tradition the *History of the Church* is usually referred to as being "written" by Joseph Smith, it was mostly dictated by him, and parts were written by contemporaries of his who presumably knew what he wanted to say. At least 20 men are known to have contributed as scribes or writers, including Oliver Cowdery, John Whitmer, and Sidney Rigdon, all important figures in the early history of the church. It was first published as *History of Joseph Smith*, then as *History of the Church of Jesus Christ of Latter-day Saints*. It has often been referred to as *Documentary History of the Church*. The earliest, brief version was written in 1832, the later, longer version in 1838–1839, and acquaintances of Smith are known to have worked on it after he was murdered. Anyone researching the book should be aware that biographers of Smith and historians of the early church often use the titles interchangeably, and sometimes do not note the multiple authorship. The church began publishing a seven-volume edition in 1902 and completed the set in 1912. Edited by B.H. Roberts, that set is today widely considered the standard edition. The *History* is available online at two sites, http://www.kristus.dk/jkk/text.php?id=90000, and http://www.boap.org/LDS/History/History_of_the_Church/.

17. For Joseph Smith ordering the destruction of the *Nauvoo Expositor* see Bushman, pp. 539–541, Brodie, pp. 372, 374–377, Remini, p. 167, and Ostling, pp. 15–16, 64, 242. The lone issue of the *Nauvoo Expositor* that was published can be read online in a facsimile edition at http://www.solomonspalding.com/docs/exposit1.htm.

18. For splits in Mormon church leadership after the murder of Joseph Smith see note 25, Chapter 5.

19. For Polk and the admission of Texas to the Union see Borneman, *Polk: The Man Who Transformed the Presidency and America*. See also Anderson, *The Conquest of Texas*, pp. 211–212.

20. See Arrington, *Brigham Young: American Moses*.

21. Heber C. Kimball's defense of polygamy was made in a speech he delivered on April 6, 1857, in Great Salt Lake City (now Salt Lake City) at the dedication of a new storehouse for grain. See Kimball, *Journal of Discourses*.

Chapter 7

1. The essay "The Significance of the Frontier in American History" by Turner appears as a chapter in Turner, *The Frontier in American History*, and in Turner, *Frontier and Section*. It has also been published as a single volume.

2. For biographical information on Turner see Billington, *Frederick Jackson Turner*.

3. For a detailed summary of the scholarly debate surrounding Turner's views, see Taylor, editor, *The Turner Thesis: Concerning Frontier in American History*.

Selected Bibliography

Alexander, Thomas. *Utah, The Right Place*. Salt Lake City: Gibbs Smith, 1995.

Ambrose, Stephen. *Undaunted Courage*. New York: Simon & Schuster, 1996.

Anderson, Fred. *Crucible of War: The Seven Years' War and the Fate of Empire in British North America, 1754–1766*. New York: Knopf, 2000.

Anderson, Gary Clayton. *The Conquest of Texas: Ethnic Cleansing in the Promised Land, 1820–1875*. Norman: University of Oklahoma Press, 2005.

Anderson, Karen. "As Gentle as Little Lambs: Images of Huron and Montagnais-Naskapi Women in the Writings of the 17th Century Jesuits." *The Canadian Review of Sociology and Anthropology*, V. 25 (November 1988).

_____. *Chain Her by One Foot: The Subjugation of Women in Seventeenth-Century New France*. New York: Routledge, 1991.

Armstrong, William H. *Warrior in Two Camps: Ely Parker, Union General and Seneca Chief*. Syracuse: Syracuse University Press, 1978.

Arndt, Karl John Richard. *George Rapp's Harmony Society, 1978–1847*. Philadelphia: University of Pennsylvania Press, 1965.

Arrington, Leonard J. *Brigham Young: American Moses*. New York: Knopf, 1985.

Axtell, James. *The Invasion Within: The Contest of Cultures In Colonial North America*. New York: Oxford University Press, 1985.

Beckwourth, James P. *The Life and Adventures of James P. Beckwourth, Mountaineer, Scout, and Pioneer, and Chief of the Crow Nation Indians, Written from his own Dictation by T.D. Bonner*. Lincoln: University of Nebraska Press, 1972 (originally published in 1856).

Beebe, Rose Marie, Robert M. Senkewicz, and Jay I. Kislak. *Lands of Promise and Despair: Chronicles of Early California, 1535–1846*. Berkeley, CA: Heyday Books, 2001.

Billington, Ray Allen. *Frederick Jackson Turner*. New York: Oxford University Press, 1973.

_____, and Martin Ridge. *Westward Expansion: A History of the American Frontier*. New York: Macmillan, 1974.

Binnema, Theodore. "Hudson's Bay Company." In *Encyclopedia of the Great Plains*. Lincoln: University of Nebraska Press, 2004.

Borneman, Walter R. *Polk, the Man Who Transformed the Presidency and America*. New York: Random House, 2008.

Bradbury, John. *Travels in the Interior of America, in the Years 1809, 1810, and 1811*. 1819 (available at Gutenberg Project website).

Brady, Patricia. *A Being So Gentle: The Frontier Love Story of Rachel and Andrew Jackson*. New York: Macmillan, 2011.

Brands, H.W. *Andrew Jackson: His Life and Times*. New York: Doubleday, 2005.

Brodie, Fawn. *No Man Knows My History*. New York: Vintage Books, 1995 (first published in 1945).

_____. *Thomas Jefferson: An Intimate History*. New York: W.W. Norton, 1974.

Brooks, Juanita. *The Mountain Meadows Massacre*. Norman: University of Oklahoma Press, 1991 (first published in 1950).

Brown, Dee. *Bury My Heart at Wounded Knee: An Indian History of the American West.* New York: Holt, Rinehart & Winston, 1971.

Burstein, Andrew. *Jefferson's Secrets: Death and Desire* at Monticello. New York: Basic Books, 2005.

Bushman, Richard Lyman. *Joseph Smith: Rough Stone Rolling.* New York: Knopf, 2005.

Byman, Jeremy. *Showdown at High Noon: Witch-Hunts, Critics, and the End of the Western.* Lyman, MD: Scarecrow Press, 2004.

California Poison Hotline, http://www.calpoison.org/hcp/2011/callusvol9no1.htm.

Calloway, Colin G. *One Vast Winter Count: The Native American West before Lewis and Clark.* Lincoln: University of Nebraska Press, 2003.

Campbell, Marjorie Wilkins. *The North West Company.* New York: St. Martin's Press, 1957.

Caren, Maren Lockwood. "Oneida Community." *Encyclopedia of New York State.* Syracuse, NY: Syracuse University Press, 2005.

Carriker, Robert C. *Father Peter John de Smet: Jesuit in the West.* Norman: University of Oklahoma Press, 1995.

_____. "Pierre-Jean De Smet." *Encyclopedia of the Great Plains.* Lincoln: University of Nebraska Press, 2004.

Carson, Kit. *Kit Carson's Autobiography.* Edited by Milo Milton Quaife. Chicago: The Lakeside Press, R.R. Donnelley & Sons Co., 1935.

_____. *Kit Carson's Own Story of His Life.* Edited by Blanche C. Grant. Taos, NM: Privately published, 1926; republished in a facsimile edition by Sunstone Press, Santa Fe, New Mexico, 2006.

Cather, Willa. *Death Comes for the Archbishop.* New York: Vintage Books, 1971, (first published in 1927).

Cerami, Charles A. *Jefferson's Great Gamble: The Remarkable Story of Jefferson, Napoleon and the Men Behind the Louisiana Purchase.* Naperville, IL: Sourcebooks, 2003.

Chambers, William Nisbet. *Old Bullion Benton, Senator from the New West: Thomas Hart Benton.* Boston: Little, Brown, 1956.

Channing, Edward. *The Jeffersonian System.* Volume 12 in the American Nation: A History. New York: Harper & Brothers, 1906.

Christian, Shirley. *Before Lewis and Clark.* New York: Farrar, Straus, and Giroux, 2004.

Chuinard, Eldon G., M.D. *Only One Man Died.* Fairfield, WA: Ye Galleon Press, 1999.

Clark, William. All quotes from Clark in this book, unless otherwise cited, come from Jackson, *Letters of the Lewis and Clark Expedition* and Moulton, *The Lewis and Clark Journals* (because even many large public and academic libraries to not have copies of the unabridged journals of Lewis and Clark, the interested reader should consult the full journals at the Guttenberg Project [http://www.gutenberg.org/cache/epub/8419/pg8419.txt]).

Clyman, James. "James Clyman, His Diaries and Reminiscences." Edited by Charles L. Camp. *California Historical Society Quarterly,* 1925. In Froncek, *Voices From the Wilderness.*

Crockett, David. *A Narrative of the Life of David Crockett of the State of Tennessee, Written by Himself,* Knoxville: University of Tennessee Press, 1973 (first published in 1834).

Cuch, Forrest S., editor. *A History's of Utah's American Indians.* Salt Lake City: Utah Division of Indian Affairs and Utah Division of State History, 2000.

Cunningham, John. "The Tin Star." *Louis L'Amour Western Magazine (May 1995),* pp. 71–78, 80, (originally published in *Colliers* in 1947).

Dary, David. *The Santa Fe Trail: Its History, Legends, and Lore.* New York, Knopf, 2000.

Deloria, Vine, Jr. *Custer Died for Your Sins: An Indian Manifesto.* New York: Macmillan, 1969.

_____. *For This Land: Writings on Religion in America.* New York: Routledge, 1999.

Denton, Sally. *American Massacre.* New York: Knopf, 2003.

_____. *Passion and Principle: John and Jessie Fremont, The Couple Whose Power, Politics, and Love Shaped Nineteenth-Cen-*

tury America, New York: Bloomsbury, 2007.
de Smet, Pierre-Jean. *Oregon Missions and Travels Over the Rocky Mountains*. New York: E. Dunigan, 1847.
Diner, Hasia R. "American West, New York Jewish." In *Jewish Life in the American West*, edited by Ava F. Kahn. Los Angeles: Autry Museum of Western Heritage, 2002.
Dippie, Brian W. "Catlin, George." In *Encyclopedia of the Great Plains*. Lincoln: University of Nebraska Press, 2004.
Donnelly, Joseph P. *Jean de Brebeuf*. Chicago: Loyola University Press, 1975.
Drury, Clifford Merrill. *Henry Harmon Spalding*. Caldwell, ID: Caxton Printers, 1936.
Edwards, William P. "Narrative of the Capture and Providential Escape of Misses Frances and Alira Hall, Two Respectable Young Women (Sisters) of the Ages of 16 and 18 — Who Were Taken Prisoners By the Savages at a Frontier Settlement, Near Indian Creek, in May Last, When Fifteen of the Inhabitants Fell Victims to the Bloody Tomahawk and Scalping Knife; Among Whom Were the Parents of the Unfortunate Females. Likewise is Added, the Interesting Narrative of the Captivity and Sufferings of Philip Brigdon, A Kentuckian, Who Fell Into the Hands of the Merciless Savages on Their Return to Their Settlement, Three Days After the Bloody Massacre," 1832. The complete Edwards narrative can be found on line at the Open Book website, http://openlibrary.org/books/OL6586564M/Narrative_of_the_capture_and_providential_escape_of_Misses_Frances_and_Almira_Hall.
Englebert, Omer. *The Last of the Conquistadors, Junipero Serra, 1713–1784*. New York: Harcourt, Brace, 1956.
Ens, Gerhard J. "Metis." *Encyclopedia of the Great Plains*. Lincoln: University of Nebraska Press, 2004.
Exley, Jo Ella Powell. *Frontier Blood: The Saga of the Parker Family*. College Station: Texas A&M Press, 2001.
Fanselow, Julie. *Traveling the Lewis and Clark Trail*. Helena, MT: Falcon, 1994.

Filson, John. *The Adventures of Colonel Daniel Boon* [sic] *Containing a Narrative of the Wars of Kentucky*, with Daniel Boone, 1793 (available at Gutenberg Project website).
Flake, Kathleen. *The Politics of American Religious Identity*. Chapel Hill: University of North Carolina Press, 2004.
Flora, Stephenie. "Whitman Massacre: The Aftermath." At Oregonpioneers.com, 2004.
Flores, Dan L., editor. *Southern Counterpart to Lewis and Clark: The Freeman and Custis Expedition of 1806*. Norman: University of Oklahoma Press, 2002.
Fogel, Daniel. *Junipero Serra, The Vatican, and Enslavement Theology*. San Francisco: Ism Press, 1988.
Fone, Byrne R.S. *Homophobia: A History*. New York: Metropolitan Books, 2000.
Frémont, John C. *The Life of Col. John Charles Frémont, and His Narrative of Explorations and Adventures, in Kansas, Nebraska, Oregon and California*. New York and Auburn: Miller, Orton & Mulligan, 1856.
Froncek, Thomas, editor. *Voices from the Wilderness: The Frontiersman's Own Story*. New York: McGraw-Hill, 1974.
Furtwangler, Albert. *Bringing Indians to the Book*. Seattle: University of Washington Press, 2005.
Gass, Patrick. *Gass's Journal of the Lewis and Clark Expedition*. Chicago: A.C. McClurg & Co., 1904.
Greene, Jerome A. *Washita, the U.S. Army and the Southern Cheyennes, 1867–1869*. Norman: University of Oklahoma Press, 2004.
Gregg, John B., and Pauline S. Gregg. *Dry Bones, Dakota Territory Reflected, An Illustrated Descriptive Analysis of the Health and Well-Being of Previous People and Cultures as Is Mirrored in Their Remnants*. Sioux Falls: University of South Dakota Press, 1987. (Available online at http://www.uiowa.edu/~anthro/paleopathology/drybones/cover.html).
Guice, John D.W., editor. *By His Own Hand? The Mysterious Death of Meriwether Lewis*. Norman: University of Oklahoma Press, 2006.

Gwynne, S.S. *Empire of the Summer Moon: Quanah Parker and the Rise and Fall of the Comanches, the Most Powerful Tribe in American History*. New York: Scribner, 2010.

Hackel, Steven W. *Children of Coyote, Missionaries of Saint Francis: Indian-Spanish Relations in Colonial California, 1769–1850*. Chapel Hill: University of North Carolina Press, 2005.

Haley, James L. *Sam Houston*. Norman: University of Oklahoma Press, 2002.

Hall, Brian. *I Should Be Extremely Happy in Your Company: A Novel of Lewis and Clark*. New York: Viking, 2003.

Hamalaimen, Pekka. "Seven Oaks Massacre." *Encyclopedia of the Great Plains*. Lincoln: University of Nebraska Press, 2004.

Hans, Birgit. "Captivity Narratives." *Encyclopedia of the Great Plains*. Lincoln: University of Nebraska Press, 2004.

Harrison, Julia D. *Metis: People Between Two Worlds*. Vancouver, British Columbia: Glenbow-Alberta Institute in association with Douglas & McIntyre, 1985.

Hausdoerffer, John. *Catlin's Lament: Indians, Manifest Destiny, and the Ethics of Nature*. Lawrence: University of Kansas, 2009.

Hayes, Derek. *First Crossing: Alexander Mackenzie, His Expedition Across North America, and the Opening of the Continent*. Seattle, WA: Sasquatch Books, 2001.

Henry, Alexander. *Travels and Adventures in Canada and the Indian Territories between the Years 1760 and 1776*. I. Riley, 1809 (available at Gutenberg Project website).

Hicks, John D., George E. Mowry, and Robert E. Burke. *The Federal Union: A History of the United States to 1877*, and *The American Nation, A History of the United States from 1865 to the Present*. Boston: Houghton Mifflin Company, 1965.

Howard, Joseph Kinsey. *Strange Empire: A Narrative of the Northwest*. New York: Morrow, 1952.

Huel, Raymond. "Louis Riel." *Encyclopedia of the Great Plains*. Lincoln: University of Nebraska Press, 2004.

Igle, Ida Rae, editor. "Affidavit of Oral Testimony." *No Rooms of Their Own: Women Writers of Early California, 1849–1869*. Berkeley, CA: Heyday Books, 1992.

———. "Charlotte L. Brown." *No Rooms of Their Own: Women Writers of Early California, 1849–1869*. Berkley, CA: Heyday Books, 1992.

Jackson, Donald, editor. *Letters of the Lewis and Clark Expedition, With Related Documents, 1773–1854*. Urbana: University of Illinois Press, 1962.

———. *Thomas Jefferson and the Stony Mountains; Exploring the West from Monticello*. Urbana: University of Illinois Press, 1981.

Jefferson, Thomas. All quotes from Jefferson in this volume come from Jackson, *Letters of the Lewis and Clark Expedition*.

Jeffrey, Julie Roy. *Converting the West: A Biography of Narcissa Whitman*, Norman: University of Oklahoma Press, 1991.

Jenkins, Steuben. "Historical Address at the Wyoming Monument." http://www.inmanfamily.org/documents/battlewyo.htm.

Jones, Nard. *The Great Command: The Story of Marcus and Narcissa Whitman and the Oregon Country Pioneers*. Boston: Little, Brown, 1959.

Journals of the Military Expedition of Major General John Sullivan Against the Six Nations of Indians in 1779 with Records of Centennial Celebrations. Freeport, NY: Books for Libraries Press, 1972.

Kelly, Fanny. *Narrative of My Captivity Among the Sioux Indians*. Edited and with a Prologue and Epilogue by Clark C. Spence and Mary Lee Spence. Barnes & Noble Books, 1990 (first published in 1871). A slightly different version of the book can be found online at Google Books at ttp://books.google.com/books?id=wn8TAAAAYAAJ&q=Your+memorialist+#v=snippet&q=in%20companionship&f=false.

Killoren, John J. "Come Blackrobe." *De Smet and the Indian Tragedy*. Norman: University of Oklahoma Press, 1994.

Kimball, Heber C. *Journal of Discourses*. v. 5, p. 22. The *Journal of Discourses* can be found online at http://jod.mrm.org/1.

Klaw, Spencer. *Without Sin: The Life and Death of the Oneida Community*. New York: Allen Lane, 1993.

Krakauer, Jon. *Under the Banner of Heaven.* New York: Doubleday, 2003.

Kukla, Jon. *A Wilderness So Immense: The Louisiana Purchase and the Destiny of America.* New York: Alfred A. Knopf, 2003.

Law, William, Wilson Law, Charles Ivins, Francis M. Higbee, Chauncey L. Higbee, Robert D. Foster, Charles A. Foster, publishers and editors. *Nauvoo (IL) Expositor*, June 7, 1844. A facsimile edition of the lone issue of this newspaper is available online at http://www.solomonspalding.com/docs/expositl.htm.

Le May, Alan. *The Searchers.* New York: Harper & Brothers, 1954. Basis for 1956 movie of the same name, directed by John Ford, script by Frank S. Nugent and starring John Wayne, Jeffrey Hunter, Vera Miles, Ward Bond, and Natalie Wood.

Leonard, Zenas. *Narrative of the Adventures of Zenas Leonard, a Native of Clearfield County, Pa., Who Spent Five Years in Trapping for Furs, Trading with the Indians, &c., &c., of the Rocky Mountains; Written by Himself.* D. W. Moore, 1839 (available at Gutenberg Project website).

Lewis, Meriwether. All quotes from Lewis in this book, unless otherwise cited, come from Jackson, *Letters of the Lewis and Clark Expedition* and Moulton, *The Lewis and Clark Journals* (because even many large public and academic libraries to not have copies of the unabridged journals of Lewis and Clark, the interested reader should consult the full journals at the Guttenberg Project [http://www.gutenberg.org/cache/epub/8419/pg8419.txt]).

MacGregor, Greg. *Lewis & Clark Revisited: A Photographer's Trail.* Seattle: University of Washington Press, 2004.

Madsen, Brigham D. *The Lemhi: Sacajawea's People.* Caldwell, ID: Caxton Printers, 1979.

_____. *The Shoshoni Frontier and the Bear River Massacre.* Salt Lake City: University of Utah Press, 1985.

Mann, John W.W. *Sacajawea's People: The Lemhi Shoshones and the Salmon River Country.* Lincoln: University of Nebraska Press, 2004.

Marks, Paula Mitchell. *In a Barren Land: American Indian Dispossession and Survival.* New York: William Morrow, 1998.

McGinity, Brian. *The Oatman Massacre: A Tale of Desert Captivity and Survival.* Norman: University of Oklahoma Press, 2004.

McLynn, Frank. *Wagons West: The Epic Story of America's Overland Trails.* New York: Grove Press, 2002.

Miller, Lee, editor. *From the Hearts: Voices of the American Indian:* New York: Knopf, 1995.

Moquin, Wayne, and Charles Van Doren, editors. *Great Documents in American History.* New York: Praeger, 1973.

Morgan, Henry Louis. *Ancient Society.* Edited by Leslie A. White. Cambridge, MA: The John Harvard Library, The Belknap Press of Harvard University Press, 1964 (first published in 1877).

_____. *League of the Iroquois.* Secaucus, NJ: Carol Publishing, 1993 (first published in 1851).

Morgan, William. *Illustrations of Masonry.* "Printed for the Proprietor" (according to the copyright page), Rochester, New York, 1827. (Available online at the Project Gutenberg website under the title *The Mysteries of Freemasonry* (http://www.gutenberg.org/files/18136/18136-h/18136-h.htm.)

Moring, John. *Men With Sand: Great Explorers of the North American West.* Helena, MT: Twodot, 1998.

Morris, Larry. *The Fate of the Corps: What Became of the Lewis and Clark Explorers After the Expedition.* New Haven, CT: Yale University Press, 2004.

Moulton, Gary, editor. *The Lewis and Clark Journals.* Abridged edition. Lincoln: University of Nebraska, 2003.

Munn, Michael. *John Wayne: The Man Behind the Myth.* New York: Penguin, 2005.

Naparsteck, Martin. "The Morgan Affair." *Genesee Country.* New York: Avon, April/May 1994.

Newman, Peter Charles. *Empire of the Bay: The Company of Adventurers That Seized a Continent.* New York: Penguin Books, 2000.

Nugent, Frank S. (screenplay) *The Searchers* (1956). Directed by John Ford, Starring John Wayne, Jeffrey Hunter, Vera Miles, Ward Bond, and Natalie Wood.

Oregon Spectator, January 20, 1848. www.oregonpioneers.com/whitman3.htm.

Osborn, William M. *The Wild Frontier: Atrocities During the American-Indian War From Jamestown Colony to Wounded Knee*. New York: Random House, 2000.

Ostling, Richard N., and Joan K. Ostling. *Mormon America*. San Francisco: Harper, 1999.

O'Sullivan, John L. "Annexation." *The United States Magazine and Democratic Review*, July/August 1845.

_____. Untitled article. *New York Morning News*, December 27, 1845.

Page, Jake, editor. *Sacred Land of Indian America*. New York: Harry N. Abrams, 2001.

Paton, Bruce. *Lewis & Clark: Doctors in the Wilderness*. Golden, CO: Fulcrum Publishing, 2001.

Plummer, Rachel. *Rachel Plummer's Narrative of Twenty-One Months Servitude as a Prisoner Among the Comanche Indians*. Austin, TX: Jenkins Publishing Company, 1977. The full *Narrative* is included in VanDerBeets, *Held Captive by Indians*. All parenthetical page references in the text refer to the VanDerbeets edition.

Powell, Mary Lucas, and Della Collins Cook, *The Myth of Syphilis: The Natural History of Treponematosis in North America*. Gainsville: University Press of Florida, 2005.

Punke, Michael. *The Revenant*. New York: Carroll & Graf, 2002 (a novel about Hugh Glass).

Purich, Donald J. *The Metis*. Toronto: Lorimer & Company, 1988.

Remini, Robert V. New York: *Joseph Smith*. Viking, 2002.

Rippy, J. Fred. *Joel R. Poinsett, Versatile American*. Durham, NC: Duke University Press, 1935.

Roberts, David. *A Newer World: Kit Carson, John C. Fremont, and the Claiming of the American West*. New York: Simon & Schuster, 2000.

_____. *The Pueblo Revolt: The Secret Rebellion that Drove the Spaniards out of the Southwest*. New York: Simon & Schuster, 2004.

Robston, Lucia St. Clair. *Ride the Wind: The Story of Cynthia Ann Parker and the Last Days of the Comanche*. New York: Ballantine, 2001.

Rolle, Andrew. *John Charles Fremont: Character as Destiny*. Norman: University of Oklahoma Press, 1991.

Rowlandson, Mary. *The Captivity and Deliverance of Mrs. Mary Rowlandson, of Lancaster, Who Was Taken by the French and Indians*. 1675, in VanDerBeets, *Held Captive by Indians*.

Russell, Osborne. *Journal of a Trapper: A Hunter's Rambles Among the Wild Regions of the Rocky Mountains, 1834–1843*. Edited by Aubrey L. Haines. New York: Barnes & Noble Books, undated (first published in 1914).

_____. Letter written by Russell to his sister, Eleanor Read, dated August 26, 1855 (with thanks to Kathryn James of Yale University Library for providing me with a copy).

Russell, William D. "King James Strang: Joseph Smith's Successor." In *Mormon Mavericks*, edited by John Sillito and Susan Staker. Salt Lake City: Signature Books, 2002.

Ruxton, George Frederick. "Life in the Far West." *Blackwood's Edinburgh Magazine*, September 1848 (available at the Gutenberg Project website).

Sagard, Gabriel. *The Long Journey to the Country of the Hurons*. Edited by George M. Wrong. The Champlain Society, 1939 (available on line at http://champlainsociety.ca/).

Sampson, Robert D. *John L. O'Sullivan and His Times*. Kent, OH: Kent State University Press, 2003.

Sanchez, Joseph P. *Explorers, Traders, and Slavers: Forging the Old Spanish Trail, 1678–1850*. Salt Lake City: University of Utah Press, 1997.

Seaver, James E. *A Narrative of the Life of Mrs. Mary Jemison*. North Haven, CT: Linnet Books, 1995 (originally published in 1823). Available at Gutenberg Project website at http://www.gutenberg.org/cache/epub/6960/pg6960.html.

Sells, Jeffery E., editor. *God and Country: Politics in Utah*. Salt Lake City: Signature Books, 2005.

Shoumatoff, Alex. *Legends of the American Desert: Sojourns in the Greater Southwest.* New York: Knopf, 1997.

Simmons, Marc. *Kit Carson & His Three Wives.* Albuquerque: University of New Mexico Press, 2003.

Sisby, Robert W. *The Holland Land Company in Western New York*, Buffalo, NY: Buffalo and Erie County Historical Society, 1961.

Smith, James. *An account of the Remarkable Occurences in the Life and Travels of Col. James Smith During His Captivity with the Indians, in the years 1755, '56, '57, '58 & '59.* John Bradford, 1799 (available at the Gutenberg Project website).

Smith, Joseph. "Translator." *The Book of Mormon.* Church of Jesus Christ of Latter-day Saints, 1981 (first published in 1830).

Smith, Joseph, et. al. *History of the Church,* Salt Lake City: Deseret Books, Salt Lake City, 1832, 1838–39, 1902–12.

Southerton, Simon G. *Losing a Lost Tribe: Native Americans, DNA, and the Mormon Church.* Salt Lake City: Signature Books, 2004.

Speek, Vickie Cleverley. *"God Has Made Us a Kingdom." James Strang and the Midwest Mormons.* Salt Lake City: Signature Books, 2006.

Sprague, Marshall. *So Vast, So Beautiful a Land: Louisiana and the Purchase.* Boston: Little, Brown, 1974.

Stack, Peggy Fletcher. "Brigham Document to Be Sold." *Salt Lake Tribune*, May 28, 2005.

Stansbury, (Captain) Howard. *An Expedition to the Valley of the Great Salt Lake of Utah.* 1852 (available at the Gutenberg Project website).

Stark, Rodney. *The Rise of Mormonism.* New York: Columbia University Press, 2005.

Starrs, Paul F. *Let the Cowboy Ride.* Baltimore, MD: The Johns Hopkins University Press, 1998.

Stein, Stephen J. *The Shaker Experience in America: A History of the United Society of Believers.* New Haven, CT: Yale University Press, 1992.

_____. "Shakers." *Encyclopedia of New York State.* Syracuse, NY: Syracuse University Press, 2005.

Stratton, Royal B. *Captivity of the Oatman Girls, Being an Interesting Narrative of Life Among the Apache and Mohave Indians.* Alexandria, VA: Time-Life Books, 1982 (reprint of original published by Carlton & Porter, New York, 1857).

Swinton, Heidi. *American Prophet.* Salt Lake City: Shadow Mountain, 1999.

Talbot, Francis Xavier. *Saint Among the Hurons.* New York: Harper and Brothers, 1949.

Tanner, John. *A Narrative of the Captivity and Adventures of John Tanner, (U.S. interpreter at the Saut de Ste. Marie,) During Thirty Years Residence among the Indians in the Interior of North America.* Written with Edwin James, M.D. 1830 (available at Gutenberg Project website).

Taylor, George Rogers, editor. *The Turner Thesis: Concerning the Role of the Frontier in American History.* Lexington, MA: D.C. Heath and Company, 1972.

Terrell, A.W. "Recollections of General Sam Houston." *Southwestern Historical Quarterly,* Texas State Historical Association, volume 16, number 2, (October 1912): pp. 113–136.

Thomas, Robert David. *The Man Who Would Be Perfect: John Humphrey Noyes and the Utopian Impulse.* Philadelphia: University of Pennsylvania Press, 1977.

Thwaites, Reuben Gold, editor. *The Jesuit Relations and Allied Documents.* Cleveland, OH: The Burrows Brothers Company, 1898.

Tome, Philip. *Pioneer Life; or, Thirty Years a Hunter, Being Scenes and Adventures in the Life of Philip Tome.* 1854 (available at Gutenberg Project website).

Tooker, Elisabeth. *An Ethnography of the Huron Indians: 1615–1649.* Washington: D.C.: United States Government Printing Office, 1964.

Trexler, Richard C. *Sex and Conquest: Gendered Violence, Political Order, and the European Conquest of the Americas.* Ithaca, NY: Cornell University Press, 1995.

Trigger, Bruce. *The Children of Aataentsic: A History of the Huron People to 1660.* Volume 2. Montreal, Canada: McGill-Queens's University Press, 1987.

_____. *Huron: Farmers of the North.* New

York: Holt, Rinehart, and Winston, 1969.

Turner, Frederick Jackson, *Frontier and Section: Selected Essays*, Englewood Cliffs, NJ: Prentice-Hall, 1961.

_____. *The Frontier in American History.* New York: Henry Holt, 1920.

_____. *The Significance of the Frontier in American History.* Ithaca, NY: Cornell University Press, 1956 (a single volume reprint of an essay with the same title first published in 1894).

Twain, Mark. *Life on the Mississippi.* Mineola, NY: Dover Publications, 2000 (first published in 1883).

_____. *Roughing It.* New York: Signet, 1980 (first published in 1872).

Udall, Stewart L. *The Forgotten Founders: Rethinking the History of the Old West.* Washington, D.C.: Shearwater, 2002.

Utley, Robert M. *A Life Wild and Perilous: Mountain Men and the Paths to the Pacific.* New York: Henry Holt, 1997.

VanDerBeets, Richard, editor. *Held Captive by Indians: Selected Narratives, 1642–1836.* Knoxville: University of Tennessee Press, 1973.

Vogel, Dan. *Joseph Smith: The Making of a Prophet.* Salt Lake City: Signature Books, 2004.

Weidhorn, Manfred. "*High Noon*: Liberal Classic? Conservative Screed?" *Bright Lights Film Journal*, February 2005. brightlightsfilm.com.

Welke, Barbara Y. "Rights of Passage." In *African American Women Confront the West, 1600–2000,* edited by Quintard Taylor and Shirley Ann Wilson Moore. Norman: University of Oklahoma Press, 2003.

Whitman, Narcissa. *The Letters of Narcissa Whitman.* Fairfield, WA: Ye Galleon Press, 2002.

_____. *My Journal, 1836.* Fairfield, WA: Ye Galleon Press, 1982.

Wilson, Elinor. *Jim Beckwourth, Black Mountain Man and War Chief of the Crows.* Norman: University of Oklahoma Press, 1972.

Wishart, David J. "Native American Gender Roles." *Encyclopedia of the Great Plains.* Lincoln: University of Nebraska Press, 2004.

Yenne, Bill. *Indian Wars: The Campaign for the American West.* Yardley, PA: Westholme, 2005.

Yount, George C. "The Chronicles of George C. Yount" Edited by Charles L. Camp. *California Historical Society Quarterly*, v. 2 (1923): pp. 26–33.

Index

Aberdeen, Lord 59
Abernethy, George 85, 87
Aespaneo 124–126
Alabama 90, 94
Alamo 93
Alger, Fanny 164
Allen, Ebenezer 117, 210n
Allen, Eliza 91, 209n
Allen County, Kansas 159
American Board of Commissioners for Foreign Missions 58
American Philosophical Society 13, 14
American Revolution 116, 161, 210n
Ancient Society 67
Andy (former slave) 133, 134
"Annexation" 5, 187–192
Anti-Masonic Party 168
Arizona 80, 81, 123, 124, 129, 165, 177
Arkansas 181, 182
Arkansas River 91, 92
Articles of Confederation 68
Ash Hollow, Battle of 159
Austin, Texas 104
Avery, Waighstill 95, 99

Bannock City, Montana 133, 198
Batavia, New York 165, 166, 167, 168, 210n
Bear River Massacre 130, 182, 211n
Beauvais, Geminien 152
Beckwourth, James 38, 49–52, 53, 54, 57, 207n
Benton, Jesse 101
Benton, Thomas Hart 33, 36, 101, 102, 206n
Bent's Fort 38
berdache 29, 205n
Bewley, Crockett 84
Bewley, Lorinda 84, 85, 87
Bexar, Texas 93
Bighorn River 43
Billings, Montana 43

Bingham, C.E. 128
Black Bear 144
Black Foot 155
Black Hawk 109
Black Hawk War (Illinois) 87, 109
Blackwell, Elizabeth 156–157
Blanchet, Bishop Magloire 85
Blynn, Clara 157
Blynn, Willie 157
Boggs, Gov. Lilburn 87, 162, 175
Book of Mormon 162, 163, 176, 178, 181
Boone, Daniel 36
Bowdoinham, Maine 52
Bowie, Jim 93
Boyeau, Mary 139–141
Brewster, James Colin 123, 126
Bridger, Jim 45–47, 48, 52
Brigdon, Philip 110–111
Brouillet, Father 85
Brown, Charlotte 121–122
Brown, Judge Henry 167
Brown, Hiram 173
Buchanan, James 35, 181
Buckner, Alexander 92
Buell, Norman 170
Buell, Prescindia Huntington 170
Bureau of Indian Affairs 72
Burr, Aaron 14, 99, 100
Bushman, Richard Lyman 171–172, 211n

Cache Valley, Utah and Idaho 182
California 10, 13, 26, 35, 52, 55, 56, 76, 81, 82, 123, 124, 125, 126, 127, 129, 132, 177, 180, 181, 187, 190, 191, 192
California Gold Rush 10, 132, 180, 181
Callis, Dona Eulalia 82
calomel 17, 26; *see also* mercury pills
Cameahwait 22
Camp Fortunate 22
Camp Wood 17
Canandaigua, New York 165, 166, 167, 168

223

Canfield, Edna Amelia 130
captivity narratives 105, 108, 110, 111, 124, 131, 134, 150, 154, 160
Captivity of the Oatman Girls 127, 130
Carlyle, Thomas 89, 209n
Carroll, William 101
Carson, Adeline 38, 39
Carson, Kit 34, 35, 36–41, 46, 48, 206n, 207n
Carson, Maria Josefa Jaramillo 39, 40
Carthage, Illinois 123, 174, 175
Casper, Wyoming 61
Castile, New York 119
Cather, Willa 40, 207n
Catherine the Great 13
Catholic Church *see* Roman Catholic Church
Catlet, Hanson 100
Catlin, George 111, 112
Cedar City, Utah 181
Census, United States 10, 133, 179, 184
Chaney, Lon, Jr. 8
Charbonneau, Toussaint 19, 20, 21, 24, 26
Cheesboro, Nicholas 167
Chief Joseph 26
Chili, New York 129
Chivington, John 38
Chuinard, Eldon 21
Church of Jesus Christ of Latter-day Saints, *see* Mormons
Cincinnati 156, 160, 185
Civil War 6, 11, 72, 132, 153, 160, 175, 179, 180, 181
Clark, George Rogers 13
Clark, Henry 168
Clark, William 2, 3, 13, 16–24, 26–30, 31, 42–43, 47, 58, 77, 78, 89, 186, 187, 195–196, 204n, 205n
Clemens, Orion 179, 180
Clinton, Gov. DeWitt 166, 167
Colorado River 123, 124, 125
Colter, John 26, 42–44, 47, 48, 88, 207n
Columbia River 25, 59, 193, 196
Columbus, Christopher 16, 24, 78, 80, 83
Commission on Indian Affairs, 72
Community of Christ *see* Reorganized Church of Latter Day Saints
complex marriage 169
Confederate States of America, 6, 94, 128
Constitution of the United States 14, 15, 68, 188, 201
Corbett, Margaret 35
Cornplanter 116–117
Corps of Discovery 16, 19, 27, 28, 42, 43, 47, 58

Council Bluffs, Iowa 46, 60, 61
Cowdery, Oliver 164, 212n
Cowper, William 155
Cox, Jacob 158
Crockett, Davy 91, 93
Cuba 6
Cumming, Alfred 181, 183
Cunningham, John 8, 9
Custer, Lt. Col. George Armstrong 60, 157
Custer Died for Your Sins 60, 207n
Custis, Peter 14

Dakota Territory 132
Davids, John 166
Davis, Jefferson 181
Death Comes to the Archbishop 40, 207n
Deer Creek Station, Wyoming 136
Defoe, Daniel 155
Deloria, Vine 60, 207n
Democratic Review 5, 187
Deseret 177, 178, 181
De Smet, Pierre-Jean 60–61, 62, 88
Dickewamis *see* Jemison, Mary
Dickinson, Angie 9
Dickinson, Charles 99
Diner, Hasia R. 10
Dixon, Joseph 43
Doctrine and Covenants 199
Donelson, Alexander 101
Doniphan, Gen. Alexander 162
Donoho, Mary 108
Donoho, William 108
Douglas, Elmore 92
Douglas, Wyoming 133
Drouillard, George 19
Duley, Laura 141
Duley, Capt. William J. 141
Dunhamn, Jonathan 175
Du Pratz, Le Page 78, 208n
Dyer, Russell 166

Edwards, William P. 109–111
Egosegalonicha 143–144
Ellsworth, Kansas 156
Elmira, New York 116
Erwin, Joseph 99, 100
Espaniola 127
Eubanks, Lucinda 155

Fages, Pedro 82
Fairchild, John Brant 129–130
The Far Horizons 23, 204n
Far West, Missouri 168
Farmington, Michigan 129
Fast Bear 158

Field, Reuben 26
Fillmore, Millard 35, 180, 181
Fisk, Capt. James Liberty 146, 147, 159
Fitzgerald, John S. 45–46
Fitzpatrick, Thomas 59, 61
Five Crows 84–85, 87
Floyd, Charles 26
Follett, King 172
Ford, John 127, 185, 211n
Ford, Gov. Thomas 175
Fort Atkinson 46
Fort Bridger 47, 181
Fort Clapsop 25
Fort Duquesne 113, 114
Fort Gibson 92
Fort Hall 53
Fort Hays 156
Fort Laramie 72, 112, 152, 155, 198
Fort Niagara 115, 167
Fort Parker 104
Fort Pitt 114
Fort Sully 132, 153, 155, 158, 199
Fort Yuma 126, 127
Foster, Robert 174–175
France 11, 14, 15, 60, 188, 192
Francisans 62, 64, 79, 80, 81, 88; *see also* Recollects
Francisco 126
Franklin (former slave) 133, 134
Franklin, Benjamin 165
Franklin, Texas 104
free trapper 52
Freeman, Thomas 14
Freemasons 165–168
Frémont, Anne 31–32
Frémont, Jessie (Benton) 33–36, 40, 102, 206n
Frémont, John C. 31–36, 40, 77, 102
French and Indian War 113, 210n
The Frontier in American History 184

Galena, Illinois 110
Galveston, Texas 93
Gardow Flats 116
Gass, Sgt. Patrick 17
Genesee River 113, 116, 120
Geneseo, New York 115, 116
Geneva, Kansas 132
Genishau 115
Gentry, Tiana Rogers 92
Gettysburg, Pennsylvania 113
Gibson, George 25, 26, 205
Gila River 123
Gilliam, Cornelius 87–88
Gilliland, Isaac 84

Glass, Hugh 45–46, 47
golden plates 163
gonorrhea 16, 17, 18, 20, 21, 22, 24, 25
Goodrich, Sills 25, 26, 205
Gordon, William 160
Grand River 16, 45
Grand Tetons 43
Grant, Ulysses S. 72, 158
Gray, John 61
Great Britain 5, 48, 59, 60, 116, 169, 177
Great Salt Lake Valley 3, 176, 178, 179
Greeley, Horace 103
Green River 53
Grey, Zane 131, 184

Haines, Aubrey L. 54–55, 56
Hale, Emma (Smith) 163, 164, 170, 171, 173, 176
Hall, Almira 109–110
Hall, Frances 109–110
Hallowell, Maine 55
Hamilton, Alexander 13, 99, 100
Hancock, Clarista Reed 170
Hancock, Forest 43
Hancock, Julia 23, 30
Hancock, Levi 170
handcart companies 179
Handsome Lake 69
Harmony, Pennsylvania 169
Harmony Society 169
Harney, Gen. William 159
Harris, George Washington 168
Harris, Lucinda (Morgan) 165
Harrison's Mill, Kentucky 100
Haun's Mills 162
Hawks, Howard 8, 9
Hays, Stockley 101
Henry, Andrew 45, 46
Heston, Charlton 23
Hidalgo, Fray Nicolas 80
High Noon 7–9
Hill Cumorah 163
Hiokatoo 115, 117, 118, 119
History of the Church 173, 212
Ho-de-no-sau-nee see League of the Iroquois
homosexuality 27, 28, 29, 30, 42, 65, 205n
Hooker, Nancy 44
Horseshoe Bend, Battle of 90
House Un-American Activities Committee 8
Houston, Margaret Moffette Lea 94
Houston, Sam 2, 89, 90–95, 102, 104
Houston, Texas 93, 108
Howard, Thomas Proctor 26
Hudson's Bay Company 55, 59, 77, 78, 79, 85, 87

Index

Hunter, Jeffrey 128
Hurley, Mary 133, 135, 136, 155, 198
Hyde, Orson 164

Idaho 18, 19, 22, 59, 130, 133, 181, 182, 211n
Idaho Territory 53, 133
Iliad 90
Illustrations of Masonry 166
Independence, Missouri 176
Indian Nations 13, 31, 48, 94, 143, 155, 210n; Apache 37, 123, 127–130; Arapaho 38; Arikara 16–18, 45; Assiniboin 139; Blackfeet 41, 43–44, 50, 53, 137, 148–149, 151–152; Brule Sioux 27, 158; Cayuga 67–68; Cayuse 47, 55, 58–60, 82–88; Cherokee 2, 90, 92–94, 102–103, 119, 128, 133; Cheyenne 37–39, 41–42, 51, 157; Chinook 25; Clapsop 42; Comanche 104–109, 111, 114, 128, 150; Creek 90, 102; Crow 43, 49, 51, 54; Delaware 42, 53, 67, 68, 103, 114, 115; Flathead 47, 48, 52–54, 60; Gro-rout 198; Hidatsa 19, 22, 24, 29, 204n; Huncpa-pa 198; Huron 62–67, 69, 77, 88, 208n; Iroquois Confederacy 49, 53, 62, 66–72, 78, 116–117, 208n; Lakota Sioux 112; Mandan 18, 20, 23, 25, 42, 48, 111; Mohave 124–130; Mohawk 67–68; Navajo 37; Nez Percé 26, 27, 59, 75, 83, 88, 205n; Oglala Sioux 131, 147–149, 155, 159, 198; Oneida 68; Onondaga 67; Paiute 182; Pawnee 72; Pima 126; Potawatomi 61; Rees 198; Sac and Fox 87; Santee Sioux 139–141; Seminole 87; Seneca 63, 67, 69, 72, 114–121, 150, 158, 208n; Shawnee 113–114; Shoshoni 18–20, 22–25, 42, 48, 130, 156, 182, 204n, 211n; Sioux 112–113, 118, 131–133, 137–139, 143, 145, 147–150, 153–156, 158–160 (*see also* Brule; Hunc-pa-pa; Lakota; Oglala; Santee; Teton; and Yankton); Snake 54; Southern Cheyenne 38; Teton Sioux 17, 27; Tolkepaya 122–123; Tuscarora 68; Ute 47, 156, 181; Western Yavapai 123; Winnebago 110; Yankton Sioux 151–152; Yazoo 78; Yuma 82
Indian Territory 92
Irataba 129
Islam 170

Jachin and Boaz 166, 212n
Jackson, Andrew 2, 89, 91, 92, 95–103, 161, 165, 168, 211n
Jackson, Rachel Robards 95–97, 99, 101–102
Jacobs, Henry 170

Jacobs, Zina Dianthia Huntington 170
Jean Baptiste (Pomp) 23, 26
Jefferson, Thomas 2, 3, 13–16, 20, 24, 28–30, 45, 78, 89, 185, 187, 192–194, 203n, 205n, 209n
Jemison, Betsey 115
Jemison, Jane (daughter of Mary Jemison) 115
Jemison, Jane (mother of Mary Jemison) 113
Jemison, Jesse 115, 119
Jemison, John 115, 118–120
Jemison, Mary 113–121, 127–128, 131, 137, 150
Jemison, Nancy 116
Jemison, Polly 116
Jemison, Thomas (father of Mary Jemison) 113, 115
Jemison, Thomas (son of Mary Jemison) 115, 118–119
Jesuits 60, 62, 64, 65, 66, 67, 77, 79, 88, 208n
Jews 10, 55, 154, 212n
John, Daniel 166–167
Johnson, Eli 164
Johnson, Gov. J. Neely 126
Johnson, Nancy Miranda 164
Jones, Dan 175
Journal of a Trapper 52
Jumping Bear 137, 152

Kansas 41, 132, 156, 159–160, 177, 197–198, 206n
Kearney, Gen. Stephen 35
Kellogg, Elizabeth 104
Kelly, Fanny 3, 131–160, 187, 187–199, 211n
Kelly, Grace 8
Kelly, Josiah (husband of Fanny Kelly) 132–134, 136, 148, 153–157, 159, 198–199
Kelly, Josiah (son of Fanny Kelly) 159
Kentucky 13, 36, 48, 96, 100, 110
Key, Francis Scott 92
Kimball, Herber C. 178–179, 213n
Kingsley, David 166–167
Kipling, Rudyard 165
Kirtland, Ohio 3, 162–165, 173
Knoxville, Tennessee 90, 97, 98

Labiche, Francis 19, 24, 26
Lake Simcoe 132
Lake Couchiching 132
Larimer, Sarah 133–134, 136, 157, 159–160, 198
Larimer, William 133–134, 157, 159, 160, 198
Law, Jane 174
Law, William 174, 175
Law, Wilson 174
Lawson, Loton 167

League of the Iroquois 53, 67, 69–72, 208n
Leavenworth, Co. Henry 46
Ledyard, John 13
Lee, John D. 183
LeMay, Alan 128, 211n
Lepage, Jean-Bapiste 26
Le Roy, New York 166
Lewis, Joe 82
Lewis, Meriwether 2–3, 13–31, 42–43, 47, 58, 77–78, 89, 185–187, 192–196, 204n, 205n
Lewiston, Idaho 59
Lewiston, Maine 55
Lightner, Adam 170
Lightner, Mary Elizabeth Rollins 170
Limerick, Patricia Nelson 185
Lincoln, Abraham 94, 140–141, 165, 177
Lisa, Manuel 43–44
Little Beard's Town 116
Lizette 23
Logan, Capt. John 154
Los Angeles Star 126
Louisiana Purchase *see* Louisiana Territory and Napoleon
Louisiana Territory 14–15
Lucas, Gen. Samuel 162
Luna, Antonia 38

Mackenzie, Alexander 78
Madison, James 14
Mahpeah 139
Making Out Road 39–42
Man-Afraid-of-His-Horses 148
Man in the Wilderness 46
Manifest Destiny 1–2, 5–7, 11, 76, 187–188
Manitoba 77
Manitoba Act (1870) 79
Marsh, Walter 84
Marsh Creek 113
Marshall, John (chief justice) 103
Marshall, John (discover of gold in California) 9
Marshall, Capt. Levi 143
Maryville, Tennessee 90
McCarthy, Joseph 8
McNairy, Nathaniel 99
McNeal, Hugh 26
measles 82–84, 86
mercury pills 18–19, 25–26, 30, 205n; *see also* calomel
Methodists 59, 79, 123, 127, 129, 133, 162
Metis 77–79
Mexico 2, 5, 10, 32, 37, 48, 59, 93, 107, 123, 165, 176–177, 180, 189–191
Mexico City 79, 81

Michaux, Andre 13
Miles, Nelson 27
Miller, David 166–168
Minto, John 112–113
missionaries 2–3, 29, 37, 53, 58–88, 89, 179, 186, 196–197, 207n
Mississippi 78
Mississippi River 13–14, 16, 32, 109, 162, 175, 179, 191
Missouri 3, 33, 36, 39, 47–49, 87, 92, 101, 108, 162–163, 165, 168, 173, 175–176
Missouri River 16, 20, 27, 32, 34, 43, 45, 46, 61, 77, 148, 192, 195, 196
Mohawk River 116
Mollhausen, Balduin 125
Moncache-ape 78, 208n
Montana 18, 19, 20, 22, 23, 43, 79, 133
Montana Territory 133, 198
Moonlight, Col. Thomas O. 155
Morgan, Henry Louis 53, 66–72, 208n
Morgan, Lucinda *see* Harris, Lucinda
Morgan, William 165–168
Mormon (angel) 163
Mormon Battalion 163
Mormon War 182–183
Mormons 3, 10, 42, 47, 87, 123, 151, 156, 161–165, 170–184, 186–187, 199–202, 211n, 211n, 212n
Moroni (angel) 163
Moss, John 129
Mount Morris, New York 119–120
Mountain Meadows Massacre 181–183
mountain men 2, 31–58, 61–62, 89, 186, 207n
Munroe, Timothy 168
mutual criticism 169

Napoleon 14–15
Narrative of My Captivity Among the Sioux Indians 131, 218n
Nashville, Tennessee 91, 95–96, 99–101
Natchez, Mississippi 96
Native Americans *see* Indians
Nauvoo, Illinois 164, 168, 171, 173, 174, 175, 178
Nauvoo Expositor 174–175
Nauvoo Legion 174
Nauvoo Neighbor 174
Neosho River 92
New Harmony, Indiana 169
New Lebanon, New York 169
New Mexico 36, 80–81, 106–108, 177
New Mexico Territory 8, 123
New Orleans 14, 15, 100
New Orleans, Battle of 102

New York Morning News 5
Newtown, New York 116
North American Review 5
North Beach and Mission Railroad 122
North Carolina 32, 36
North Platte River 61
North West Fur Company 78
Noyes, John Humphrey 169

Oak Orchard Creek, New York 168
Oatman, Charity Ann 123
Oatman, Lorenzo 123, 126, 127, 129, 130
Oatman, Lucy 123
Oatman, Mary Ann (daughter) 122, 124, 125, 126
Oatman, Mary Jane (mother) 123
Oatman, Olive 122–130, 154
Oatman, Roland 123
Oatman, Roys 123
Oatman, Roys, Jr.
O'Bail, Old John 116–117
Ogden, Peter 85–86
Ohio River 114
Oklahoma 2, 92, 102, 130, 157, 177
Old Faithful 43
Omnibus Railroad Company 122
Oneida Community 169
Ontario, Canada 62, 77, 132
Oolooteka 90, 92
Ordway, John 26
Oregon 31, 59, 60, 61, 177, 181, 192, 210n
Oregon Territory 5, 47, 53, 55, 58, 73, 76, 78, 82, 84, 87, 112, 127, 133, 176
Orilla, Ontario 132
O'Sullivan, John 5–6, 187–192
Ottawa (Sioux chief) 133, 139–140, 142–144, 146, 148–149, 152, 153
Ottawa, Canada 79
Otter Woman 19–20
Overton, John 96
Overton, Thomas 100

Palmyra, New York 161–163, 169
Parker, Benjamin 104
Parker, Cynthia Ann 104–105
Parker, Ely 67, 72, 158, 208n
Parker, John 104
Parker, Quanah 105
Parker, Samuel 58
Peta Nacona 104–105
Philadelphia 15, 21, 35, 68, 117, 159, 165, 179
Pierce, Franklin 181
Pierson, George Wilson 185
Pittsburgh 112–113, 185, 195–196
Placerville, California 55

Plummer, James Pratt 104–106, 108
Plummer, Luther (son of Rachel) 106
Plummer, Luther Thomas Martin (husband of Rachel) 106, 108–109
Plummer, Rachel 104–110, 114, 127, 130–131, 137, 150, 209n
Plummer, Wison 108–109
plural marriage 3, 163–164, 172–174, 186–187, 199–202; *see also* polygamy
Poinsett, Joel 32–34
Polk, James 35, 59, 93, 177, 180, 183
polygamy 2–3, 42, 60–61, 67, 82, 87–88, 111–112, 118, 143, 151, 164, 172–177, 180–184, 186–187, 199, 201–202
Porcupine 143–144
Portland, Oregon 59, 86
Potts, John 43
Prairie Flower 105
Pratt, Julius 6
Pratt, Sarah 168
Presbyterian Church 47, 53, 58, 60, 79, 85, 88, 162
Preston, Idaho 182
prostitution 1, 54, 205n
Pryor, John 31
Pryor, Nathaniel 26
pueblos 80–81
Puritans 10
Putney, Vermont 169

Quebec, Canada 32, 79
Quincy, Illinois 144, 196–197

Rath, Charles 41–42
Read, Lemuel 55
Recollects 62, 64–66, 79; *see also* Franciscans
Red Cloud 158
Reed, Donna 23
Regina, Saskatchewan 79
Remington, Frederick 184
Reorganized Church of Latter Day Saints 176
Richmond, Virginia 31, 46, 96
Riel, Louis 79
Rio Bravo 7–9
Robards, Lewis 95–96
Robertson, James 99
Robinson Crusoe 155
Rochester, Nathaniel 165
Rochester, New York 118, 129–130, 161, 165–168, 208n, 210n
Rockwell, Porter 175
Rocky Mountain Fur Company 52
Rodgers, Andrew 84

Rogers, Will 92
Rogue River 127
Roman Catholic Church 2, 27, 34, 60–65, 79–80, 85, 87–88, 170, 186
Roughing It 179–180
Rousseau, Father 85
Russell, Osburne 52–57

Sacagawea 18–26, 30, 42, 48, 204n
sachems 68
Sager, Frank 84
Sager, John 84
Sagers, Harrison 173
St. George, Kansas 156
St. Louis 16, 23, 26, 43–44, 111
Sales, Amos 84
Salt Lake City 156, 165, 176, 179–182, 201, 213n
Sand Creek Massacre 38, 130
San Diego, California 177
San Francisco 10, 78, 122, 128, 178, 192
San Jacinto, Battle of 94
Santa Anna, Antonio Lopez de 93, 107
Santa Clara, California 129
Santa Fe, New Mexico 108, 123, 177
Santana 157
Saunders, L.W. 84
Sawyer, Col. Samuel 167
Scott, Sir Walter 33–34, 40, 207n
The Searchers 127–128, 211n
Selkirk, Alexander 154–155
Serra, Junipero 79–82
Seven Oaks, Battle of 78
Sevier, James 98
Sevier, John 97–99
Shakers 169
Shamans 63, 65
Shannon, George 26
Sheninjee 114–115
Sherman, Texas 130
Sherman Station, Wyoming 157, 159
Shields, John 26
"Significance of the Frontier in American History" 184
Sil'aid 125
Silver Horn 158
Sioux Uprising (Minnesota) 139–141, 147–148
slaves 6, 11, 17, 19, 22–24, 35, 48–49, 61, 80–81, 87, 93–94, 108, 113, 116, 121, 124–125, 129, 133, 140, 155, 174, 177, 181
smallpox 16–17, 25, 41, 66, 83
Smith, Don Carlos 174
Smith, Hyrum 175–176
Smith, Jedediah 44, 47–48

Smith, Joseph 123, 161–165, 168–176, 178–179, 183, 187, 199–200, 211n, 212n
Smith, Joseph, III 178
Snow, Lorenzo 172
South Dakota 16, 27, 44–45, 130, 209n–210n
Southwest Point, Virginia 98
Spain 6, 11, 14, 48, 81, 191
Spalding, Eliza Hart 59
Sparks, Richard 14
Spaulding, Henry 59
Spotted Tail 158
Stanberry, William 92
Stark, Rodney 170, 212n
Steptoe, Edward 181
Stockton, Richard 35
Stratton, Royal 127–130
Sullivan, Gen. John 116–117, 121
Sully, Gen. Alfred 138, 148, 159
Sutter, Johan (John) 10
Swann, Thomas 99
Swift Bear 158
Sylvester, Charles 144–145
syphilis 17–18, 20, 24–25, 26

Tall Soldier 152
Taos, New Mexico 36, 38–40, 80
Taylor, Zachary 180
Te-lou-ki-ke 74
Tennessee 67, 90–92, 97–101, 177
Terre Haute, Indiana 168
Texas 2, 5, 11, 14, 90, 93–95, 102, 104, 107–108, 128, 130, 170, 176–177, 187–192, 210n
Texas Rangers 105
Three Forks 45
Tilaukait 83–85, 88
"The Tin Star" 8
Tomahas 83–84, 88
Topeka 125
Trail of Tears 2, 92
transcontinental railroad 10, 187
Travis, William 93
Tsayahha 27
Turner, Frederick Jackson 3, 184–185
Twain, Mark 179–180
Two Face 155
two-spirited 29, 205n
Tyree, William 92

Unita Mountains 157
United Society of Believers in Christ's Second Coming *see* Shakers
University of the Pacific 129
Utah 3, 123, 156, 165, 176–183, 201, 211n
Utah Commission 201

Vandyke, Thomas 98
Van Sice, John 115
venereal disease *see* gonorrhea; syphilis
Virginia 15, 28, 31, 46–47, 49, 90, 96, 98, 113, 205n

Waanibe (Carson) 37–41
Wade, Richard C. 185
Waiilatpu, Oregon Territory 59, 76, 85, 197
Wakefield, Gardner 133, 198
Walla Walla, Oregon Territory 47, 55, 58, 74, 76, 86–87
Walla Walla River 82
War of 1812 90, 93, 109, 165
Warsaw, Illinois 174–175
Warsaw Signal 175
Wasatch Mountains 156
Washington (state) 31, 58–59, 177
Washington, George 13–14, 68, 113, 116, 165
Washington, D.C. 28, 33, 40, 92, 117, 158, 160, 192, 194–195, 210n
Washington Territory 133
Washita Massacre 130, 182
Washita River 157
Watervliet, New York 169
Wayne, John 8–9, 128
Weaver, Duff 126
Wechela 134
Werner, William 26
Whipple, Lt. A.W. 125
White Tipi 144
Whitehouse, Joseph 26

Whitman, Marcus 3, 53, 55, 58–61, 72–73, 76, 82–88, 187, 196–197
Whitman, Narcissa Prentiss 58–59, 72–77, 82–85, 87–88, 196–197
Wiggins, James 132
Wilkinson, James 14
Willamette River 86
Willamette Valley 77
Willson, Marcus 139
Windsor, Richard 26
Winnipeg, Manitoba 78
Wirt, William 168
Wood, Natalie 128
Woodruff, Wilford 183, 201–202
Worcester, Massachusetts 130
Workman, David 36
Wounded Knee, South Dakota 130, 182, 209n
Wyeth, Nathaniel 52
Wyoming 34, 37, 43, 47, 53, 61, 112, 131, 133, 157–159, 177, 179–182
Wyoming Massacre 116, 131
Wyoming Valley, Pennsylvania 116

Yellow Bird 138, 148
Yellow Hair 158
Yellowstone River 43
Yerka, California 127
York (William Clark's slave) 17, 23
Young, Brigham 47, 123, 162, 170–171, 173, 176–183, 212n
Young, Steve 178
Yuma, Arizona 123, 126

www.ingramcontent.com/pod-product-compliance
Ingram Content Group UK Ltd.
Pitfield, Milton Keynes, MK11 3LW, UK
UKHW041945140426
5217IPUK00014B/667